LANCASHIRE'S HISTORIC HALLS

Lancashire's Historic Halls

DAVID BRAZENDALE

Carnegie Publishing, 2005

To Hilary
with love and thanks

Lancashire's Historic Halls
David Brazendale

First published by Carnegie Publishing Ltd, 1994

This revised, second edition published in 2005
by Carnegie Publishing Ltd,
Carnegie House
Chatsworth Road
Lancaster LA1 4SL
www.carnegiepublishing.com

ISBN 1-85936-106-4
EAN 978-1-85936-106-1

Typeset and designed by Carnegie Publishing
Printed in the UK by Alden Press, Oxford

Contents

Preface

I N RECENT YEARS visiting country houses has become an increasingly popular pastime for many thousands of people to whom a whole new world has been opened by the mobility provided by the car. Any summer weekend finds the car parks of National Trust and other properties crowded, and often an almost continuous crocodile of visitors wends its way through the rooms. One must wonder what it is that attracts so many and so diverse a cross section of the population. Some are earnest students of the architecture, or the fine arts that are on display. Some no doubt are driven by a curiosity about how the 'other half' lived. Some are there because it is somewhere to go to give purpose to a week-end 'run' in the car; they have heard it is a pleasant place and that the tea shop is highly recommended.

The administrators and custodians of these houses face the almost impossible task of trying to preserve the buildings and their contents and yet at the same time to interpret the building and its history for the visitors whose interests and tastes are so different. Many different solutions are in use to try to recon-cile these conflicting aims, and they achieve their goals with varying degrees of success.

One aspect of the history of any property that is often badly neglected in most cases, is the way in which that house, either in its architecture, the history of its family or some incident connected with it, reflects the wider history of a county or even of the nation. The aim of this book is to try to fill a part of this gap by telling the story of some aspect of the history of ten Lancashire houses, all of which can be visited by the public. At some point in their history these houses reflect some important theme which might not otherwise be apparent. It is hoped that it will in this way make a contribution to a deeper understanding and interest for visitors to the properties and at the same time give an insight into the development of the historic county of Lancashire from the Middle Ages until the coming of industrialisation in the eighteenth century.

The preparation of a work of this nature is the result of the contributions of many people and it is impossible to record one's gratitude to them all. However, I must specially acknowledge the debt which I owe to the staffs of the Lancashire Record Office, Sefton Libraries and of Chetham's Library for their unfailingly courteous assistance. Alistair Hodge of Carnegie Publishing and Dr Alan Crosby, my editor, have saved me from myself on numerous occasions and provided constant help and guidance. I must record my debt to John Champness, Lancashire County's Historic Buildings Conservation

Officer, for his advice on Samlesbury Lower Hall and in the same context Gary Miller gave me the benefit of his research. Susan Bourne of Towneley Hall Museum was most helpful in sorting out the complex building history of that house and in providing illustrations. Mr Robinson-Dowland and Mr D. Morris have made important contributions to the chapters on Turton and Hall i'th'Wood. Father M. O'Halloran SJ, Rector of Stonyhurst, Mr C. Parker of Browsholme and the Ven. W. D. Robinson, Archdeacon of Blackburn, have provided invaluable help. My gratitude goes to the Brigadier Commanding Liverpool District and to the range staff at Altcar for their help in visiting the Grange. My friends Roger and Jennifer Haynes have encouraged, helped with the word processing and with photography. The late Professor William Kershaw and Mrs Lois Kershaw are owed a special debt of gratitude for their insistence, without which the book might remain unpublished, and to their names I must also link all those other students in my classes for their support and encouragement. Mr Bottomley-Wise of HW Partnerships of Crossgates, Leeds has drawn the maps with meticulous care and my thanks go to the Rev. Richard Littledale for the title suggestion. Finally I must express my appreciation and gratitude to my proof reader extrordinaire and critic, my wife, to whom I dedicate this book. I hope it is some consolation for the time she has spent looking after the present while I was living in the past. In spite of the contribution of all these people, the blame for the mistakes is entirely mine.

Notes

Quotations have been modernised in spelling and punctuation where the original might prove difficult to understand. These instances are noted in the text. Otherwise they are in the original form. Dates before 1753 are given in the old-style calendar and the year is assumed to commence on 25 March. Where a date occurs between January and March during this period the form '1752/53' is used. Spelling of place names is taken from the Ordnance Survey map Land Ranger series.

Preface to the Second Edition

I N THE TIME SINCE the first publication of this book there has been no indication that visiting historic houses has become any less popular than it was. Consequently, I am glad to have had the opportunity to make some amendments to the text and to greatly increase the number and quality of the illustrations. A new section is also included, in which a number of other houses – all of which can be visited but which were omitted previously – are described and an indication given of their historical importance.

As always, my debt is to innumerable people. To the institutions and libraries mentioned before must be added the Library of the Liverpool Athenaeum and Liverpool University Library. Additional pictorial matter has been provided by my friends and students, Len Fender, Netta and Bernard Dixon. Again, my many thanks go to Alistair Hodge of Carnegie Publishing and to his staff, especially Claire Walker and Adam Gregory for patiently sorting it all out. My family have been, as always, a tower of strength and encouragement and invaluable in proof reading. None more so than my wife, Hilary, to whom this edition like the other is dedicated.

In spite of all the people who have helped I am sure that there are errors and omissions and for these I take the responsibility.

David Brazendale
Crosby, September 2004

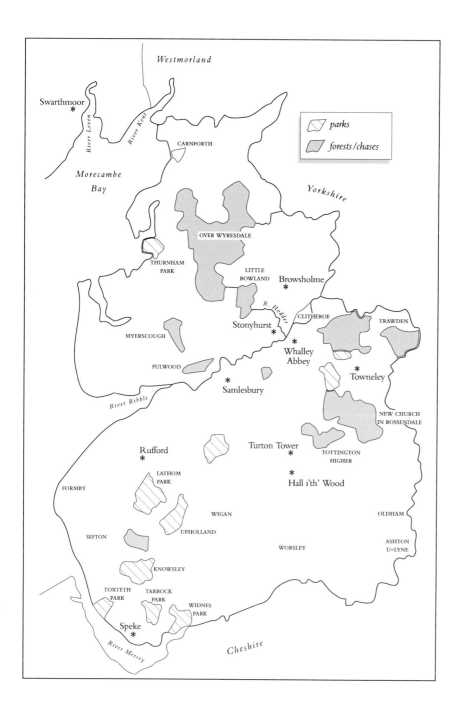

Westmorland

Swarthmoor
*

River Leven

River Kent

CARNFORTH

Morecambe
Bay

Yorkshire

parks

forests/chases

OVER WYRESDALE

THURNHAM
PARK

LITTLE
BOWLAND

Browsholme
*

R. Hodder

CLITHEROE

TRAWDEN

MYERSCOUGH

Stonyhurst
*

Whalley
Abbey
*

FULWOOD

Samlesbury
*

Towneley
*

NEW CHURCH
IN ROSSENDALE

River Ribble

Rufford
*

Turton Tower
*

TOTTINGTON
HIGHER

LATHOM
PARK

FORMBY

Hall i'th' Wood
*

WIGAN

OLDHAM

SEFTON

UPHOLLAND

WORSLEY

ASHTON
U-LYNE

KNOWSLEY

TOXTETH
PARK

TARBOCK
PARK

WIDNES
PARK

Speke
*

River Mersey

Cheshire

CHAPTER I

Browsholme Hall and the Lancashire Forests

T HE DESIGNATION of large areas of Lancashire as 'forest' in the Middle
Ages had a great influence on the structure of life and society within
the boundaries of the county. To find a house which exemplifies the
forest areas in the county, though, we have to go outside the historic boundaries
of Lancashire into that area which was until 1974 part of the West Riding of
Yorkshire. In the medieval period the term 'forest' did not necessarily imply
the existence of extensive tracts of woodland. Instead, the term referred to those
areas of the countryside which were designated as hunting preserves in which
the sport was reserved to the monarch. Within these bounds a special code of
law was enforced, its aim being the protection of both the game and the
environment to ensure the well-being of the deer and other beasts of quarry.
The laws of the forest were often harsh and uncompromising and had severe
effects on the lives of those who dwelt within the forest and around the
boundaries of the actual hunting preserve.

Everything about Browsholme Hall at Bashall Eaves speaks of the days when
much of the region was designated as forest. The name of the house refers to
an area where the deer of the forest could come to browse in safety on the
herbage and fodder provided for them. Ever since the fifteenth century
Browsholme has been the home of the Parker family, whose name means 'one
who tends a Park' – an artificially created safe refuge and breeding area for
the deer. The family's arms of three stags' heads, and its colours of green and
gold, remind us of their forest past. The house is bedecked with the antlers of
quarry long past and no visitor can forget the family's claim to the hereditary
post of 'Bowbearer of Bowland'. As a result, no other house so clearly evokes
the days of the county's forests.

Even before the Norman Conquest, many areas of the region later to be
known as Lancashire were included within the estates of Edward the Confessor.
Large tracts were at that time designated among the hunting preserves of the
king, though it must be doubtful if he ever took advantage of them personally.
These royal forests extended down the western coastal plain from Myerscough
and Fulwood in the Fylde, south through West Derby Hundred where there
were several hunting areas, of which the most important were Simonswood and
Toxteth Park. After the Battle of Hastings the district between the Ribble and

the Mersey, which was then administered as part of Cheshire, became the nucleus of the feudal landholdings of Roger de Poitou. To this area were later added the hundreds of Amounderness, the area between the Ribble and the Lune, and Lonsdale, which included the Lune valley and as far north as the sands of Morecambe Bay. In addition Roger received the peninsulas of Cartmel and Furness. Thus was created the curious division of the later county into Lancashire north and south of the sands.

Among Roger's principal henchmen were the de Lacy family of Pontefract and Chester. To them was given the Blackburn hundred and this, together with other estates, went to form what became known as the Honour of Clitheroe, because it was on the rocky limestone knoll at Clitheroe that the de Lacys built their castle. Eventually, in the reign of Henry II, Lancashire was recognised as an independent shire, the last English county to be created.

The de Lacys continued to grow in importance and wealth, with vast estates in Yorkshire and Cheshire as well as the lands of Clitheroe. Their importance was recognised when they were created earls of Lincoln. Like many Norman noblemen they delighted in the pastime of hunting, which not only gave them the opportunity to enjoy the thrill of the chase but also provided a welcome supply of fresh meat and allowed them to practise the vital skills of horsemanship. The frequent passage of the hunt past their door must have served as a permanent reminder to the peasantry of the ever-present power of their new landlords. In their desire to improve the sport on their lands they decided to develop the potential of their East Lancashire estates. At this time, the early thirteenth century, the region was sparsely populated and had little agricultural value. On the other hand, with its mixture of open grassland on

Browsholme Hall exterior from the south west. This view shows the four major building phases of the house. The central hall block and the former service wing to the right of the façade date from the original construction in 1507. On the extreme right is the new kitchen wing added in the early eighteenth century. The three-stage decorative entrance was built by Thomas Holt for Thomas Parker in 1604. The new state rooms added by Wyatt comprise the left-hand wing and are easily distinguished by their more regular masonry and sash windows.

the slopes and bare moorland on the tops of the hills it was ideal hunting country. The river valleys were thickly wooded to provide shelter for the deer and in the trees eyries of hawks could be found: it must be remembered that to the Norman nobles falconry was almost as popular and important as the chase. The existence of these varied landscapes encouraged the de Lacy family to turn much of their estates in Lancashire into hunting preserves.

As noted earlier, the hunting areas and their laws were designed to protect game and to prevent damage to their environment. The well-being and livelihood of the human inhabitants of the area were subject to this imperative. The methods of agriculture, the enclosure of farmland and the way of life of the people were therefore regulated minutely. Any activity which might be seen as imperilling the deer was prohibited and infringement was punishable with brutal and drastic penalties. The most serious of all offences was to poach the deer. An added problem for the local people was that the forest law did not only apply within the designated forest itself but also in the adjoining bands of territory into which the deer might stray, known as the 'purlieus'. The purlieu might be several miles in width and where the forests were closely set they and the purlieus might come to form a continuous belt of land in which the forest laws applied.

As might be expected, suspension of the common law was not a privilege allowed to a subject – however powerful – and strictly speaking the term forest should only be applied to Crown lands. When members of the aristocracy set up hunting preserves they were known as chases: the common law continued to run but the imposition of special bye-laws and administrative procedures was permitted. However, long custom and the fact that they eventually became royal property allows us to use the traditional name of forest for the preserves established by the de Lacys. These forests were not continuous but the lands which remained outside the purlieus formed only narrow strips. South of the Ribble almost the whole of the Blackburn hundred was taken up by the forests of Rossendale and Accrington, to which was added the park at Musbury. Between the Ribble and the Calder lay the Forest of Pendle. This was much more extensive than just Pendle Hill, and included the lower ridges within the loop of Pendle Water. Across Colne Water to the south and east of Pendle was the forest of Trawden. North of the Ribble and between the valleys of the rivers Loud and Lune was the great mass of Bowland which extended to adjoin the forest of Over Wyresdale and the park of Quernmore to the north and Bleasdale Forest to the west. It is on these eastern forests that this study will concentrate, rather than on the demesne forests of the coastal plain.

By the beginning of the fourteenth century the ownership of the de Lacy estates in east Lancashire had passed to Thomas, Earl of Lancaster. He was the grandson of Henry III by his youngest son, Edmund, who had been created earl of Lancaster in 1295. Thomas married Alice de Lacy, the daughter and heiress of Henry, earl of Lincoln and at the death of his father-in-law in 1314 the Honour of Clitheroe passed to Thomas, by then Earl of Lancaster. Thomas became involved in the corrupt politics of the reign of Edward II. The king appointed him Steward of England, a post equivalent to the king's deputy and commander-in-chief. Thomas opposed the influence of Piers Gaveston, the royal favourite, and played a major part in bringing about his downfall and execution. Gaveston was replaced in Edward's affections by Hugh de Spencer and in disgust Lancaster refused to serve in the Bannockburn campaign. His relationship with Edward remained uneasy until, finally, in 1322, he led a revolt against the king. Widespread support was forthcoming in the North, but the rebels were defeated by the king's army at Boroughbridge, in Yorkshire. Lancaster was taken prisoner and executed at Pontefract Castle. The traitor's lands were confiscated by the Crown and the properties in Lancashire given to Queen Isabella.

In the reign of Edward III the lands of Lancaster were returned to Thomas' younger brother, Henry, and with them came the revived title of earl of Lancaster. His son, also Henry, was rewarded for his support of the king during the Hundred Years War by having his earldom elevated to a dukedom and he was given palatine powers in the county. This conferred on the duke the powers usually exercised by the king. Henry had no sons and at his death the lands were inherited by his two daughters. One daughter, Blanche, married John of Gaunt, the king's fourth son. Their son, Henry, eventually overthrew Richard II and came to the throne as Henry IV. From that time onwards the dukedom of Lancaster was retained by the Crown and the chases of the Honour of Clitheroe became royal forests.

Although each of the forests in Lancashire was administered individually, the system was similar in every case, though the titles given to the various officers and institutions varied. For each forest a chief steward or master forester was appointed to have overall supervision. This was a post of some consequence as the master forester enjoyed a number of privileges in the forest which he could exercise on his own account. He was permitted to use the forest for his own hunting and he could graze his own animals or rent out grazing within the confines of the forest – a practice known as agisting. He could authorise the felling of timber and also controlled the use of the woodland to provide firewood. Though a proportion of this income would be expected to go to the Crown, holding the office of master forester gave many opportunities for self-enrichment. Because of the value of the appointment it was reserved for families of importance in the hope that they would be bound to the Crown; thus we find names like Stanley, Towneley and Shireburne among the lists of master foresters.

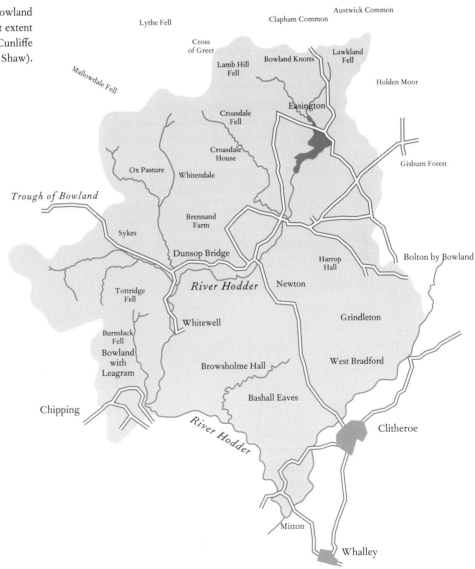

Sketch map of Bowland at its greatest extent (based on R. Cunliffe Shaw).

It was not expected that the master forester should exercise any personal supervision of the forest itself, though on occasion some did become involved. In general, the day-to-day running of the forest and supervision of its staff and institutions was left to a deputy, who in Bowland was known as the 'Bowbearer'. By the middle of the sixteenth century the upwardly mobile Parker family were claiming this as their hereditary office.

Control of the forest was imposed principally through the two forest courts of 'woodmote' and 'swainmote', which met thrice yearly at the court house in Whitewell. These courts dealt with offences against *vert* and *venison*. Vert included all the green things of the forest – trees, shrubs, bushes, grass and undergrowth. Venison had a less specialised meaning than it does today and included all the animals of the forest which were considered possible quarry, although the main emphasis, of course, was on the herds of deer. For Bowland there exists an almost complete set of court rolls from 1554 to 1663, and they record how the courts dealt with offences such as deer poaching, the felling of timber and the illicit clearing of land. At Browsholme is preserved a grim relic in the form of the dog gauge, a hoop of metal through which, at least according to legend, a dog owned by a resident of the forest had to be able to pass. If it was too large for the gauge it was considered a danger to the deer and had to be crippled to make it useless for hunting.

The hamlet of Whitewell became the administrative headquarters of the forest due to its central location and the presence of the steward's house, now included in the hotel building. The dignity of the place was enhanced by the

Whitewell Chapel, the Forest church. Originally in the cure of the Chapel of St Mary in Clitheroe Castle, the pastoral care of Bowland passed to the monks of Whalley Abbey, who, in 1422, established the chapel at Whitewell. The present early nineteenth-century building contains a carved oak pulpit from the earlier chapel.

The Forest Steward's House, Whitewell. The central location of Whitewell dictated its choice as the administrative capital of the Forest of Bowland. In this seventeenth-century building, refurbished in the 1830s, the steward held the Courts of Woodmote and Swainmote, which regulated the affairs of the area. (See engraving from Whitaker, p.8.)

PHOTOGRAPH, AUTHOR

founding, some time before 1422, of a chapel to serve the forest. Originally the spiritual welfare of the forest people had been the responsibility of the chapel of St Michael in Clitheroe Castle and a small chapel existed at a remote location in the Brennand valley: traces of this building have been found in the lower barn at Brennand Farm. Early in the fifteenth century the monks of Whalley acquired control over the castle chapel and the forest was included within the vast parish of Whalley. It was after this that the Whitewell chapel was built. The present building is of early nineteenth-century date, but contains an unexpected treasure in the shape of a very fine Elizabethan carved oak pulpit.

For administrative purposes the forest was divided into four wards. These were Slaidburn Ward in the north, where the court room survives in the Hark to Bounty; the south-western or Lancashire part of the forest made up Chipping Ward, together with the park at Leagram; the south-eastern quarter was known as Bashall Ward; and there was also a detached portion called Harrop Ward. Each ward was supervised by a resident keeper, who would have had a number of underkeepers as his staff. Very often, as well as giving general help, these underkeepers had some special responsibility for a particular area or some aspect of keepering. In 1662, for example, one was designated as the keeper of the fallow deer; he lived at Whitewell in a house that was provided for him and he was also equipped with two horses. The keepers of the wards seem to have found the post lucrative and the holders were able to build themselves official houses or lodges, the only surviving one being at Harrop Hall above Slaidburn.

Physically separate from, but included within, the forest were the parks. Parks were enclosed sanctuaries for the deer, in which they could be fattened and in which they could breed in safety. The parks were surrounded by a ditch and bank on which was mounted a wooden fence or pale. These were arranged so that although it was easy for the deer to jump into the enclosure, it was impossible for them to escape, except when special gates were opened so that the animals could be driven for the hunt. The fences encircling these parks were often very considerable works. The perimeter of the 1,400 acres of Leagram Park was six and a half miles (10 km) in length, and for this thousands of paling stakes were needed. In 1304 when the Earl of Lincoln fenced Musbury Park in Rossendale, the pales had to be brought from Tottington Woods and their transport required the purchase of eighteen oxen at a cost of £8 17s. 9d. The whole project cost £74 0s. 5½d. to give a total cost for four and a half miles of fencing of £82 18s. 2½d., a vast sum for the period. A park was under the supervision of an officer known as a parker and the care and repair of the fences was the work of the palliser. In the West Derby hundred forests in 1314 this official was paid 5d. a week. At a similar period the weekly cost of repairs to the fences of Ightenhill Park near Burnley was ½d. per perch, a measurement of about 5½ yards. In Bowland there were two parks: Leagram in Chipping Ward, and Radholme, in the vicinity of Whitewell and the wooded lands of the Hodder valley.

Within the parks areas were cleared of trees and scrub to form open grass-land pasture or 'launds' on which the deer could graze undisturbed. The launds

Whitewell and the Keeper's Lodge from Whitaker's *History of the Original Parish of Whalley*, 1872. This engraving by Basire shows the old administrative heart of the Forest of Bowland as it appeared at the end of the eighteenth century. The Keeper's Lodge (now part of the Inn at Whitewell) is in the centre, while the earlier chapel building is to the left of the house. The farm house in the middle distance behind the lodge is New Laund. The river Hodder is crossed by stepping stones.

WHITAKER'S HISTORY OF THE ORIGINAL PARISH OF WHALLEY (ROUTLEDGE, 1872 EDN)

would be enclosed by hedges or, as they were known in the area, heys, a word which in Lancashire was transferred to any hedged field. In winter hay, tree trimmings and other fodder would be put out so that the animals could browse – hence the name Browsholme, a safe feeding area for the deer.

It can be seen that the forest provided considerable employment and needed a large staff of men who could work in at least a part-time capacity on the tasks connected with the hunting of the area. Medieval hunting techniques required a considerable number of helpers, as the area to be hunted was first closed off with brushwood barriers. The deer were then driven by huntsmen and packs of dogs – the Lancashire hounds had a specially high reputation – to pre-selected killing grounds. Here the quarry were driven into nets hung between trees, and when they became entangled the huntsmen would approach on foot and kill the animal. The men required for a hunt would be drawn from among the foresters and from the inhabitants of the small and scattered hamlets within the forest, settlements which had often existed before the creation of the hunting preserve.

Though both the de Lacys and the Crown valued the recreational possibilities of the forests, and though these areas provided a source of game, they realised that the forest lands were too extensive not to be used and exploited in other ways. While the provision of sport was the primary purpose of the forests, it was possible to devise other uses which would not interfere unduly with the hunting. Henry de Lacy, the last earl of Lincoln, in particular, pursued a vigorous policy of exploiting the potential of the land.

Cattle grazing had always taken place in the region but under his direction a system of intensive cattle rearing was introduced. Each forest was divided into a number of units, called 'vaccaries' (from the Norman French *vache*, a cow). The extent of the vaccaries varied but the number of cattle seems to have been fairly standard: presumably the quality of the grazing and the natural conditions were taken into account when fixing the boundaries of each farm. Originally there were eleven ranches in Pendle, fourteen in Bowland, eleven in Rossendale and one in Accrington. Over the years the number tended to increase as the original vaccaries were sub-divided. Each vaccary and its stock were leased out to a Herdsman or Boothsman for about £3 per year. He was entitled to the dairy produce of the herd, but for this he had to pay an additional fee known as 'lactage', which was usually similar in value to the rent. The main purpose of the vaccary herds was the breeding of cattle. These could either be taken down to kinder country for fattening and slaughter to provide meat for the lord's table or could be sold in local markets. Even more valuable were the oxen produced on the vaccaries, as these were the principal draught and burden animals of the Middle Ages.

These vaccaries were a form of commercial farming on a large scale, and were in sharp contrast to our usual picture of the medieval peasant ploughing his strips in the common fields and producing a crop sufficient for his family's needs but with little or no surplus for sale. The vaccaries were much more closely related to the techniques of modern industrial farming. In 1295 the thirty

vaccaries outside Bowland were grazed by 2,417 head of cattle, made up of 35 bulls, 1,197 breeding cows, 186 steers (young male beasts due to be gelded as oxen), 169 heifers (young cows who had yet to breed), 378 yearling animals and 470 calves, which gives an average figure of 80 animals per vaccary. The low number of calves reflects the poor breeding record of cattle in the period – only about 40 per cent.

The day-to-day running of a vaccary was in the hands of its resident tenant, or boothsman, but the whole operation was controlled on behalf of the earl by the chief instaurator, whose title was derived from the Latin *taurus* – a bull. This was a senior and important post which was held by a gentleman of quality and influence. For example, one of the ancestors of the Towneley family laid the foundations of their fortune in the post. There was an instaurator for each forest and he was assisted in his work by the 'geldherd', who was an animal husbandry and veterinary expert. Each year the geldherd and the instaurator would visit each vaccary to inspect the herd and receive the accounts of the herdsman. The geldherd would examine the animals and ensure that they were receiving proper care. Any failure on the part of the herdsman was punishable by heavy fines. In his accounts or 'compotus', the herdsman had to be able to account for every animal in his charge. If any beast had died he had to be able to produce the hide, hooves and horns, and to show the sale of the meat in his accounts.

The herdsmen built themselves a house and cattle sheds near the centre of their territory and these became known as 'booths' – hence the alternative name of boothsman given to the tenants of the vaccaries. The name Booth still survives in several places in the former forest lands. In village names such as Barley Booth and Roughlee Booth in Pendle, and Crawshaw Booth in Rossendale, the word also has a more general application as the name of the forest townships.

Boundary fence on the vaccary of Wycoller. This rough stone fence, made of slabs of cleft stones, marks one of the boundaries of the vaccary of Wycoller near Colne. These fences seem to have been a customary field divider in those areas where suitable stone was available. They provided a quickly erected and durable method of land division.

PHOTOGRAPH, AUTHOR

An activity which was related to the work of the vaccaries, although quite distinct, was the creation of stud farms. At Ightenhill the de Lacys converted the former deer park of Filly Close into a horse breeding station, although it is quite possible that it still remained in use as a deer park, with the horses and the deer co-existing. It was stocked with forty brood mares and two stallions and produced about twenty foals a year. It will be noticed that, as in the vaccaries, the breeding rate was low. The young foals faced hazards from disease and from attacks by wolves, which took several animals a year.

In the Middle Ages timber was a most valuable commodity, the essential raw material for building and furnishing homes, for shipbuilding, for the making of machinery in watermills and windmills and for fuel, both domestic and industrial. Though the forests were not essentially woodland, there were large tracts of timber and this was too valuable a resource not to be exploited. Provided that felling was accompanied by planting, and that the cutting of trees was strictly controlled and limited, this could be done without detriment either to the timber reserves or the hunting. Timber from Bowland was used for the repair of Clitheroe Castle and in building the houses and court houses in the forest. At Slaidburn it was used to build a fulling mill and it was frequently required for the various corn mills belonging to the Earl, both in the forest and in the other demesnes. However, not only was there the official cutting of timber but illicit depredations were made by the forest residents and, in some cases, by the forest officers. Edward Braddyll, for example, had cut timber for use on his own estates and sold the surplus to the corn mill at Chipping.

It was not only timber which had an economic value: the underwood and brushwood was needed both for domestic fuel and for charcoal burning. The residents of the forest had a right of 'estovers', that is to take, dry and fallen

The Court Room of
Slaidburn. The upper
room of this wing of
the intriguingly named
Hark to Bounty was
built in the early
seventeenth century to
house the Court Room.
Originally entered by
the exterior stairs, the
room, though it retains
some of its original
furnishings, had new
windows installed in the
nineteenth century.
PHOTOGRAPH, AUTHOR

wood for domestic use. Demand tended to outstrip supply, and as a result 'fallen wood' was often helped on its way. In some places the tenants had the right to lop trees provided that only branches out of reach of the deer, but accessible 'by hook or by crook' to a man standing on the ground, were taken. In Rossendale and Quernmore and in other parts of the forests there were pockets of lead and iron ore which were mined from time to time, which required large quantities of charcoal for smelting. On these occasions there was almost indiscriminate felling of woodland. For domestic fuel most of the forest people enjoyed the right – known as 'turbary' – to cut peat or turf: the areas from which peat could be cut were carefully defined and rigorously protected.

Under the direction of Henry of Lincoln the forests yielded a considerable income (£732 in 1305) but his policies began a period of change which, in time, completely altered the way of life. Many factors helped to bring about this change, but it was accelerated by the death of Henry. Not only were his talents as a successful entrepreneur lost, but the forests now became a part of the vast duchy and Crown lands and the personal interest and involvement that he had shown disappeared as well. The new overlords seldom, if ever, visited their properties or took advantage of the forests. The use and administration of these large areas were left in the hands of officials who were more anxious to exploit the resources for their own benefit than to pursue a policy of development. As far as is known the first and only monarch to make use of the hunting of the Lancashire forests was James I, during his brief visit in 1617, by which time the herds were in decline. He is reputed to have hunted in Bowland and certainly visited Fulwood and Myerscough, where his activities are described in the diary of Nicholas Assheton of Downham. Thus in the later Middle Ages, although the forest laws and administrative machine remained in place, the imperative of direct personal control was lost. Abuses of power became more common, and the Crown remained indifferent to, or ignorant of, the peculations of the forest officers. The most common infringement was the permitting of excessive agisting. Though letting the pasture land of the forest for grazing was a traditional practice, its extent had been strictly controlled. Now more and more land was leased to local farmers and cleared for grazing, while the foresters and the lesser officials exploited their powers by authorising extensions to the pasture land and pocketing the rents. The spread of these illegal pastures or preprestures was to the detriment of the deer, yet simultaneously these same officials were rigidly enforcing prohibitions on fencing or enclosure of existing farmland in the forest. The fencing was intended to protect the farmland from the depredations of the grazing deer, but it was forbidden because enclosure interfered with the hunting. Another source of friction between the local peasants and farmers and the forest officials was the right of the latter to claim free overnight accommodation for man and horse when they were on duty – something that seemed to occur all too frequently to their unwilling hosts.

Even the boothsmen benefited from the slackening of control by the central authorities. The vaccary system fell into desuetude, but the tenants seem to have acquired a lease or copyhold right to the lands of their booth. As their families became established the holdings were sub-divided to provide an inheritance for their children, or portions were sublet to land-hungry outsiders. More and more land was farmed, the cattle and sheep from the farms competed with the deer, and the laxity of the officers ensured that it was the cattle which were favoured. The deer found that the undisturbed areas which were available to them were shrinking year by year. Timber was felled and not replaced, and brushwood – a vital food for the stags and hinds – was cleared and burned as domestic fuel. As a result in hard winters death by starvation decimated the herds: during the winter of 1571 in Bowland 273 deer died of hunger.

The Justice Room in the 'Hark to Bounty' Slaidburn. This interior view of the room formerly used for the Forest Courts shows the seats of the officers of the courts who would have dealt with offences against the Forest Law and infringements of the custom of the ward.

PHOTOGRAPH, AUTHOR

The best areas for cattle pasture were the existing parks and gradually these were used for agisting. The fences were neglected and the launds were no longer reserved for the deer but let, and enclosed, and lost to the wild animals.

Another threat to both the economy of the area and to the deer came from the indiscriminate felling of the large timber trees. Periodic surveys by the Crown show the rate of loss: in 1556 1,327 trees were counted, by 1587 the number had declined to 372, and by 1662 only 96 trees of any size could be found. In this way the environment which provided the essential food and shelter for the deer was destroyed.

The clearest indication of the changing attitude to forest land came in 1507. Henry VII was anxious to increase the Crown's revenue to its maximum extent. He took little personal interest in field sports, especially if these were to be prac-tised far away from the centres of power, as in remote Lancashire. It seemed more profitable to turn these areas (which could be regarded as waste land) into a source of rents and fines, than to preserve them for game. In 1507 Bowland was surveyed and the decision was made to deforest the district partially. The rents on existing vaccaries and pastures were raised considerably but by way of compensation the conditions on which they were held were made much easier. Tenants were to be free to enclose their lands to keep out the deer, they were allowed to take wood and underwood, and – perhaps most important of all – they were to be allowed to encroach on and enclose the waste and thus extend the size of their holdings. It was laid down that each encroachment was to be reported to the woodmote court and there enrolled. In fact, if not in name, the tenants of the forest lands had become copyholders, with a rent fixed in perpe-tuity and with the right to transfer the holding of the land upon payment of a fine equivalent to an extra year's rent. Those areas not taken over by the new copyholders stayed as forest and the administrative machinery remained in place.

The appearance of the new copyhold tenancies led to a population explo-sion in Bowland during the next century. This seems to have had three causes. First, the whole country went through a period of general population growth: the reasons for this are matters of debate among demographers but they are agreed that during the sixteenth century the population of Lancashire more or less doubled. The second reason for the population growth in Bowland was that those who were already tenants or occupiers of the vaccaries and farms now felt themselves secure, and were encouraged to put down roots in the area. As their children grew and married there was sufficient land to divide the holdings to provide a home for the newly married couple. In addition, there seems to have been a local custom of partible inheritance, whereby the lands of the father were divided on his death equally among the children, including daughters. It has been suggested that this was a survival in a remote area of ancient Celtic custom. While it might seem more equitable than primogeniture it had the economic disadvantage of reducing an estate to many small units which could not provide a viable farm. Some individual holdings make this process clear and show how sub-letting was also used and could produce a handsome profit for the original tenant.

Bowland, looking north
from Longridge Fell.
This view across the
valley of the River
Loud towards Chipping
emphasises the sharp
difference in the land
use of the valley bottom
and the fellside. The
park of Leagram lies to
the north-east of
Chipping and the area
to the east of this is the
Lancashire or Little
Bowland portion of the
Forest. The clear
dividing line between
the cultivated lands of
the valley bottom and
the fell slopes is very
distinct.

PHOTOGRAPH, AUTHOR

In 1498 the former vaccary of Burnslack, to the north of Chipping, was occupied by Agnes Parker, at a rent of 10s. 4d. *per annum*. By 1527 it was held by Brian Parker, who paid 5s. 2d. rent and Ellis and Anthony Parker, who held a quarter of the tenement apiece and thus paid 2s. 7d. each. It must be presumed that these were the three sons of Agnes and that they were quite content to share the rent equitably among themselves and not to profit at each other's expense. A more complicated and obvious division had taken place at Sykes, on the road through the Trough of Bowland. Thomas Bond held it in 1498 at a rent of 53s. 4d. a half year, but by 1527 it was divided into nine separate holdings. The major shares were occupied by Richard Bound (sic) – probably the son of Thomas – who paid 13s. 10d, as did Giles Parker, who was perhaps a son-in-law. The wife of Thomas Huntyngdon paid 5s. 2¼d., and so did Thomas Herling, while the wife of James Huntyngdon and Thomas Bound, each paid 10s. 4½d. Giles Bound and Edmund Parker each paid 1s. 8¾d., while Oliver Merton's rent was 3s. 5d. Some unspecified 'others' paid one penny. The frequency of the appearance of the name Bound or Bond among the tenants would suggest that these were family members, perhaps the younger sons of Thomas, the original tenant.

A calculation shows that the total rent being paid at Sykes in 1527 was 65s. 9d.: as the rent paid to the Crown on the whole property remained at 53s. 4d., someone was making a half-yearly profit of 12s. 5d. An even clearer example of the profits produced by sub-letting comes from that portion of the former Ightenhill stud farm, which was known as Filly Close. In 1507 Lawrence Towneley took a tenancy of this land at an annual rent of £10 13s. 4d. By 1527 it had been divided and sub-let at a total rent of £16 11s. 4d a year, and by 1688 the rent return was £115. The Towneleys continued to pay the fixed rent of £10 13s. 4d. to the Crown. By such means were the fortunes of the Towneleys increased and those of the Parkers made.

The third factor which extended the areas of land available for cultivation and settlement was the practice of encroachment on the waste lands. This right, given to the tenants in 1507, ensured that gradually, by piecemeal nibbling at the boundary between their properties and the residue of the forest, new farm lands were created. The privilege began to be exploited by incomers to the district, who were drawn by the magnetism of the availability of land. Everyone concerned seems to have been willing to turn a blind eye to this attrition of the moorland, provided the encroachments were not too large or too blatant. It was expected that enough waste would be left to allow its use for communal rough grazing and to provide some sort of feeding area for the much reduced herds of deer, which might now only be hunted by the forester and his cronies. The other condition under which encroachments were allowed was that they had to be reported for enrolment on the manorial rolls: in his turn the pioneer became a copyholder. It may be supposed that the manorial overlords in fact encouraged the practice as it was a useful way of increasing their rent roll at no cost to themselves. The records of Slaidburn show that in the century between 1520 and 1620 there were registered, on average, two new encroachments each year. It is true that in general each was very small, but these were early days and it is apparent that from this base the new tenants would continue the process of eroding the last wild areas. During the same period it has been shown that the number of surnames recorded in the parish registers doubled and that the new names are ones unfamiliar in the area. This seems clear evidence of migration to Bowland, brought about by the promise of readily available land.

In this climate the importance of the forest for sport sank into insignificance, the numbers of deer declined, and the Parks disappeared. Leagram was disparked in 1553 and the profitable exploitation of other resources became the priority. A circle of decline and decay began. There was less interest in sport, the parks and the maintenance of a congenial environment were neglected, the deer declined in numbers, and in consequence the quality of the sport deteriorated further. There was less interest in its potential, so more farming and enclosure was allowed, and the spiral of decay became ever deeper. As a result, by the early seventeenth century even that devotee of the chase, James I, was prepared to use Bowland as a source of rent rather than a place of resort. Oxfordshire and the Home Counties were sufficient to provide recreation for a monarch who was unwilling to move too far from London. The first Stuart king, like the first Tudor king, was always anxious to increase his revenues in the hopes of solving his chronic cash crisis. In the case of Bowland he decided to use the same techniques that had been successfully employed before. Copyholds were revised and fines increased but rents were left at their original level so that the situation remained unchanged. Some copyhold properties were sold to become freehold tenements.

By the mid-seventeenth century, Bowland presented a very different

The Last Keeper of Bowland Forest. Robert Shaw, of New Laund, Whitewell, was appointed to the post of Keeper in 1774 and held it until his death in 1804. By this time the decision had been made to deforest Bowland and no successor was appointed. This painting, based on a portrait by Northcote, shows Shaw near the end of his life. Northcote was one of a group of contemporary artists who was patronised by Thomas Lister Parker and may well have been painted during a visit to the hall. The original portrait was included in the 'Below Stairs' exhibition at the National Portrait Gallery in 2003–4.

PHOTOGRAPH COURTESY OF MR C. PARKER

landscape to that which would have been seen two hundred years earlier. Most of the woodland had gone, though thin fringes of trees still clung to the banks of the rivers and the more inaccessible corners. Where once the forest had spread was now mainly pasture land, with the cattle trampling down the ditches around the parks and rubbing themselves on the decayed remains of the palings. On the sites of the vaccaries small hamlets and clusters of houses had sprung up. Few of these now remain intact, but at Harrop Fold there is a good example. Even as late as 1841 the Census returns show that over sixty people lived in the Fold, which now has just a handful of permanent residents. In most other cases these folds have now reverted to a single farm house.

Between the hamlets spread a network of small, irregularly shaped fields enclosed by hedges or stone walls, the results of enclosure and encroachment. In the hamlets and on the fields of the farms an increasing number of stone farm houses were being built, a mark of the growing prosperity of their owners.

These houses were somewhat old fashioned in design but represented a tremendous advance in domestic comfort. They took the place of hovels built of timber and turf, often with only a single room and with the cattle byre as an integral part of the house. These new yeomen's houses are perhaps more evident in the kinder setting of Pendle than of Bowland but they can be found throughout the area. Plain and functional, but sturdy and restrained in design, they are two storeyed and often have a porch to protect the front door. Their windows are small and square headed with mullions of stone, and over the head of the window is a square ended dripstone moulding.

The houses now had a number of rooms which could be used for specialist functions. The kitchen and dining room were combined in a hall which was a relic of the medieval great hall. In addition there was a parlour at one end of the hall and several chambers or bedrooms on the upper floor. Instead of there being only a single central fireplace several other rooms would have had a fire and the prosperous yeomen could enjoy the benefits of a boarded rather than a stone flagged or beaten earth floor. The floor boards, or threales as they were known, were so highly valued that they were sometimes left as bequests in wills, and, on occasion were taken away by departing tenants.

These houses exude an air of comfortable prosperity, and this impression has been substantiated by research into the wills and inventories of their inhabitants, especially those who lived in Pendle in the seventeenth century. Though on average the level of wealth indicated is below that of men of a similar station in the south east of England, certain yeomen achieved considerable prosperity. For example James Hargreaves of Higham Booth at his death in 1652 was possessed of an estate valued at £585. It was also found that of the 121 inventories examined only thirty-five had a total value below £50, the bench mark set by contemporary opinion as the minimum income for anyone claiming yeoman status. Not all this wealth was derived from farming. In the same research there was found ample evidence that many farmers in Pendle Forest were engaged in the making of textiles. Then, as now, the area was not a zone of rich soils and friendly climate and it was necessary for the farmers to try to develop an alternative source of income. The preparation of the yarn, either of wool or flax, and the weaving of cloth were trades that could easily be accommodated in farm houses and fitted into the routine of farming. One of the findings of the research is at first sight unexpected; it was the wealthier farmers who developed textile manufacture. Much less evidence was found among the poorer men, who might be thought to be in greater need of a by-income, that they took part in the making of textiles. They could not afford to employ extra labour outside the family, and their whole energies were taken up by trying to wrest a living from the unpromising soil. Other investigation has found a similar pattern in the Forest of Trawden and it is likely that work on Bowland would reveal the same. Some hint of the possible prosperity that could result from the making of textiles in the area can be seen in the school and alms houses, at Chipping, endowed in 1683 by John Brabin, a local linen draper or merchant in the second half of the century.

Bowland continued to change and evolve through the seventeenth and eighteenth centuries, with agriculture becoming the predominant occupation and a steady decline in its sporting use. In spite of this the courts of Woodmote and Swainmote were held, even though they were frequently adjourned due to absenteeism or lack of business to be discussed. The Forest Officers were still appointed, until in 1774 Robert Shaw of New Laund, Whitewell was appointed as Keeper. He continued to serve until his death in 1804 and his portrait by Northcote hangs in the gallery at Browsholme Hall.

With the death of Shaw the maintenance of the Forest of Bowland as a hunting reserve came to an end. In the year following his death the remaining herds of deer were exterminated and the whole area was turned over to sheep and cattle. Later in the century, with the growing popularity of grouse shooting, the high moorlands recovered a degree of importance and August of each year saw parties of guns intent on obtaining a large 'bag' of birds. Some deer survived and are to be glimpsed even now, though they are roe deer, the smaller and less valued species.

It is perhaps appropriate that the largest concentrations of these animals are to be found in the vicinity of Browsholme Hall, as the history of the Parker family mirrors in many aspects the history and development of Bowland. The family seems to have originated at Alkincoates near Colne and the early generations were associated with the Forest of Trawden. At some time in the middle of the fourteenth century Edmund Parker came to Bowland as Parker of Radholme Park. He was the younger son of a family, which might have been considered to be on the fringe of the gentry, but even so he had to make his way in the world. At his death his duties as Parker of Radholme were jointly assumed by his sons Richard and John. In 1380 they became the tenants of the vaccary of Nether Browsholme, where in 1326 a herd of forty-three cattle had been located. In 1400 the lease for the vaccary of Browsholme was renewed and it is likely that at this time Richard built the first house, or at least replaced the previous timber and thatch booth with a stone-built dwelling. In 1411 Richard was pensioned off as the Deputy Keeper of Radholme and the post was taken up first by his son and then by his grandson, Edmund. It was he who in 1507 at the time of the granting of copyholds secured that of Browsholme at a rent of 32s. 3d. *per annum*. Now secure in their copyhold tenancy he began to build a new family home.

His building is still the nucleus of the house. It was a very conventional house of the period, built from random pieces of local stone, now mostly covered by a later facing in ashlar. There was a central great hall, and wings at either end were set at right angles to the axis of the hall. Of these the southern wing was the service area, with kitchens and food store, while the wing at the

The Great Hall, the oldest portion of the house, and originally the central communal living and dining room of the household. The doors visible in the end wall led to the kitchen and food storage rooms. Most of the furnishings reflect the 'gothic' taste of its early nineteenth-century owners. The dog gauge or stirrup is visible on the left of the bellows; by tradition dogs too large to be passed through this hoop were mutilated to prevent their use for hunting.
PHOTOGRAPH COURTESY OF MR C. PARKER

The main entrance, Browsholme Hall. This remarkable and early display (for the area) of classical columns was added in 1607 by Thomas Parker, probably to commemorate the purchase by the family of the freehold of Browsholme. His mason, Thomas Holt, was undoubtedly inspired by the gatehouse of Stonyhurst, of which it is a naive copy. The ensemble is an interesting example of neighbourly rivalry and emulation.

PHOTOGRAPH, AUTHOR

northern end of the hall contained the private rooms of the family, made up of a parlour and a number of chambers where they could live in some privacy. The house had two upper floors, and a range of garrets in the roof that were used as accommodation for servants. An inventory of 1591 shows the house to have had twenty-three rooms. One of the inconveniences of the house at this time was the absence of any direct communication between the service and the family wing except through the hall. Furthermore on the upper floors it was

necessary to pass from one room to another by a series of connecting doors. This phenomenon was by no means confined to Browsholme, and was one of the reasons for the popularity of curtained beds.

In 1607 Thomas Parker, the grandson of Edmund, bought the freehold of Browsholme from the Crown and it seems likely that in celebration of this event he decided to give a greater air of consequence to the house, by building a more imposing entrance and thus signifying his and his family's pride in their social achievement. Through their involvement in the forest administration the Parkers had first found employment. Then they had been able to take advantage of the change from a hunting preserve to a farming area by exploiting the development of the vaccary system. This had raised them to a moderate level of prosperity which had allowed them to benefit from the deforestation of 1507. They had obtained the copyhold of their lands and could then have been considered to have entered the ranks of the minor gentry. Now in the latest reorganisation they had undoubtedly entered the ranks of the land-owning gentry and had become a family of consequence in the area.

In 1591, Sir Richard Shireburne of Stonyhurst had begun building an imposing and splendid house at Hurst Green to demonstrate the pre-eminence of his family in the district. The first part of the house to be completed was the Gatehouse, with its semi-circular Roman arch, classical busts set in roundels and its four orders of columns, Doric, Ionic and two stages of Corinthian rising in smooth progression according to the latest principles of Palladio. This structure was the first in Lancashire to be completed in the newly fashionable Classical style, and must have been an endless topic of conversation, comment and wonder among the local families. It is no surprise that when Thomas Parker decided to renovate Browsholme he gave directions that his mason, John Holt, should take the Stonyhurst gatehouse as his model. It is quite apparent that the Browsholme porch is a direct, and naive, copy of the other, the details of the entablature with its garlanded bulls' heads, the carving of the capitals and their rather uncertain decoration, and the break in the fluting of the columns, all show how Holt copied even the minor details as he struggled to meet his client's demands while working in such an unfamiliar style. His main architectural problem was that, while the Stonyhurst Gatehouse was a building in its own right and a self contained unit, Holt's work had to be attached to an existing structure with which it had nothing in common. This can best be seen in the way the Browsholme porch, after three orders of columns simply stops at the entablature, although it is true that when it was built the porch culminated in one of the several gables of the roof, which gave it a more finished, if still incongruous appearance. An eighteenth-century drawing of the hall shows this original façade. The gables and dormers disappeared during a re-roofing of the house in the mid-eighteenth century.

This rather eccentric but charming adjunct to the house is a clear expression of the way in which the Parkers viewed their rise to social distinction with the purchase of the freehold of their estates. The Shireburnes were the unrivalled

The Kitchen Wing. The kitchen wing was added to the east end of the Hall in 1704 to replace the earlier kitchen attached to the Great Hall. Its sash windows and hipped roof are typical of the period. The effectiveness of the block as a kitchen was enhanced by the provision of the long corridor to link it to the dining room. This block remained the main cooking and food preparation area of the Hall until the late twentieth century.

PHOTOGRAPH, AUTHOR

first family of the area and the parvenu Parkers could not hope to compete in prestige. However, the porch is a statement that they saw themselves in terms of equality with Sir Richard, whom they regarded not as a superior but as *primus inter pares*. They were determined that their house should have all the appearances and appurtenances of a gentleman's seat.

The next phase of building at Browsholme was at the beginning of the eighteenth century, when a new service wing was added to the existing kitchen. This annexe, with its sash windows and its hipped roof, is concealed from the main frontage. It is likely that it was at this time that the service passage, running behind the great hall, was added to link the two subsidiary wings of the house. In 1754 a portion of the now redundant great hall was partitioned off to form the library. This room was later lined with remarkable diagonal panelling brought from Parkhead, the Kenyons' house in Whalley. Only two other examples of this type of panelling exist, at nearby Towneley Hall and at Norbury Hall in Derbyshire.

Once every hundred years the Parkers seem to have been seized with an urge to build and it was in 1804 that Thomas Lister Parker began the extension and refurbishment of the house. Whereas the previous generations of the Parkers had been content to take their place among the local gentry, Lister Parker had other and grander ideas. He became a friend of the Prince Regent and his brother, the Duke of Clarence, and lived among their set of extravagant friends at Court, at Carlton House and the Royal Pavilion. As well as being known as a dandy, Parker also acquired a reputation as a patron of artists and a connoisseur of painting.

He commissioned works by fashionable artists of the day, including Romney and Northcote, and he was one of the first to recognise the talent of the young Joseph Turner. Turner was persuaded by him to make his North of

England tour. Parker introduced the artist to Charles Towneley and to
Thomas Whittaker, for whose *History of the Parish of Whalley* he provided
the illustrations.

It is said that Thomas Lister Parker planned his new building at Browsholme
in anticipation of a visit from his royal friends, a visit that never took place.
The fashionable architect Jeffry Wyatt, who was later knighted by George IV
as Sir Jeffry Wyatville, a reward for his work at Windsor Castle, was called
in and commissioned to design two state rooms. The old family wing was
demolished and rebuilt with a drawing room in high Regency style as its main
component. Wyatt's drawings, which were always known for their wealth of
detail, survive and it is clear that the room remains virtually unaltered in
furnishings and decoration. Alongside the drawing room a single storey annexe
was built to serve as a dining room and gallery for Parker's collection of
modern paintings. The distance between this room and the kitchen ensured that
it was far more suitable for the second of these uses. It was at this time that an
effort was made to refront the house. Some of the mullioned windows on the
lower floor were replaced by sashes and the clock and bell cote were added.

It was unfortunate that the promise of distinguished visitors was not fulfilled,
and Lister Parker found himself in financial straits as a result of his lavish way
of life and the expensive building projects he had undertaken. His recompense –
to be appointed as Sergeant Trumpeter to the King – was not enough to pay
the bills and he was forced to sell Browsholme to his cousin Thomas Parker.
The new owner was a great admirer of the new taste for the Gothick and for
old oak furniture. Having acquired a Tudor house he now set out to furnish
it in what was thought to be an appropriate style. Furniture of the sixteenth
and seventeenth centuries was acquired from a variety of sources, some being
gifts from friends and neighbours who searched their attics and outhouses –

The Drawing Room (*top*) and the dining room, Browsholme. These two rooms, the work of Jeffry Wyatt, were commissioned by Thomas Lister Parker in anticipation of a royal visit by George IV which never took place. They are still decorated to the patterns of Wyatt's designs. Though strongly classical in their style, the doorcase of the drawing room pays tribute to the original style of the house by its decorative version of Elizabethan strap-work. The dining room was unsuitable for its purpose because of the distance from the kitchens but made a fine gallery for Parker's collection of paintings.

hence items like the carved medallion of the Towneley arms above the fireplace in the library, and the composite dresser in the great hall. In his taste Thomas Parker was one of the pioneers of the Victorian Gothic Revival, and as such the decor of the house has a special interest as being one of the earliest to exhibit the revolution against the Classical model that had dominated taste for so long. To complete the illusion of antiquity Thomas Parker had the sash windows of the main block, so recently installed, removed and replaced with stone transoms.

Since the time of Thomas Parker, Browsholme has changed little, apart from essential modernisation and maintenance. The continuity is best illustrated by

Browsholme Hall: Portraits of members of the Parker family by Arthur Devis. Robert Parker (shown on the left) was a member of the Alkincoates branch of the family and, after an education at Cambridge and training as a doctor, lived at the family house. From there he pursued for seven years a passionate courtship of his cousin, Elizabeth – 'Parky' as he affectionately called her – to whom he was eventually married in 1751. Her portrait is shown above.

Edward Parker (on the right) was the brother of Elizabeth and did not favour her marriage. His dress in boots and spurs, his tilted hat and the riding crop he carries all symbolise his sporting interests. He married Barbara Fleming and he appears with her in another Devis painting.

a comparison of the watercolour of the great hall painted by John Buckler in 1807 and the room itself today; even the buff-coat of Captain Whittingham, killed at the battle of Newbury in 1643, hangs where it did in 1807.

A visit to Browsholme has several specially rewarding features. The house, though not architecturally outstanding, is well proportioned and its pink sandstone radiates a feeling of warmth. Apart from the bizarre flourish of the porch it gives an impression of strength, stability and solid down-to-earth respectability. Its setting in the beautiful countryside of Bowland adds to its charms, especially when the house is seen through the gothic arches of the lodge added in 1806 by Thomas Lister Parker. The house gives the visitor a feeling that it is not a show place but a home, one inhabited by the same family for over five hundred years, and this feeling is strengthened by the fact that visitors are shown round not by some impersonal guide, regurgitating a remembered litany, but by a member of the family to whom the builders and occupants are not just names but distant ancestors. As one walks through Browsholme there are constant reminders of its forest past and the way in which the house, the family and the area around it reflect the very origins of Lancashire.

CHAPTER 2

Whalley Abbey and Monasticism in Lancashire

I N MOST PEOPLE'S MINDS the mention of a medieval monastery conjures up one of two pictures. The tall elms, filled with cawing rooks, shade the mellow stone work of the cloisters in which monks stroll sedately, their minds set on higher things and lost in contemplation. The sound of plainsong drifts on the evening air, a bell tolls melodiously and the brothers are using their superlative craftsmanship and infinite patience to produce sumptuously illuminated books and manuscripts. All is calm, holiness and peace. The other picture is of fat, red-faced, jolly monks sitting round the refectory table on which are heaped good food and plentiful supplies of wine and strong ale. The implication is that though these indulgences are infringements of the monastic rule, the brothers are so happy and gaze at us with such obvious enjoyment that one can only be tolerant and overlook their little lapses.

Like most popular misconceptions there is perhaps an element of truth in both these pictures, but what they do not reveal is the central place played in the life of the Middle Ages by the monasteries and the widespread ramifications of an abbey's influence, not only in the religious but also in the secular life of its district.

The monasteries came late to Lancashire and, due to the poverty of the county and the absence of wealthy patrons, they never became as dominant in its affairs as they did in other places: they tended to remain among the smallest and least important houses of their Orders. The first monastic foundation in the county was at Lancaster in 1094, when Roger of Poitou established a daughter house of the Abbey of Séez in Normandy. This eventually found itself the victim of the Act of 1414 by which the lands of foreign monasteries were transferred to the Crown. Those of Lancaster were given to the nunnery founded by Henry V at Syon and the Priory fell into disuse, except as a parish church. During the twelfth century the Benedictine priories of Evesham and Durham inherited lands in Lancashire and each founded a small house on their new estates. These were at Penwortham and Lytham respectively. In 1319 another small Benedictine house was established at Upholland. The Orders of Canons, though not originally intended as monastic organisations but as communities of priests serving a single church became, in all but name monastic orders which followed a rule based on that of St Benedict. The Augustinians

Cartmel Priory Church. Of this Augustinian priory founded in 1188 there are only fragmentary remains of the conventual buildings. The church survives to give an impression of its original magnificence. At the time of the Dissolution of the Monasteries the church was spared because it was also the parish church of the area. The striking angled upper stage of the tower was added in the fifteenth century and carried a beacon to guide travellers benighted on the sands of Morecambe Bay.

PHOTOGRAPH, AUTHOR

Whalley Abbey House from the abbey ruins. The remains of the abbey church and cloister can be seen in the foreground. The west wing of the house is part of the building constructed by the Asshetons, but there are two clearly marked sections of this wall of the house, the southern half being the older. This originally contained the kitchens of Abbot Paslew – three massive stone-arched fireplaces survive. During the Assheton rebuilding a long gallery was constructed over the kitchen; of this only the large, square, double-transomed windows survive.

PHOTOGRAPH COURTESY OF THE WALLEY ABBEY MANAGEMENT

seem to have found Lancashire a congenial area, perhaps because the paucity of existing religious houses ensured that land was freely available without conflict with some neighbouring establishment. This Order founded four houses in the county, at Burscough, Conishead, Cockerham and Cartmel. Of these the last became the largest and most successful. The Priory church, largely rebuilt in the fifteenth century and refurbished in the seventeenth is probably the most beautiful of the parish churches of the historic county of Lancashire. In 1189 the Order of Premonstratensian Canons founded a house on the windswept marshes at Cockersand. Today only the lonely but beautiful chapter house remains on the edge of the Lune estuary. The same Order also had a small house at Hornby. The other minor monastery in the county was a tiny, Cluniac cell at Kersal which had been established by the Nottinghamshire priory of Lenton. In addition to the houses of the 'Regular Orders' the orders of friars also established houses in Lancashire. In contrast to those of the other orders the friars chose urban sites for their houses. The Franciscans built at Preston, the Dominicans at Lancaster and Warrington was chosen by the Augustinians or Austin Friars.

The only two houses of any size or consequence in the county belonged to the Cistercian Order who, in their desire to live the life prescribed by St Bernard based on the Rule of St Benedict, shunned populous districts and built their monasteries in the most remote places, far from the distractions of the world. Their largest house in Lancashire was the Abbey of Furness. Founded originally by the Savignac Order, it became a Cistercian establishment in 1147, some twenty years after its foundation. The abbey owned or controlled large areas of Furness and Cartmel, and much of its income was derived from the export of wool and from the iron mining and processing that went on on its various estates. The blooms, as the semi refined lumps of iron were known, were sent out by sea from the abbey's fortified harbour on the Piel of Foudray, off the coast of the modern town of Barrow. The abbot also had an important part to play in the defence of the North against Scots' incursion, and in 1537 was deemed to be capable of turning out 850 armed horse and foot from its extensive properties.

Though at most of these sites some evidence of the former monastic buildings can be seen, and at Furness extensive remains of the conventual buildings and the church survive, these do not qualify for inclusion in this work. At only two of the Lancashire abbeys, Whalley and Furness, were the buildings, after the Dissolution, converted into dwelling houses which brings them within the compass of this study. The house at Whalley is now used by the diocese of Blackburn as a conference centre and retreat house but is sometimes open to public access, while the monastic ruins can be visited at most times.

Whalley Abbey had its origins in 1175 but not at its present site. The original house was founded by John de Lacy, Baron of Halton, and Constable of Chester Castle.

His motives in making the foundation were probably very mixed. Undoubtedly, men of this period were driven by a deep and genuine piety. Additionally, creation of a monastery was a substantial donation to the Church, it would count to the credit of its founder at the Last Judgement, it would ensure continuous prayers for his soul's well-being, and those of his family and descendants, and a livelihood might be open to any members of the family who were prepared to take their vows. It could also provide a refuge. It was not unusual for ageing noblemen, when life became too much for them, to hand their estates to their heir and to enter a monastery.

He gave to the Order a site at Stanlaw on the Cheshire side of the Mersey estuary and extensive estates, mainly in Cheshire, for its maintenance. The house built at Stanlaw proved unsatisfactory, often flooded and extremely cold so that life became too difficult even for the hardy monks. Later members of the de Lacy family had given the monks further lands from their extensive Lancashire estates in the Honour of Clitheroe, and by the end of the thirteenth century the monks were seeking permission to move to this more congenial area. Henry de Lacy agreed to the move in 1283 and added to the endowments of the monastery the appropriation of the parish church of Whalley, with the possibility that the attached glebe land would provide a site for their new premises. However, it was not until 1296 that the first party of twenty monks, led by Abbot Gregory of Norbury, arrived at Whalley. An unfortunate party of five monks was left at Stanlaw, which was retained as a cell and grange until the Dissolution of the Monasteries.

Whalley was one of the first of the larger monasteries to be dissolved and its property dispersed by King Henry VIII: the abbot, John Paslew, having been involved in the abortive protest against the closure of the lesser monastic houses in 1536. The Pilgrimage of Grace, which had originated in the North of England, found strong support in north Lancashire. On 12 October 1536 the 'Pilgrims' of the rebel army had re-established the monks at nearby Sallee or Sawley Abbey and a few days later took over Conishead Priory and restored the monks who had been turned out a few weeks earlier. Burnley and Colne were occupied by a force of rebels under Sir Stephen Hammerton and a larger force of several hundred men commanded by Nicholas Tempest, of Bashall Hall, marched on Whalley, took over the town and demanded that Paslew and the Whalley monks should join the insurrection. Paslew was at first reluctant to throw in his lot with the Pilgrims, though this unwillingness may have been feigned for political purposes so that he could claim 'force majeur'. Tempest was well known to Paslew as he served the abbey as Deputy Steward for Blackburn and Accrington and was well aware of the abbot's real sympathy for the aims of the rebels. Eventually Paslew and eight monks took the Pilgrim's Oath, even though Paslew knew that the county's forces under Lord Derby were approaching. Conflict was avoided when the main body of the Pilgrimage, under Robert Aske, entered into negotiations. Having achieved peace the King went back on his undertakings and the leaders of the rebels, including Paslew and his monks were rounded up and put on trial. Commissioners were sent to close the two major Lancashire monasteries which had supported the Pilgrimage, Whalley and Furness, and these were dissolved in April 1537.

On the dispersal of the abbey's property much of its land passed into the hands of John Braddyll of Brockhall, who had been acting as Bailiff of the lands during the process of dissolution, and to Richard Assheton of Lever near Bolton. Assheton was a wealthy lawyer and had bought the Manor of Downham and other extensive properties in the area. In the division of the spoils between the two men, Assheton was given the actual site and buildings of the abbey. Here he began to build a new house, incorporating some of the former monastic buildings (notably the abbot's house) and using stone and other material taken from the monastery.

Today, the exterior of the house gives an overall impression of being Elizabethan-cum-Jacobean and parts of it, notably the porch with its steps and columns, do indeed date from this time. So do some of the windows on the east range, with their double transoms, but according to Nikolaus Pevsner much of the surrounding masonry is much older and may even predate the building of the abbey. At its southern end are the ruins of a medieval chapel which, it is suggested, may have been part of the house of Peter of Chester, the last rector of Whalley before the arrival of the monks. It was his long awaited death which cleared the way for the monks to move from Stanlaw and take up residence at Whalley. On the north side of the house, almost hidden by the later work, is a thirteenth-century doorway and there is a vaulted undercroft. In the 1840s the possession of the house passed to a wealthy textile manufacturer named Hargreaves, who made extensive refurbishments and 'improvements' to it: as a result, most of the interior shows few signs of the

Whalley Abbey House from the courtyard. The architectural history of this house is complicated. Pevsner suggests that the oldest parts of the building pre-date the building of the abbey and gives a thirteenth-century date to the eastern wall and the remains of the chapel. The square Elizabethan windows were inserted by the Asshetons when this wing was redeveloped. The north front contains medieval masonry and a fine door gives access to a vaulted undercroft; much of this wall was refaced and refurbished about 1840. The two wings and the porch with their characteristic dutch gables and blind oval decorations date from the late seventeenth century.

past but many signs of the Victorian conception of how a medieval house would have looked. Visitors to the abbey should certainly not ignore the house, which provides an interesting architectural puzzle and a good example of a late Tudor residence.

Preserved in the grounds are those monastic ruins that survived the robbing of materials to build the house, and the depredations of later years. Today they give a clear picture of the layout and appearance of the conventual buildings in the last days of the Monastery.

The entire area of the abbey, which was much more extensive than the portion that we see today, was enclosed in a stone wall with crenellations. The purpose of the wall was not, as is popularly imagined, to keep the monks in but to keep the world out. It also provided a defensive perimeter in a county which was still subject to periodic Scots raids: one of the most serious being in 1316 when the forces of Robert the Bruce ravaged much of Lancashire north of the Ribble and burned Preston. The curtilage of the abbey was pierced by the north-west or outer gate. This still stands astride the road some half a mile from the abbey itself. In style it is of the early fourteenth century and is the oldest standing portion of the abbey. Over the vaulted roadway tunnel and its smaller footway stood a dwelling and oratory for the Vicar of Whalley, the monk designated to serve the Parish Church. A small door outside the gate allowed him and his parishioners to have contact without having to enter the

Whalley Abbey: The Outer Gateway. This is the oldest building of the Abbey which survives, and dates from the early part of the fourteenth century. It opened into the outer court of the monastery, where the secular buildings and fishponds were located. The upper floor contained a room and oratory for the monk who served as Vicar of Whalley. A postern door and staircase gave him access to his parishioners. In the background can be seen the remarkable railway viaduct of 1850, built of some seven million bricks.

PHOTOGRAPH, AUTHOR

precincts of the abbey. It would have been at this gate that the Almoner distributed doles of bread and ale to travellers who sought refreshment.

Passing through the gate a traveller, who had asked for and been given overnight accommodation would have been within the outer court of the abbey. As well as the now vanished guest house this court was surrounded by the secular buildings of the abbey – the workshops, smithy, brew house, bakehouse and dairy – where the everyday work of the community went on, often carried out by the lay brothers and servants. Also in this outer quadrangle were found the stew ponds, in which living fish from the abbey's fisheries on the Calder and the Ribble were kept ready for use. Today, unfortunately, no trace remains of the buildings in the abbey's outer ward.

The inner part of the abbey was entered through the north-east gate. This is still the main entrance to the abbey ruins and remains as a vivid reminder of the splendid buildings that have been lost. It used to be thought that it was part of the building programme of Abbot Paslew, but its construction is now dated to about 1480. It reflects the style of the period, with its crenellated parapet and angled buttresses. The door tunnel divides in two to give vehicular and pedestrian entrance and the porter's lodge is still intact. Harrison Ainsworth created the popular legend that this gateway provided a sumptuous scaffold for the hanging of Paslew. In fact we know that he met his fate on Lancaster Moor, but Ainsworth perhaps had in mind the execution of the abbot of nearby Sawley Abbey. Lord Derby was ordered by the king to hang the offender 'On long pieces of timber ... out of the steeple'. No doubt Paslew, who was jealous of the prestige and rights of his community, rejoiced in the strength, solidity and defensive nature of the gatehouse. Apart from the utilitarian value of the defences, they would be seen as tangible evidence of the

Whalley Abbey, the Chapel of Peter de Chester. This is thought to have been the oratory of the Rector of Whalley before the arrival of the Cistercian monks in 1296. The two lancet windows date from the thirteenth century. Though usually described as the former Rectory, there are suggestions that it may, in fact, be the remnants of the original manor house.

importance and aristocratic nature both of the abbey and its abbot.

Today the gate leads us into an enclosure divided into two halves. To the left is a large courtyard, with the house on its south side, enclosed by buildings such as former stables, barns and coachhouses which are mainly of nineteenth-century date, though their walls incorporate many stones derived from the abbey. To the right a wall separates this entrance yard from the abbey ruins. The original despoilation of the abbey and the subsequent demolition carried out in the Restoration period, to enlarge the garden of the house, has left only partial walls and foundations but the plan of the monastery as it existed in its final years can easily be seen to follow the conventional plan.

The buildings are ranged around the central square of the cloister and the cloister garth. Of the cloister arcades nothing remains and we have no idea of their original appearance, but on the east side the inner walls remain standing to some considerable height. Originally the northern side of the cloister was closed off by the church, but this portion of the building has been razed more thoroughly than any other. Sufficient excavation has been carried out to show that it was a cruciform building of fourteen bays, about 260 feet (78 metres) long. It follows the usual plan of Cistercian churches in having a small sanctuary with an ambulatory which was used by the monks of the abbey, about thirty in number at the height of Whalley's fortunes. This was separated by a solid screen from the long nave which was the portion of the church used by the lay brothers and the local community. The church must have been a building of considerable splendour and magnificence. Enough of it remains to show that it was floored with tiles of an orange-red and slate-blue decorated with heraldic and other patterns in a creamy yellow slip. The stalls and misericords, which were transferred to and preserved in the parish church, show that the craftsmanship displayed in the furnishings was of a high order.

There was a central tower and among the additions made by Paslew was a Lady Chapel and a chapel dedicated to the 'martyred' Henry VI. This ineffectual monarch inspired considerable devotion in the North West, and doubtless some of the inhabitants of Whalley were aware that he had been finally captured by his enemies at Brungerley Hippings (or stepping stones) near Clitheroe. From there he was taken to imprisonment and murder in London. During the early sixteenth century unsuccessful attempts were made to have the unhappy king canonised. The work on these additions so impressed the people of Burnley that when, a few years later, they were rebuilding their chapel, it was ordered that the gargoyle waterspouts of Whalley were to be copied by the masons. It is a very significant point, one to which we will return, that even as late as the 1520s when, according to popular history, the monasteries were sunk into dissolute decline, there was at Whalley a sufficient interest, devotion and desire to add considerably to the extent of the buildings. This fact might suggest a more vigorous spiritual life than is usually supposed for monastic establishments at this time.

The south transept of the church connected with the buildings of the eastern range of the cloister. The buildings on this side of the quadrangle comprised, on the ground floor, the sacristy where the vestments and communion vessels of the abbey were stored, a library, a wide passage way or slype leading through to the chapter house and the parlour where the monks could receive occasional

visits by members of their family. The whole of the first floor of this building was taken up by the dorter, or monks dormitory. When the abbey was in use this long room was probably subdivided by wooden partitions to provide cubicles in which the monks slept. At either end was a staircase. At the north end were the night stairs which gave direct access to the church via the south

above Fourteenth-century doorway. Typical of the difficulties in unravelling the complex building history of the Assheton house at Whalley is this doorway, which is surrounded by work which appears to be of the seventeenth and nineteenth centuries but which includes earlier masonry. This door leads into a vaulted undercroft, now used as a chapel.

PHOTOGRAPH COURTESY OF LEN FENDER

transept. These stairs were used when the monks were roused from their beds in order to attend the nocturnal services. At the other end of the dorter were the day stairs for access at other times.

The chapter house at Whalley was an octagonal building with a tiled floor. If it matched the standard of the entrance passage it must have been a very handsome building. The slype is entered through a door in the Decorated style ornamented by crockets and fleurons. It is flanked by windows of two lights with a central shaft, which are marred by loss of their tracery. The chapter house was the daily meeting place of the monks, when a chapter of the Rule was read (hence the name), business was discussed and decisions made about the running of the abbey and its estates. Here also those monks who had offended against the 'Rule' were disciplined.

The southern range of the cloister was made up of the now vanished refectory and kitchen building. Apart from a few fragmentary remains the most visible part of this block is the cloister wall. Originally the refectory would have appeared like a typical medieval great hall but with the addition of a wall-mounted pulpit from which readings would be given during the meals, which otherwise would have been taken in silence. The exterior of the refectory at Whalley gives us an interesting reminder that in the monasteries there survived in the Middle Ages something of the Roman world's obsession with plumbing: most monastic houses had provision of running water and flushed sanitation at a time when secular houses had none of these facilities. On the refectory wall is a large arched recess in the masonry. In this can be seen the battered remains of a stone trough. Originally a constant stream of fresh water would have poured through the trough, which was used by the monks to wash before meals.

Monks were so keen to have a good water supply that they would carry out very elaborate works to ensure this. At Chester, for example, water was carried from Christleton by an aqueduct of lead and earthenware pipes to a conduit in the cloisters of the abbey.

No such construction was necessary at Whalley, with its riverside site. A weir on the Calder, east of Whalley Bridge, provided a head of water that was diverted along a culvert, firstly to drive the abbey mill, which still stands in an alley way in the village. The culvert then passed through the abbot's kitchen. At some point water was diverted into smaller channels and probably pipes to carry, it to the kitchens and to other places where it would be needed throughout the buildings. It then passed through the extremely elaborate lavatories, coyly dubbed the 'rere dorter' by Victorian antiquaries. The example at Whalley, where stone cubicles were corbelled out over the stream, is one of the most complete to survive. The culvert then re-entered the river some way downstream from the abbey.

The best preserved building at Whalley actually lies outside the area open to the public. The western range of the cloister was made up of the lay brothers' dormitory and a store room or *cellarium*. This building still stands to its full height and is roofed. Though now in a bad state of repair, and not open to the public, the view from the cloister gives a good idea of the original appearance of the abbey. The lay brothers, whose accommodation was on the upper floor, were those members of the community who followed the Rule of the house and lived a monastic life, but who lacked the educational qualifications to be

The Lay brothers' dormitory and Cellarium. This is the only remaining part of the Abbey which stands to its full height; it lies outside the areas open to the public. This western range appears to be of the fifteenth century and had a dual use. On the upper floor was the sleeping acommodation for the Lay Brothers while the ground floor was used for storage. The wall facing into the cloister would have supported the pent house roof which surrounded the central open area of the cloister.

PHOTOGRAPH, AUTHOR

Whalley Abbey, the parish church of St Mary and All Saints. This ancient church probably began as a Minster church in Saxon times and the presence of three pre-Conquest crosses in the churchyard would seem to confirm this. Fragments of Norman work still survive in a church which mostly displays the Early English style. The furnishings of the church are remarkable and include two unusual family pews, a chained library and a Roman altar.

PHOTOGRAPH, AUTHOR

ordained and to take the monastic vows. They provided many of the craftsmen and manual workers of the abbey.

Before the closure and demolition of the abbey there were two other major portions of the building. The site of the infirmary is completely lost. It would have provided a home for sick monks or those who were considered too old and frail for the rigours of the life. In the infirmary they had more warmth and comfort, and the advantage of good medical treatment. Part of the abbey's charitable work was the maintenance of twenty-four old and infirm men from the community, and they would undoubtedly have had close acquaintance with the infirmary. It would have been like a miniature version of the abbey with its own chapel and cloister.

The other block of buildings separate from the main block were the abbot's lodgings. Little trace remains of these, and it is certain that parts were incorporated into the Assheton house. For example the extensive kitchen wing, where the huge fireplaces remain, was incorporated into the later building and the long gallery extended over it. The foundations of the great hall of the abbot's house and the remains of its spiral staircase can also be seen. The abbot lived in some state, but this was justified on the grounds that he was not only the head of the community but also a great feudal magnate, who might find it necessary to entertain noble or even royal guests: it was important for him to be seen to live and entertain in an appropriate style.

Stones and ruins do not give any sort of picture of the abbey at its height,

Remains of Chapter House and the eastern range of the cloister. The eastern range of the cloister contained the warming room and the library, whose traceried, square-headed window can be seen. In the foreground are the remains of the Chapter House, of which nothing survives except some fragments of the tiled floor. At Whalley the Chapter House seems to have been octagonal in shape rather than rectangular, the customary Cistercian practice.

PHOTOGRAPH COURTESY OF THE WHALLEY ABBEY MANAGEMENT

The barn, Altcar Grange. Given to Whalley Abbey in 1238 by William Blundell of Ince, the Altcar lands included a mill. After the Dissolution the Grange became the house of a branch of the Mollineux family, but they maintained its connection with the church and the large barn, built c.1550, was used as a Catholic chapel. The fragments of masonry in the footing of the wall are relics of the monastic buildings.

PHOTOGRAPH, AUTHOR

when these buildings were filled with bustling life. Nor do they give one any idea of the many activities of the abbey and its multifarious interests, not only in Whalley but all over the North West. We can begin to put some flesh on the stone skeleton of Whalley by an examination of the written records which still exist. Particularly useful for this purpose are the bursar's accounts surviving from the end of the fifteenth century (1478) and from the last years of the monastery in 1520 and 1521. The fact that three sets of accounts survive, relatively close in date, is useful in allowing a comparison to be made and trends detected. A further view of the abbey in its final days is given by the inventory and valuation carried out at the time of the Dissolution by the King's Commissioners. It is not clear whether in every case the accounts represent actual expenditure, or if they are more in the nature of a statement of predicted spending, but this is of little importance for our purposes.

Even a cursory glance at the accounts shows that vital to the finances of the

House was its position as a landowner. In some cases its lands were part of the original endowment of the monastery from the de Lacy family. Others were gifts given by later patrons, often in the hope of buying salvation. The abbey owned some thirty-nine secular estates, which brought in rents and profits varying from the £24 11s. 11d. from their lands in Rochdale to the 3s. 4d. from the mill at Croptrod in Spotland, also in Rochdale parish. This was one of the five mills owned by the abbey: the most valuable was at Acton in Cheshire, which brought in an annual income of £1 6s. 8d. When the abbey owned a mill the local population might be required to use it, and to pay for the privilege by donating a portion of their flour. This flour, and perhaps grain as well might be stored in an adjoining barn like the one at Staining near Poulton: the barn was valued at 1s. and the mill at £1. Other benefits of a miscellaneous nature brought in by the lands of the abbey were fisheries on the River Weaver at Acton, producing an income of £1 10s. 0d. and, in the same place, the right of turbary (to dig peat for fuel) was valued at £1 0s. 0d.

In earlier times these outlying lands were usually cultivated by the abbey, which would have sent lay brothers to run its farms. The brothers would have worked under the supervision of one or two monks. The centre of such an estate was known as a 'grange' and comprised a house with barns and storage buildings. Whalley established granges at Stanlaw, Staining and at Altcar. The latter was on land given by William Blundell of Ince and the gift included a mill, but this seems to have disappeared by the 1520s. Remains of the Alt Grange survive in a house of that name located within the Ministry of Defence

training area. These remains include a very substantial brick built barn with a queen post trussed roof of which some of the purlins are rough hewn tree trunks. This barn is dated to about 1550 but the walls include fragments of masonry which are presumably derived from the original buildings. By the sixteenth century these outlying lands were usually let to tenants.

However, the most important source of income for the abbey was not these lands, which produced a combined revenue of £281 1s. 2d. in 1520, and £281 7s. 10d. in 1521, but its ecclesiastical patronage of some of the most valuable parishes in Lancashire. It was the gift of the advowson of Whalley which had inspired the move from Stanlaw: this entitled the abbey to appoint the vicar of Whalley and to take the tithes of the parish. One of the monks could be appointed to serve the parish church and apart from a few minor running expenses the revenue of the parish could be diverted to the abbey. By 1520 this amounted to £224 15s. 3d. The abbey had also acquired the advowsons of Blackburn parish, and of Eccles (which then included the later parish of Deane). They had also gained the living of Rochdale parish. Thus it drew the income from four of the largest and most lucrative of all the Lancashire parishes. In 1520 Rochdale brought in £104 16s. 10d., Blackburn £132 1s. 0d., while Eccles contributed £120 0s. 0d., a total revenue of £581 12s. 3d. This income varied slightly: in 1521 it amounted to £592 3s. 1d. due to slight increases in the tithes of Whalley and Rochdale. Tithe income did not always prove easy to collect; five men of Marsden refused to pay tithes on corn and hay and it took a two year battle in the ecclesiastical courts between 1532 and 1534 to obtain the money.

Remains of the abbey church. The excavated remains of the church extend to the modern boundary wall, beyond which were two further bays. The two transepts are visible and contain the excavated remains of medieval tombs, including one of the de Lacy family. At the crossing was a bell tower, supported on the massive piers whose bases remain. A stone screen or pulpitum divided the eastern portion of the church used by the monks from the nave used by the lay brothers, townspeople and visitors.

PHOTOGRAPH, AUTHOR

If the lands and ecclesiastical patronage brought in the greater part of the abbey's income, it also received money from a bewildering number of sources which are listed in the accounts as *De Perquisites* (From Profits). They include 1s. 4d. from the offertory box in the Chapel of Our Lady and the Blessed King Henry: if King Henry VI was popular in the North West his memory does not seem to have been a money spinner in the area! The monks let winter and summer pasture on their lands to local farmers (*agistment* as it was called) and this brought in £3 4s. 0d. They were able to sell the lees – the dregs – of their wine and beer for £1 13s. 4d. More income was generated by activities with an agricultural base. The abbey had a tannery, and leather surplus to its requirements was sold to bring in £3 6s. 8d., with a further £4 10s. 0d. coming from the sale of extra hides and 5s. from selling tan bark. The management of the estates and enterprises was delegated to lay stewards. These men were drawn from the local gentry, a fact which tied the well-being of the Abbey to the interests of the local elite. In some way which was not made clear by the form of the accounts the monks seem to have made a profit on the daily running of the abbey. A surplus is recorded in the accounts of the cellarer and the sub-cellarer (the monks responsible for the provisioning of the abbey), on the account of the vicar of Whalley and on his budget for the purchase of bread and wine. It may be that these represent underspending of previously apportioned amounts, or the surplus may result from the sale of stock. However it was achieved, these items contributed a valuable £10 18s. 4d. to the revenue.

The absence of weathering on this arch, compared with its exterior counterpart (see p. 36) shows that it has always been in the interior of the building. It dates from the fourteenth century. The size of the stones used in the voussoirs of the arch are very remarkable, and must reflect the easy availability of good building stone in the area.

As a feudal landlord the abbey was entitled to various incomes from its estates apart from rents. We have already seen how the mills were a valuable source of revenue. The abbey also received fines levied in the manorial courts in those places where it held the lordship of the manor: this source contributed 13s. 4d. in 1520. As the overlord of several manors, the abbey was entitled to receive heriots, a custom whereby a landlord, on the death of a tenant, was permitted to claim either his best beast or any chattel of the deceased man. In 1520 both Peter Dunblayn and Thomas Cole had made such involuntary contributions to the abbey, worth 16s. and 16s. 8d. respectively. An unusual and unexpected source of income in both 1520 and 1521 came from the estates of Robert Cunliffe. He was a 'gentleman' from Wilpshire who was held responsible for the murder of Elias Wood of Dinckley. In 1514 he had been outlawed and his lands were forfeited to the abbey: they produced a revenue of 14s. 8d. in 1520 but by the following year the income from them had declined to 4s 8d.

From all these and from other sources the abbey enjoyed an annual income of around £900: £895 14s. 6d. in 1520 and £908 2s. 9d. in 1521. This income, though adequate, was well below that enjoyed by the richer houses in the country. However, one might well ask how it was that the monks whose life was supposed to be one of frugality and asceticism spent an income which in modern terms represented several million pounds each year. In many ways the expenditure side of the accounts gives the best insight into the life of the monastery. We find, for example, that in 1520 they were £64 15s. 6d. overspent. Some of the items of expenditure, such as £2 4s. od. paid to the minstrels and 10s. paid to the bearward (the man who led a performing bear), might suggest that the picture of the lax, luxurious and corrupt life in the monastic houses at this time may very well be an accurate picture of Whalley. But we know from the support given to the monks by the local community during the Pilgrimage of Grace that the monasteries and the monks were personally popular and from this we might infer that they were regarded as living up to expectations. Therefore, it is worth examining these records to see if we can obtain a view of how the abbey at Whalley met its spiritual and temporal commitments.

We have seen how the abbey gained from its feudal landholdings, but the system also carried with it concomitant expenses. Except for the Crown, everybody had a landlord, and that was as true for the peasant farmer, such as Alice Morcel in Swinton who paid a rent of 3s. 4d. as it was for Abbot Paslew, who in turn had to pay rents to his feudal overlords. In earlier days this would have been in the form of military service, but now a cash payment was made. These ranged from the 14s. 1d. to the lord of Elland, for lands in the parish of Halifax to 2d. paid to the King for lands in Burnley. These rents accounted for an expenditure of £8 7s. 11d. An interesting item included in this category is the 2s. paid for suits of court and castle guards at the King's castle of Liverpool. As one of the great territorial magnates in the county the abbey was expected to contribute to the defence of the area.

Another drain on the abbey's resources is listed under the heading *In Donis* (In Gifts). The nature of the services which were rewarded are not recorded, but we know that many of the local landowning families performed various secular functions for the abbey. For example, Edward Stanley, 3rd Earl of Derby, was serving as the abbey's steward at the time of its dissolution; and the Towneley family of Towneley Hall had been secular officers of the abbey for several generations. So in the list of recipients of gifts we find many well-known local names – such as Thomas, Earl of Derby, Lord Mounteagle of Hornby, Talbot, Shireburne, Hesketh, Fairfax, Fleetwood, Standish and Starkie – alongside the names of such obscure men as William David, who received 6d. Some gifts were obviously intended to buy favours or services, or to give a means of access to their masters by 'sweetening' the servants of important men. The 10s. paid to the 'Servants of our Lord the King in the Wine Cellar' or the 13s. 4d. to the 'Servants of the Lord Bishop' fall into this category. Others seem to be gifts for a particular service, such as the 1s. 8d. paid to a servant of Lord Mounteagle: was he a messenger from Hornby? The messenger to 'Our Lord the King' was more generously rewarded, with 8s. 8d.

Another group of payments are to religious organisations and to individuals seeking help. The gift of 4s. to the four Orders of Friars seems paltry, but perhaps reflects the hostility between the the monastic orders and the itinerant friars. The 1s. 8d. paid to 'A monk of Louth' was probably a payment to a member of their own order who was either bringing a message or was on a journey. The 5s. sent to the monks of Citeaux must have been a donation, however stingy, to the mother house of the Cistercians.

Another group of payments included in this section of the accounts are what seem to have been bonuses paid to the abbey's own secular servants. The foresters got £1 10s. 8d., the bailiffs or farm managers, of Aston and Wirral 1s. each. In some cases the payments were for the professional services of outsiders: thus 'a Doctor of Lancaster' was paid 3s. 4d. and Doctor Adrian and the apothecary received 7s. In total forty-one payments of gifts were made at a cost of £27 1s. 7d.

It might be expected that, as a large landowner, the abbey would have found that it was able to supply most of its own needs and that there would have been little need to buy in everyday items. However, the accounts show that the monks bought many items and from a large number of sources, often quite distant; for example 7s. was spent on buying bread at Wakefield.

We can deduce a great deal about the diet of the monks from the accounts. The importance of bread is emphasised by the fact that a special section of the account is dedicated to the purchase of grain, mostly from outside the area. During 1520 this item totalled £282 17s. 6d., or roughly one third of the abbey's annual income. In 1521 the sum was reduced to £190 13s. 8d. and it may be that there was a dearth of corn in Lancashire in 1520 which had the effect of greatly increasing grain prices and thus the expenditure on this commodity. The consignments purchased included wheat, oats and barley, the latter being bought both as grain and as malt. Pease were also bought, eighteen shillings' worth in 1520. These pulses must have provided an important part of the monk's diet. It is apparent that the bread was made from wheat flour: 268 quarters were bought (of which only 4 quarters and 3 bushels were grown locally) at a cost of £169 8s. 4d. To supplement the bread £22-worth of butter and cheese was bought.

The Cistercian monks were required by their Rule to abstain from meat, and no general purchase of meat is recorded. If any was eaten it may have been supplied from the Abbey's own farms. However, in the section devoted to the needs of the abbot we find the purchase of beef to the value of £72 4s. 6d. recorded. This seems a huge amount, but it was not exceptional as in 1521 a very similar expenditure was made. In addition to this £11 16s. 8d. was spent on mutton, £8 13s. 10d. on veal, £2 1s. 6d. on pork, 17s. 2d. on sucking pigs, £1 1s. 7d. on lambs, £2 4s. 8d. on game and £37 8s. 10d. on fresh fish, for which the fishermen were paid £3 in wages: a total for the abbot's kitchen of £139 8s. 9d. This gives the incontrovertible impression that the abbot lived a life of extreme luxury. This is particularly so as it cannot be claimed that the year of 1520 was untypical, and that special purchases were being made: in the following year the bill was, in fact, slightly higher. It can be argued that as an important local figure the abbot was constantly required to entertain important visitors, and that this food was provided for their needs rather than his own. Perhaps this is the explanation for the previously mentioned payments to the minstrels and the man with the performing bear. Nevertheless the impression of comfort and luxury is clear.

Even if no meat was bought for the monks, there were certainly adequate supplies of fish, £34 was spent on this commodity. This was the expenditure on sea fish and there were probably fresh water fish used which do not appear in the accounts. The abbey bought red herrings of both cheap and good quality (these were cured by smoking). The white herrings which are mentioned were salted, as was the 'hard fish'–dried and salted cod or ling–which was bought. There were also purchases of unspecified salt fish and of salted salmon and eels. A sturgeon, the royal fish, cost 10s. It might be thought that this was destined for the abbot's table, but it is included in the list of items purchased as general provisions, and is by no means the only luxury item to appear in this section. A major item of expenditure for the preservation of both the meat and the fish was the twenty-five crannocks of salt bought each year – a crannock being a measure of about twenty-eight pounds. The source of supply was the coastal salt pans and the carriage cost the community £1 9s. 2d.

The medieval craving for spices is well known, and the monks were not exempt from it. The accounts contain a long list of spices and such foreign exotica as figs, currants and raisins. There are payments for pepper and saffron, for ginger and for sugar, for nutmeg and mace and cloves among others. Some idea of the extent of world patterns of trade ending at Whalley is given by the 10d. spent on the appropriately named Grains of Paradise. These were capsules of extract from the West African plant *Amomum Melguetta*, which was in use both as a spice and as a medicine. This may give a clue as to the reason for these purchases, which in general seem to have been bought in small quantities. Though they had a culinary use, they were also thought to have medicinal properties and were, perhaps, intended for the infirmary.

Although the abbey consumed large quantities of wine, this must not be seen as an indication of undue debauchery for at the time wine was commonly drunk. In 1520 £31 5s. 0d. was spent on wine and a further £4 1s. 8d. on sweet wine. We know that at this time at Durham Abbey wine cost between £1 10s. 0d. and £2 per hogshead (54 gallons). If a similar price obtained at Whalley it puts the abbey's consumption at somewhere between 1,000 and 1,500 gallons a year. If we assume a total population of the abbey including monks, lay brothers and servants of 100, at the higher cost figure it gives an annual consumption of 15 gallons, about a third of a pint per man per day, hardly excessive. In addition to wine large quantities of beer would have been brewed but no estimate of the quantity can be made as only the malt purchased appears in the accounts.

In theory, the clothing of the monks belonged to the Order and not to the individual, but it seems that at this time each monk was paid an annual sum for the upkeep of his wardrobe. There seems no other explanation of the identical payment of £47 6s. 8d. 'To the convent for their habits' made in the years for which we have accounts. The abbot in 1520 was paid £5 for his habit but there is no entry in the following year. At least some of the habits and possibly vestments were made on the premises, as items for the purchase of linen and woollen cloth, and black and white thread were entered and the sewing woman was paid 2s. Other garments were bought: £17 was spent on garments for the servants and 13s. on shoes for the poor.

As well as these domestic details we can deduce from the accounts a great deal about the every-day mechanics of running the abbey. We know, for example, that the monks kept horses, though whether these were saddle or pack animals we cannot tell, as the entries are ambiguous. 'For looking after the horses'; 'For horses' nails'; for horses' girlses'; 'For saddles and that sort of thing'; 'For halters, bridles and ropes'. Perhaps the last item might be thought to suggest pack animals. On the other hand, we know that during the course of a year members of the community travelled quite widely, in many cases to visit distant parts of their estates. A whole section of the accounts is devoted to these journeys. They include visits to Hornby, Lathom, Chester, Acton, Hull and Warrington. The most splendid journey of 1520 was that of Abbot Paslew to London, which cost £26 5s. 0d. No doubt he had travelled with a considerable entourage, as Paslew was always anxious to impress the world with the dignity of Whalley. Some idea of the difference in the state held by the abbot and the other members of the community can be realised by the fact that a journey by the abbot to visit Lord Mounteagle at Hornby cost £1. Christopher Smith, the prior, whose grave is to be seen in Whalley parish church, did the same journey for 10s. 6d. and the journey of Lawrence Forest, the receiver of the rector of Whalley, to Hornby cost a mere 2s. As travellers themselves the Monks tried to help others on the road and spent 10s. on Stanlaw bridge and 2s. on a bridge at Bury.

While some of the monks or their secular agents were traversing the county others were occupied with the maintenance and repair of the large building complex in which they all dwelt. In the accounts we can find references to the purchase of materials for this constant building programme. Single and double nails, stonebrodes (the nails used for fixing slates), strebrodes (the pegs used for fixing thatch), slatestones, bitumen, lime resin and canvas were all bought and used in the repair of the buildings. In 1520 £3 was spent on the carriage of stone. This stone may have been needed for the work being carried out on the Church, which cost an additional £22. It was at this time that Paslew was building the Lady Chapel and this item, with the £23 spent the following year 'On the fabric of the Church', may record this new construction. The supervision of this work was by the master of the works, who was paid 3s. 4d. The same amount of money was paid to the keeper of the clock and the keeper of the chimes. Heating in the monastic buildings was restricted to the one fire in the warming room, but there would be others in the kitchens, the abbot's lodging and the infirmary. The main fuel for all these fires would have been wood from the abbey's lands. The forester was Edward Fish, who was paid

2s. 4d. There is no mention of the purchase or carriage of turf in the accounts, though one would expect it to have been used. The item '*Pro carbonibus marini*' refers to sea coal, or coal in the modern sense, and not to charcoal which was often so described in the Middle Ages. It is an interesting illustration of the early use of coal, which presumably came from the Burnley area, the nearest source of supply. There is an item of 10s. for the carriage of fuel, which may refer to the transport costs of the coal. The Whalley accounts are an interesting confirmation of the early use of coal for domestic heating.

The accounts, while fascinating in themselves and in the insights they give into monastic life, do not apparently tell us much about the way in which the monks were fulfilling their spiritual functions. A more careful examination, however, does give some indication that they were not sunk in the lethargy and debauchery of which they were accused. To some extent it is likely that the Cistercian system of accounting tends to obscure some of their work. In the Benedictine houses the accounts are much more specific and allow a more accurate judgement to be made. For example, according to the accounts, the monks of Whalley only spent a total of £2 11s. 0d. on gifts to the poor and the distribution of thirteen pairs of shoes to paupers. This amount seems so trivial that it might be seen as indicative of the charge laid against the monks, that they failed to fulfil their charitable commitments. However, we know that by the terms of their foundation the monks were to maintain twenty-four aged and infirm men, and the expenses of this are simply absorbed in the general costs of the abbey. Much the same applies to the regular donating of alms of food, drink and clothing. The Valor prepared at the Dissolution, which might be thought to be a hostile source, puts the annual expenditure on charity at £120 and Canon Knowles, the great historian of the English monastic movement, considers that in general the *Valor Ecclesiasticus* undervalues by two or three times the charitable outlay of the monasteries. If this is the case at Whalley, and we can therefore multiply the figure of the *Valor* by three, we get an annual expenditure on charity to the poor of over £300 or about one third of the income of the abbey. In contrast, Fountains gave only 1.7 per cent of its income to charity, Westminster Abbey 2.7 per cent and Chester 1.3 per cent. These figures puts things in a very different light, and may help to explain the popular esteem in which the monasteries of Lancashire seem to have been held.

Another activity traditional on the part of the monastic houses was the provision of education. There is some evidence that the monks of Whalley ran a school, either in the abbey or in the parish church, but its existence is not indicated by either the accounts or the *Valor*. One might suppose that the purchase of paper and materials for making ink might have been for a school, but they might equally have been for use in the abbey. However, Whalley did contribute to education, making an annual payment of £2 to St Bernard's College, Oxford: this was the Cistercian college within the University. In addition they made a payment to support a student at the University in the form of a bursary. In 1520 they paid him £5 and in the following year an additional £9 6s. 8d. for the graduation fees for his bachelor's degree. Just before its suppression one of the graduates sponsored by the abbey was ordained as vicar of Whalley

One of the most damaging accusations made against the monks at the time of the Reformation was that, in the monasteries, the few men who were still prepared to enter the religious life ignored the rule and lived in luxury and licentiousness. It is impossible to make a judgement about this from a set of accounts whose evidence can, as we have seen, be ambiguous. Perhaps the clearest indication comes from the dietary information that we can extract. It seems that for the ordinary monks and lay brothers the food at Whalley may have been very adequate if not lavish. Bread, the staple, was made from wheat, most of which was purchased rather than being garnered from the abbey's own lands. This is not necessarily a sign of inattention on the part of the estate managers. Wheat bread was of a superior quality to the oat cakes which were the food of the ordinary folk but it was not a great indulgence. Wheat was purchased because it was probably realised that the local climate was unsuitable for its cultivation and it may well have been more economical to lease the land and use the profits to buy in supplies. The items such as spices and imported luxury goods, like rice and olive oil, only appear to have been bought in very small quantities, a few shillings' worth at a time, and were probably mainly intended for use in the infirmary.

If an accusation of luxurious living, beyond the limits imposed by the Rule, is to be made it might perhaps be directed at Abbot Paslew. We have seen the apparently profligate spending made on his behalf in the purchase of meat – something over an eighth of the total expenditure. It has already been pointed out that Paslew would be required to provide entertainment on a lavish scale, and this was in an age when a man's status in society and his importance tended to be assessed by his degree of conspicuous consumption. The Abbot of Whalley was a very considerable man in the county community of the period and in the extent of the lands that he controlled. The influence he could wield was perhaps more important than any other landlord in Lancashire with the exception of Lord Derby. Paslew by nature was a man who wished to make his influence felt, and was very conscious of the dignity of the Abbot of Whalley. In order to do this he had to play the part of the lavish host and generous entertainer. Yet it was, of course, possible that this public display concealed a private simplicity of life. This latter impression is supported by the details of the furnishings of Paslew's own quarters as described in the inventory. 'The Abbot's Dining Chamber: There 1 cupboard, 1 dozen of old cushions of verdure (a quilted material with a pattern of foliage), a long settle, 2 chairs, 3 carpets, a hanging candlestick in the midst of the room'. This does not sound a particularly elaborate room even by the simpler standards of the day, and his parlour was a room that might be used by his guests. His bedchamber – 'there his own bed, 1 mattress with blankets and a little covering' – sounds suitably ascetic.

The accounts, taken by and large, give a picture of a community which was prosperous, and in which the standard of living was reasonably comfortable, but there is no evidence of any undue lavishness. It seems that the monks were making substantial donations to charity and were involved in other good works in connection with education and the repair of bridges – a traditional role of the monastic communities.

Another accusation made at the time, and repeated ever since, was that the monasteries were finding it increasingly difficult to recruit novices and that in many cases the community consisted of a handful of monks, attended by large numbers of servants. This may have been true in some houses: for example, the priory of the Augustinians at Burscough had only five canons who were served by twenty-three servants. Another accusation frequently made – that the monks were guilty of sexual misconduct – seems to have been based on the survey carried out by Leigh and Leyton on the orders of Thomas Cromwell with the aim of justifying the closure of the monasteries. It is worth noting that very little criticism is made of Whalley in this report except rather wild and prurient accusations against the monks. For the houses of north Lancashire, including Whalley, the proportion of monks accused on these grounds is much lower than for those in the softer south of the county. At Whalley only Richard Wood, of the twenty-four monks in residence, was accused of misconduct. It might be suggested that in the harsher districts the monasteries had continued to fulfil the expectations of behaviour. To generalise on the state of monastic life based on Leyton and Leigh is rather like compiling an account of contemporary life only from the pages of the *News of the World*.

A positive indication of the health of the monastic communities in Lancashire comes from the evidence that they could recruit both regular and secular clergy. For the monasteries there are clear indications that the abbeys were able to maintain their complement of monks. Indeed there are some signs that they were actually increasing the size of their communities. At Upholland the complement of four monks in 1517 had increased to five by 1522, and at Burscough two additional canons had joined in the same period. Between 1508 and 1521 twenty-three new monks were ordained at Furness Abbey alone. Even in the last days of the monasteries new entrants to the religious life were coming forward: Whalley had ordinations in 1535 and 1536, Cartmel two ordinations in 1535 and Cockersand three.

It might be argued that it is not surprising that new entrants could be found for an existence that guaranteed food, shelter and a high degree of comfort for life, but the experience of poverty-stricken, bleak Cockersand gives the lie to that. This small Premonstratensian priory, in one of the most remote locations, was finding no difficulty in attracting novices. In 1388 there were thirteen canons in residence there, by 1488 this had increased to seventeen with two novices, four years later there were twenty canons and two more novices, and by the time of its Dissolution in 1536 there were twenty-three canons. The success of this priory in gaining recruits would seem to indicate that there were, in Lancashire, a number of men who could still be attracted to the monastic life at its hardest. The names of the ordinands suggests that they were, in the

Remains of the Chapter House of Cockersand Priory. Founded in 1190 by the Canons of the Premonstratensian order, the ruins of the abbey stand on the edge of bleak marsh, right on the mouth of the River Lune. This is all that now remains of a religious house which was successful until the time of the dissolution of the lesser monasteries in 1536. The Chapter House, the daily meeting place of the monks, is small and dates from c. 1230. Parts of the building were renovated in the early nineteenth century when it was used as a burial chapel of the Dalton family.

main, local men: it was not that the devout from the whole country were being attracted to the rigours of Cockersand. To judge from their ages at the time of the Dissolution, assuming they were ordained at the correct canonical age of twenty-four, they were young men. Five of the ten canons of Cartmel and eleven of those of Cockersand had taken their Orders in the previous ten years, nine in the previous five.

This is not to say that nationally there had not been a decline in the number of entrants to the monastic life, at least partially due to a disillusionment in society with the standard of life set by the monks. Rather, it is to suggest that this decline was less sharp in remote and rather backward Lancashire than it was in other parts of the country – and may even have been reversed.

To what extent does the picture of a declining standard of morality, adherence to the Rule, and a simple life apply to Whalley in the last days of the abbeys? As we have seen, in the diet and pastoral work of the Whalley monks there is little evidence of dereliction. Can we find any indication that they had made an unseemly pursuit of wealth a first priority? If this had been the case the inventory prepared by the king's agents in 1537 would surely have made ostentatious wealth plain for us to see. But in this, too, we can perhaps see some indication of the assiduity of the monks in carrying out their religious duties.

The inventory, prepared by the Earl of Sussex, William Leyland, Henry Farrington and the priest John Clayden, is a revealing document, though whether it fulfils the remark of its first editor, M. E. Walcott, writing in 1866 that 'The monks of Whalley had ... departed widely from the ascetic rule laid down by their ancients', is more doubtful. As a source it has the disadvantage that no actual values are given, and it may be rather like an estate agent's publicity material, setting out to make everything sound as impressive as possible. In the bursar's room, which was probably the abbey's strong room,

The parish church of St Mary, Whalley. The chancel of the parish church contains the magnificent set of carved oak stalls, dating from the early fifteenth century, rescued from the Abbey at the time of the Dissolution, though they found it was necessary to mutilate them to fit below the chancel roof. The stalls include a set of miserichords, described by Pevsner as 'one of the most rewarding in the country', which survived intact.

PHOTOGRAPH COURTESY OF B. & N. DIXON

various items of plate and precious metals are listed. There is 'A standing cup with a cover and an eagle on the top gilt', a 'ewer double gilt with a dragon upon the top', 'a basin parcel gilt' and many other objects – perhaps one of the most interesting being '2 nuts harnessed with silver gilt with two covers though one without a knoppe [knob]'. One wonders how two silver-gilt bound coconuts made into drinking cups ever found their way to distant Whalley.

On the other hand others among the objects listed, 'a little piece of silver', or '2 spoons broken and 1 whole', or 'another dozen spoons with ragged knoppes' do not seem to indicate great wealth. The inventory also provides us with a clue that some of these more valuable articles were not of the monks choosing but were gifts, perhaps unwanted, from wealthy patrons and visitors. Hence the 'Large standing pounced [decorated with a punched design] bowl with a cover, parcel gilt of my Lord Mounteagle's gift' or among the vestments there is 'The Cope Venice gold with my Lord Mounteagles arms' and another from the same source of cloth of gold. Perhaps the presence of a 'mitre of siver and gilt sett with saphires, emeralds and rubies with turquois and pearls' and another all of needlework reflect Paslew's ambition to have Whalley raised to the status of a mitred abbey. This honour, accorded to the largest and most influential monasteries, gave to the abbot equivalent rank to a bishop and the right to a place in the House of Lords. However, if the vestry next to the library contained these splendid robes it also had in it the 'old vestment of old blue copper tinsel' and 'the sixteen vestments of Dornyx [cloth from Doornix] and fustian that were daily used in the church'. It should also be remembered that many parish churches possessed vestments and vessels of precious metals, and therefore their presence at Whalley is not necessarily an indication of unseemly luxury.

How, then, can we assess the position and activity of Whalley Abbey at the time of its dissolution? We have found little conclusive evidence that the usual accusations about the wealth, and luxurious and unlicensed life of the monks is applicable. The services seem to have been carried out, the poor relieved, the bridges repaired, the scholars encouraged. Life was, perhaps, a little more comfortable than had been intended by St Bernard, but there is no evidence of out and out flouting of the Rule. Perhaps the main reason why the abbey had failed to attain an ideal condition was the generosity of others, by which it had become an extensive and important landowner in the North West, and from whom many rich gifts had come to sustain its life and to glorify the worship and enrich the hospitality that it offered. The fact that the community was active in building and extending the abbey, and that it was drawing in new members, is significant. Perhaps also the fact that on his death in 1523 Thomas Hesketh of Rufford felt that he could send to Whalley Abbey his 1,400 pounds' weight of gold and silver plate and all his wealth in coins, to be held in safe keeping for his son, is a good indication of the esteem in which the abbey was held and of the respect felt for the integrity of the monks.

The pressures that led to the closure of the monasteries in England were social, economic and political and only in part religious. Undoubtedly many in the Church were greedy and dissolute and paid scant regard to the standards expected of them. For them clerical status was merely a path to profitable employment. One of the most flagrant examples of this type of churchman makes a fleeting appearance in the accounts of Whalley: 'For a gift to the Lord Cardinal ... £22 0s. 0d.' Even in remote Whalley the overweaning pride and avarice of Thomas Wolsey had to be placated, though in the end such generosity was to bring the abbey little protection from the gathering storm.

CHAPTER 3

Sir Richard Shireburne of Stonyhurst and the Lancashire Recusants

THE DATE WAS 31 July in the year 1569. In the dining chamber of Lathom House the scene was set for one of the strangest events that was to take place there in its long history as the unofficial administrative capital of the county. The sumptuous room was filled with spectators, many of them gentlemen of the Earl of Derby's household; others were lawyers, clerics and neighbouring gentry who had come to witness the bizarre trial which was to take place. At the high table the court were preparing to take their places. In the centre sat Edward, third Earl of Derby; on his right was the Bishop of Chester, William Downham; and arranged on either side of them were Richard Shireburne of Stonyhurst, Edward Fitton of Gawsworth, Richard Assheton of Middleton, Edward Holland of Manchester, William Gerrard and Robert Leck. Soon, one at a time, the delinquents were brought in. They represented some of the best and oldest landed families in the county. Francis Tunstall, John Talbot, John Rigmaiden, Edward Osbaldeston, John Westby, John Towneley and John Mollineux of the Wood were not the sort of people who were customarily brought before the courts — indeed they belonged to the group from which Justices of the Peace were recruited. A strange combination of fortunes had brought both justices and accused to this moment, and none of them can have felt it more intensely than Sir Richard Shireburne.

Perhaps his mind went back to another justice room some fifteen years before, when as a young man, he had been at the first examination by Lord Derby of one of the earliest Protestant missionaries to set foot in Lancashire. George Marsh had been a prosperous farmer in the parish of Deane near Bolton. On the premature death of his wife he abandoned the farm and in 1551 entered Christ's College, Cambridge, where he studied for a year. In this time he seems to have absorbed much of the Protestant theology which was rife in the University, and on his ordination he moved to London as a curate and schoolmaster who favoured the ideas of the continental reformers. We know little of his activities in the next two or three years

Stonyhurst from the air. Sir Richard Shireburne's original house plan can be perceived among the wealth of later building. The great hall can be seen immediately behind the gatehouse towers. The family wing of the house, with its long gallery, extends to the Blind Tower, with its gothic window. The frontage of the house, up to and including the gatehouse, dates from this original phase of building, but at this point Sir Richard's work came to an end.

but it is certain that he, together with John Bradford, another powerful, Protestant polemicist, had visited the area around Bolton and Manchester. These visits laid the foundations of reformed religious thought in that area, mainly among his friends and family. Such activities were approved of during the reign of King Edward VI but the accession of Mary, who was resolute in her determination to undo the reforms of her father and her brother, made these missions highly dangerous. Bradford returned to the south and was eventually arrested in London, but Marsh seems to have courted the martyr's crown and surrendered himself to Mr Barton of Smithills Hall. His defiant attitude and apparent determination to force the authorities to act harshly against him is remembered in the indelible 'Martyr's Footprint' in that house, made as he was carried from there to trial and eventual execution at Chester. In spite of the bishop's efforts to avoid the severity of the law Marsh went to the stake at Spital Broughton, just outside the boundary of the city, on 24 April 1555. Among the spectators at Marsh's preliminary hearing before the Earl of Derby was Richard Shireburne who, in the account given by Foxe in his *Book of Martyrs*, is described as professing himself ignorant of the scriptures but intervening to demand why 'A well favoured young man and one that might have a good living and do good would so foolishly cast himself away, sticking so hard to such foolish opinions.' This view is reflected in Shireburne's later career when, rather than run the risks of openly adhering to what he believed right, in his case the Roman Catholic faith, he put security and prosperity first.

Fifteen years later, as the first session of the High Commission for Lancashire settled down to hear the accusations and responses of those who now appeared before it charged with stubborn adherence to the Church of Rome, Sir Richard Shireburne must have reflected on the irony and the chaos which had now brought him to defend and support the Protestant ideas which, only a few years before, he had dismissed as foolish.

The Shireburnes were among the foremost families of Lancashire, and from their home at Stonyhurst wielded great influence in the lands around the lower Ribble and in the Forest of Bowland. Their power was based on the lands of this district, acquired by a marriage in 1377 between Richard Bailey of Stonyhurst and Margaret Shireburn of Hambleton in the Fylde. The children of this marriage adopted and retained the Shireburne name. As well as his lands in the immediate area of Stonyhurst and the Fylde properties, which still remained in the family, Sir Richard had estates in Yorkshire and in the Upper Lune Valley at Twistleton. By 1571 Shireburne's rental shows the various properties in Lancashire yielding an annual income of £245 0s. 3d. and a further £178 19s. 10d. was derived from his properties across the county boundary. This made him, in local terms at least, a very wealthy man. Sir Richard Shireburne had inherited his fortune on the early death of his father in 1536 when it seems he, Richard, was only ten years of age. However, the year of his birth is unknown and the age may have been understated. Despite his tender years he was soon a married man. His wedding is recorded at Farnworth Chapel in Widnes on 26 October 1539. It is significant of the low regard in which women were held that his wife's name is not given, but she was Maud Bold of Bold, whose family chapel it was. Though we do not know the form of the service used at Shireburne's wedding we do know that it was at a time when the church in Lancashire was entering a period of uncertainty and change.

At the time of Richard's childhood, north Lancashire had been threatened by the armies of the Pilgrimage of Grace, and both Whalley and Sawley Abbeys had been centres of the insurrection. The call to rise in arms to defend and restore the monasteries had met a ready response in the area and the enthusiasm for the monastic houses was but one facet of the genuine piety which seems to have existed in the County Palatine.

Lancashire was not well served by any aspect of the pre-Reformation Church. It was a remote and backward county where ecclesiastical organisation had been slow to develop. Poverty and a small population had prevented the creation of a close-knit parochial structure, and the deficiencies in the provision of worship and of an adequate force of clergy were not compensated for by direction from a diocesan level. The county was divided between two dioceses. North of the Ribble it fell within the bounds of the Archdiocese of York, by

John Bradford, the Protestant martyr. Born in Manchester, John Bradford trained at the Inner Temple in London, where he absorbed Protestant ideas from Latimer and Sampson. After studying at Cambridge, he became the most effective Protestant preacher in London. He maintained close links with Lancashire and not only visited on preaching tours but sustained an active correspondence with his converts. Burned at the stake at Smithfield in June 1555, Bradford was one of the most important avenues through which the reformed religion reached Lancashire.

PHOTOGRAPH COURTESY OF CHETHAM'S LIBRARY, MANCHESTER

which it was allocated to the Archdeaconry of Richmond. The southern half of the county fell under the control of the Bishop of Coventry and Lichfield and the Archdeacon of Chester. Difficult of access because of natural hazards and far from the administrative centres of either diocese or archdeaconry, Lancashire was largely ignored by its ecclesiastical supervisors. Neither bishops nor archdeacons made very much effort to carry out visitations and much of their power was delegated to local deans who were often men of little influence and poor standing, lax and venal in their work.

The parochial clergy worked under severe difficulties. Lancashire parishes were among the largest in the country. In the whole county there were only fifty-six parish churches. In the fourteen counties making up the Midlands and the South East the average area of a parish was four square miles: in Lancashire it was thirty-three square miles, though Whalley was over one hundred square miles in area and contained thirty townships. While a priest in the diocese of Salisbury had an average population of 167 souls within his cure, in Lancashire the average was 1,700. To attempt to meet these impossible demands, made all the more onerous in a society where weekly attendance at Church was considered obligatory, many parishes or individuals had at various times established chapels in the outlying parts of their territory. Some were built at the behest of the local family and others by the painful and painstaking collection of funds by the parishioners but, whatever their origins, these chapels of ease were of vital importance to the community. If they had not existed many parishioners would have lived too far from the parish church to have received any spiritual guidance or pastoral care, or to have had the opportunity for worship.

It was unfortunate that many of these chapels were so poorly endowed that they were nothing more than a last hope for many inadequate and unsatisfactory clergymen. Little could be expected of a priest who received less than £1 a year, the salary paid to nineteen out of a hundred North Lancashire clergy in 1524. The average over the county was a stipend of £2 9s. 6d. It is no wonder that many turned to alternative and additional occupations to make life possible, though few went as far as the curate of Singleton who turned the chapel yard into a dungheap and kept an alehouse with 'a nowty woman in it'. In many cases their superiors in the parish church were little better off. Lancashire livings (as opposed to curacies) had become desirable as a result of a huge rise in tithe income during the sixteenth century. As the population of the county doubled during that period, and its prosperity was greatly enhanced by the growth of textile manufacture, the income for the huge parishes and their enormous populations increased. Winwick, for example, became the wealthiest benefice in England. As a result of this transformation these rich livings became the targets both of ambitious local families and of institutions which would retain the title to the living and appoint a poorly paid vicar to carry out the clerical functions. For example, we have seen how the Abbey of Whalley had acquired the right to draw the tithe revenue from the parishes of Whalley, Blackburn, Rochdale and Eccles. This became the main element in the income of the abbey. To carry out the pastoral duties a vicar was appointed. At Whalley the tithes were worth £91 6s. 8d. but the vicar received only £6 3s. 4d., at Blackburn the comparable figures were £74 6s. 8d. and £8 1s. 6d. Nor were secular impropriators (lay persons who had acquired the Living and right to the tithe income of a parish) more generous. In the 1520s the Duchy of Lancaster paid the vicar of Ormskirk £10 per year, a salary determined two hundred years earlier. Where a local family held the impropriation, the living was either used as a source of income or the appointment to the church was seen as being a useful and rewarding occupation for a member of the family. For example, between 1500 and 1550 the rectory of Winwick was twice held by members of the Stanley family, on both occasions in conjunction with other desirable ecclesiastical plums. The Halsall family controlled the living of the eponymous parish and on one occasion the living was presented to Hugh Halsall at the age of seven. Between 1462 and 1557 the rectory of Sefton was held by five members of the Mollineux family. Similar examples can be found all over the county.

The vicars and curates appointed to carry out the ecclesiastical duties of these parishes were often men of no learning and of scandalous behaviour. Thomas Kirkby, curate of Halsall in 1530, was one of the most notorious. His seizure of the possessions of the rectory, his constant litigation in pursuit of claims for land, his terrorising of the parishioners with threats of everlasting damnation if they did not richly reward him for his services, provoked his flock to attack and set fire to his house, while he was in it. Kirkby managed to escape and as late as 1550 was still in trouble for embezzlement and forgery.

The provision of places of worship in Lancashire would have been even more scanty had the parochial clergy not been supplemented by chantry priests. Chantries existed in most, if not all, of the parish churches. A fundamental aspect of the piety of Lancashire was a preoccupation with prayers for the dead. For the poor this might be no more than an injunction on their grave marker to 'Pray for the soul of'; the more prosperous would endow a priest to say a number of masses – thirty, or a 'trental', was a popular number – for the release from purgatory of either their own soul or the souls of relatives. The expense of such a trental might be shared, along with the efficacy of the prayers, by those who could not afford the whole outlay. The most prosperous would leave an income in perpetuity for the establishment of an altar, usually in the parish church, and for the salary of a priest to say a daily mass for the well-being of the deceased. Once this daily duty was done, that priest became available for parochial duties and many a chantrist served as curate or as schoolmaster. For example, the priest of the altar of St Katherine, founded by John Crosse in the chapel of Liverpool served as master of the school which the Crosse family had also endowed. It is notable that though the popularity of the custom of chantry endowment had declined sharply in the rest of the country, in Lancashire they were still being founded until 1547, when all were closed by an Act of Parliament, an action that had serious consequences for the many people in Lancashire who lost the services of their priest.

In spite of the inadequate provision and deplorable standards of churchmanship in the county, the ordinary people of Lancashire retained a high regard for religion and for the church in the abstract. They seem to have been unusually devout, and due to the difficulties of communication and the isolation of the county, remained largely untouched by the flood of new ideas and the bitter anticlericalism which pervaded more sophisticated regions of England. It was in this atmosphere that Sir Richard Shireburne had been brought up and the deep loyalty to the Church of Rome which existed in Lancashire was to be a pervading influence in his life and career. It was a tradition that he seems to have fully absorbed, and our first record of his expression of religious views during the interrogation of Marsh confirms that he had little sympathy for any who would challenge the status quo. However, he, like many others, must have found difficulty in knowing what was the status quo.

The reign of Henry VIII had seen cataclysmic changes – allegiance to the Pope rejected, the supremacy of the Church transferred to the Crown, the closure of the monasteries and the discontent which that provoked, the substitution of English for Latin in the most important parts of the service, and the introduction of an English Bible. Despite these devastating upheavals Henry still clung to his reputation as 'Defender of the Faith' and desperately tried to resist the more revolutionary doctrines of the reformers. Even so, in the conservative fastness of Lancashire the reforms that were made received scant sympathy: it is probable that they were largely ignored in many places and caused protest and uproar in those churches which followed the injunctions. Any preacher speaking against the Pope could expect a hostile reception.

One move by the government designed to help the introduction of the new ideas was the creation of the Bishopric of Chester. Founded in 1541, the new diocese was the third largest in England and comprised the most northerly parts of the diocese of Coventry and Lichfield, together with the Archdeaconry of Richmond, formerly within the diocese of York. It extended from the southern boundary of Cheshire to south Cumberland and over the Pennines to include the North Riding of Yorkshire. To provide adequate episcopal supervision over such a large area would have been impossible in Tudor England. The problem was exacerbated by the inadequate financial provision made for the bishop. He was expected to meet many of the administrative expenses of the diocese from his income of £473 4s. 8d. Only one bishop, that of Rochester, whose diocese was less than a tenth of the size, received a smaller emolument. As might be expected, Bishop Bird, the first incumbent of the see, skimped on the appointment of administrative officers and it is doubtful if the quality of supervision was much improved in the short term. However, inadequate though the diocese may have been, the North West now had the advantage of the attention of a diocesan bishop.

The reign of Edward VI saw a national move to introduce a more Protestant element into the Church of England and one by one the fundamentals of Catholic theology and practice were swept away. Purgatory and prayers for the dead, the use of images and clerical celibacy were all rejected and replaced by Protestant views on justification by faith and predestination. A Protestant form of service, embodied in Cranmer's two prayer books, replaced the traditional mass. In Lancashire many of these things were deeply offensive to the majority and the situation was made worse by the closure of chapels and the confiscation of their property, and the loss of revenues to the church through the closure of chantries. In 1552 twenty-five Lancashire chapels found themselves under attack and many were closed and the buildings sold. At Tarleton the chapel was bought by Sir Thomas Hesketh for 12s. 4d.; at Billinge the chapel was turned into a barn; and in other cases, such as Littleborough and Accrington, the parishioners had to buy back their property from the Crown. In 1553 Sir Richard Shireburne, who had been knighted in 1544 as a reward for his military service against the Scots and at the siege of Edinburgh, sat as one of the two county members of parliament: it would be interesting to know whether he brought to Westminster the views of his constituents, or expressed his personal opposition to the new doctrines.

That he did oppose the reforms can be judged from his subsequent career. He served in parliament throughout Mary's reign, first as a member for Preston, then for Liverpool and then (between 1557 and 1558) once more for Preston. One may guess that he gave his support to the legislation of the unhappy queen's reign designed to turn back the clock and return England to the Roman fold. This task did not prove difficult in Lancashire, where apart from the handful of converts made by Bradford and Marsh in the Bolton area the new theology had made no impression. All the evidence is that the return to traditional practices and services was widely welcomed. During the first Marian visitation only one case of heresy was discovered in the seven Cheshire deaneries and only fourteen in Lancashire: it is notable that these were clustered in the area where the influence of Marsh and Bradford had been strongest, and it is interesting that in several of these cases the initiative for prosecution came not from the clergy but from the horrified neighbours of the heretics.

Several important new ecclesiastical appointments were made. Bishop Bird was replaced by George Coates and, perhaps more significant in the long term history of the county, the college of priests attached to Manchester Parish Church (now Manchester Cathedral) was refounded after its dissolution under Edward VI. Initially the former warden, George Collier, was reinstated, but of greater importance was the appointment of Lawrence Vaux, first as a Fellow and then, after the death of Collier in 1558, as Warden. Vaux was to become one of the most important figures in the history of Lancashire Catholicism. Born at Blackrod, he was an Oxford graduate and had served at Manchester before its suppression. He has been described as a popular and compelling figure, and in the words of one of his successors 'a man well beloved and highly honoured among the generality ... many thereabouts were lother [more loth] to be reclaimed from Popery'. The main effect of the reign of Mary on Lancashire was to reinforce the values and ideas of the majority in the area and to stamp out the smouldering sparks of heresy. However, Vaux's appointment came only months before the queen's death and the accession of her religiously ambiguous half-sister, Elizabeth. The child of the break with Rome, Elizabeth herself was thought to incline towards the conservative church that her father had created, in which many aspects of the traditional pattern of worship were retained. However, for political reasons it was appreciated that some concessions had to be made towards the new and more radical theology. This was appreciated even in remote Lancashire: Thomas Leyland, a Catholic conservative Justice dealing with the mother of Geoffrey Hurst, a Protestant, said 'Thou old fool, I know myself that this new learning shall come again; but for how long? – even for three months or four months and no longer'. This view point reflects the feeling of impermanence that had come to pervade views on religious matters in a period of some twenty years which had seen revolution, counter revolution and now a new upheaval.

The Elizabethan Settlement of 1559 reinforced the position of the monarch within the Church and required the acceptance of royal supremacy, but many of the most contentious theological issues were deliberately left vague in order that the settlement might be as widely accepted as possible – ideally by Catholic and Protestant alike. However, this expectation was reinforced by a requirement on all adults of regular attendance and reception of communion in their parish church. Those who refused or failed in this were known as recusants. Though, in theory, this term could be applied to Catholic or Protestant recalcitrant, in fact it came to be almost exclusively applied to those who retained their Catholic beliefs. In Lancashire there seems to have been almost no direct, immediate opposition to the new proposals. In a county where little had changed it must have seemed that little change would take place in the future. It is true that a number of the clergy found the new settlement unacceptable: Vaux, Coppage and Hart, from among the Fellows of Manchester, refused to take the Oath of Supremacy and were eventually dismissed. However, the majority of the clergy accepted the new Oath, and only about one in ten refused. The majority of these were from among the unbeneficed clergy who had least to lose by intransigence. The new bishop, Downham, treated these defectors with leniency, perhaps in the vain hope that they might be enticed back into the Church, but it was these deprived clergy who were to play a vital role in the survival of the Catholic church.

At first attitudes on both sides were far from extreme. Many Catholics sincerely believed that it was possible to comply with the law by attendance at the parish church and to avoid compromising themselves by finding excuses for being absent or to refrain from taking communion by saying that they were not in charity with their neighbours or not in a state of repentance. They would therefore meet the letter of the law by their physical presence, but save their conscience by mental reservations. They were then able to receive the ministrations of the itinerant, deprived priests who provided a widespread network of pastoral care. These priests have been termed 'recusant priests' and it was in this role, as ministers to a basically Catholic population, that they made the most important contribution to the survival of their faith.

That this network of recusant priests existed was well known to the authorities, but local officials proved either unwilling or – more probably – unable to deal with the situation. Their failure was due to the inadequacy of the law enforcement organisation in the county, and to the widespread popular support enjoyed by the priests, who could rely on the protection of a sympathetic laity.

Sir Richard Shireburne was among the most prominent men in Lancashire to find himself faced with the dilemmas of the period, and he, like others, had links with both sides. There can be no doubt that he himself inclined towards the Catholic church. What we have seen of his career until 1559, the reports that circulated about him during Elizabeth's reign, the fact that his new house included a chapel that was deliberately secluded, and the behaviour of his wife and his children all make this clear. Against his personal inclinations, however, many other factors had to be balanced.

The Shireburne family held a position of wealth, power and prestige in the county, being among the small group or elite which provided the judicial, administrative and political core of the community. Sir Richard himself was a justice of the peace and, as such, was expected to gather information and to proceed against any Catholic activity which came to his notice. While this might go against the grain, it was even more repugnant to him to sacrifice not only his position but the standing of the Shireburne dynasty by opposing the new religious settlement. He may also have thought that he could best protect his co-religionists by retaining his post and pursuing a policy of masterly inactivity. He was later described as 'An intelligencer for Papists in Lancashire'. It is indicative of the prestige he enjoyed that, in spite of his known opposition to the Protestant cause, he could not sensibly be omitted from the High Commission which was designed to propagate the reformed Church and to eliminate the recusant Catholics. The position of men like Shireburne was made even more difficult by the prevailing religio-political climate of the day.

In a world in which only one Church existed religion had played a small part in national politics, but the appearance of dissent and the emergence of new Churches raised major problems. The ideal persisted that the entire population of a single state must follow a single way of worship. This view had been enshrined in the Treaty of Augsburg, which had brought an end to the religious wars in Germany engendered by Luther's teachings. The treaty enshrined the principle whereby each prince had the power to make a decision on religious adherence on behalf of all his subjects and the right to enforce unity by secular means. To the sixteenth-century mind the vision of a number of Churches peacefully co-existing within one nation was inconceivable – hence the provisions of the Elizabethan settlement which equated failure to attend and be a communicant member of the state church with disloyalty and treason. During the reign of Elizabeth this view received new impetus from the actions and attitudes of outside agencies. Though the majority of English Catholics proved time and time again that they were loyal to Elizabeth, and were fully prepared to accept her temporal supremacy, the threats to English integrity

Cardinal Allen, 1532–94. William Allen was born at Rossal, near Fleetwood. He earned an early reputation for scholarship, but was most celebrated as a polemicist for the Roman Catholic church. He founded a seminary at Douai to train Englishmen as priests for the Mission. He directed and ordered the translation known as the 'Douai' Bible and was instrumental in organising the first Jesuit mission to England in 1580. He was a firm advocate of the Spanish invasion attempt of 1588, hoping to become Archbishop of Canterbury when it succeeded. He was created a Cardinal in 1587.

Si decem millia Pædagogorum habeatis in Christo. sed non multos
Patres. nam in Christo Iesu per Euangelium ego vos genui. 1. Corin.

posed by Spain, Scotland and the Papacy itself reinforced the conventional view that they were a hostile, internal group acting against the interests of the state.

To the Catholic powers Elizabeth was not only a Protestant, but also an illegitimate usurper of the throne, whom it was considered a Christian duty to destroy and replace with a Catholic prince. This was the motivating force behind the harebrained assassination plots of Mary, Queen of Scots, and her supporters; behind the more serious threat of the Armada and Spanish invasion; and behind the Papal Bull *Regnans in Excelsis* by which Elizabeth was declared a heretic and excommunicated, and her subjects relieved of the obligation of loyalty, and by which, at least tacitly, the assassination of the queen was condoned. As Philip II himself feared, this only had the effect of hardening opinion against the Catholic Church in the country at large and provoked the government into harsher methods to bring about the extirpation of Popery. By the Statute of 1571 (13 Elizabeth, Cap 1&2) any attempts to make a convert to the Roman Church or to become converted oneself were to be treated as high treason and to be punished with death and the confiscation of land and property. Anyone aiding or comforting a priest was to suffer a praemunire, by which entire estates were forfeit. The price for recusancy had been raised considerably, provided that the law could be enforced.

This was by no means a simple task in Lancashire. Throughout Tudor England the enforcement of the law depended on the vigilance and wholehearted co-operation of those unpaid drudges, the justices of the peace. In return for the doubtful honour of the post they were expected to be the administrative and executive arm of the government, acting individually in their home areas and collectively within the quarter sessions for the county as a whole. It was customary to select magistrates from among the most prestigious families and those whose loyalty and concurrence with the ideas of the government could be assumed. The selection and control of the justices depended on the lord lieutenant and his deputies and the sheriff of the county. The Lords Lieutenant of Lancashire throughout our period, and for a great many years after, were the earls of Derby, assisted by a number of deputy lieutenants selected from among the greatest gentlemen of the county.

Sir Richard Shireburne was a deputy lieutenant of Lancashire, Lord Derby's lieutenant for the Isle of Man, Master Forester for the Forest of Bowland and a justice of the peace. All these were posts which might be expected both to indicate and to guarantee his loyalty to the Crown. There is no evidence that

Shireburne's loyalty to the Crown was ever shaken except over matters of religion. The Chancellor of the Duchy had no option but to retain him in the Commission of the Peace, in spite of his well known leanings to recusancy, because it was impossible to find anyone else of sufficient prestige and stature in the Ribble valley to take his place. Shireburne was to show that he was not too concerned with the niceties of the law. His zeal outran his discretion on a number of occasions. As a result he was accused of several abuses of power. Between 1585 and 1588 there were complaints of his levying excessively high local taxes for the recruitment and maintenance of soldiers. It was also implied that the money had been retained by him and not accounted for, and that when difficulties arose over the collection of these monies he had threatened to use martial law to hang the constables who jibbed at his demands. All this might, perhaps, be attributed to over-enthusiasm at a time when the threat of Spain was ever present. Complaints were also made that he retained funds which should have been distributed to the people. One Simon Haydock had refused to sell him land at Haydock and Shireburne threatened to use his deputy lieutenancy to extract vengeance.

Shireburne's private life was far from being a model of domesticity: he was accused of adultery and incest and he was certainly the father of a number of illegitimate children. One of these, a daughter Jane, was to marry into the family of Southworth of Samlesbury. Her story is told in Chapter Four.

The problem confronting the government in trying to find a more suitable candidate to hold a magistracy is neatly summed up in a document of 1583 which listed among the Lancashire magistrates three recusant justices, fourteen so-called 'Church papists' who had made a nominal conformity to the Church of England and eight men who had families well-known to be Catholic. In 1587 twelve of the justices were removed from the Commission but several had to be reinstated because no suitable replacements could be found. A justice had to be a man of substance and one regarded as a natural leader of his community. In Lancashire all too often this meant one who was either a Papist or had intimate connections with the Roman Church. We find names like Shireburne, Hesketh, Scarisbrick and a dozen others who were known or suspected of being recusants. Even those who might be considered 'well affected' in religion often had members of their families or friends or neighbours who were unashamedly Catholic. As a result they were inclined to ignore all but the most flagrant breaches of the law. Ferdinando, fourth earl of Derby, was in such close touch with the Catholic members of his own family and with other leading recusants that he was thought to be a covert Catholic himself. He was approached by agents to see if he could be persuaded to be converted and put himself forward as a claimant to the throne. To be fair to these dilatory justices, they were well aware that the recusant community posed no threat to the regime and they were fully prepared to act in cases where a real danger was perceived. For example the vast majority of Lancashire recusants gave sincere support to the Loyal Association, formed in 1584 to protect the queen from her enemies and to take revenge in the event of her assassination.

The same attitudes prevailed at the lower levels of office, to the churchwardens and township constables who had the primary responsibility for seeking-out and reporting absences from church. Even if a report was made, it was an easy charge to refute. The large parishes and many chapels of Lancashire made it very easy to claim that one attended service elsewhere and in the absence of any co-ordination this was virtually an unshakeable excuse. If the gentry clung to the old religion it was easy for their tenantry to follow their example. In other parts of the country – for example in the West Midlands – recusancy was confined to certain distinct areas surrounding the manor house of recusant families. In Lancashire, because there were so many more Catholic gentry, there were almost continuous bands of Catholic territory in areas like the South West Lancashire plain and in the Fylde. It has been suggested that a recusant priest could travel the length of the county without ever leaving Catholic ground.

If the lord lieutenant of the county could be thus perceived as sympathetic to Catholicism, it is no wonder that the anonymous author of a report for Lord Burghley in 1591 was to say of Shireburne that he and his family were recusants 'and do not go to Church, or if they do, stop their ears with wool least they should hear; that he kept a priest in Queen Mary's time'. It should be noted that the last accusation was not an offence in Mary's reign, the spy was simply throwing in any available scrap of information, whether relevant or not. The report continues; 'He had had one [a priest] brought to confess his wife when ill; relieves Richard Startevant, who is conversant with Dr Allen and other Jesuits and is suspected to be a Jesuit and for that reason he had put Richard Startevant out of the book for the payment of this subsidy'. The informant also pointed out the reluctance of Shireburne to 'lend' money to the queen 'though worth more than £1000 a year'. It is a matter of doubt whether this should be attributed to disloyalty on Shireburne's part or merely to his unwillingness to part from hard-earned money, in view of the queen's notorious failure to repay.

By the 1580s three developments strengthened the resolve of the Catholic recusants and hardened the attitudes of the authorities. The first was the return to Lancashire of Lawrence Vaux. After his dismissal from the Wardenship of Manchester, Vaux had fled to the Continent. In 1566 he had an audience with the Pope and was commissioned to convey to England, and supervise the enforcement of, a Papal decree which prohibited attendance by Catholics at the services of the Anglican Church. This was in furtherance of a decision made in 1563 by the Roman Inquisition and the Council of Trent. On Vaux's arrival in England he came north to circulate the news of this decree. His policy was to visit the leading recusant gentry, and so he spent some time with Sir Richard Mollineux and Sir William Norris, as well as meeting with other south-west Lancashire gentlemen. He also ensured that the information was passed to the recusant priests of the area. Vaux's message caused consternation among those 'Church Catholics' who believed they had found an acceptable solution to their difficulties. They questioned his message until Vaux was driven to make an unequivocal statement: 'I am charged to make a definitive sentence, that all

such as offer children to the baptism now used or be present at a communion service now used in churches in England ... do not walk in a state of salvation ... there is no exception nor dispensation can be had for any of the laity, if they will stand in a state of salvation'.

It was the news of this mission, and this categoric denial of the practice of occasional conformity that, at last, stirred the authorities to action against recusants. Seven of the principal recusant gentlemen were arraigned before the commission at Lathom, and, as we have seen, Sir Richard found himself sitting in judgement on his friends and neighbours. The affair turned out to be something of a damp squib, as all the accused except Westby, who had said he would willingly loose blood in these matters, agreed to attend church, to conform to the statutes and were bound over on a bond of 300 marks (£200). However, this affair marked a crucial turning point in religious relationships within the county. Until this time some form of compromise had been possible, but now no loyal Catholic could be in any doubt about his duty. Furthermore the current myth that the Catholic would put obedience to the Pope before his duty to his queen was confirmed in the eyes of the government.

While Vaux was to have great influence within the county, another Lancashire man was to become the driving force of the Catholic Counter-Reformation in England. William Allen was a son of the squire of Rossall Hall at the mouth of the Wyre. After a brilliant scholastic career at Oxford, which culminated in his appointment as Principal of St Mary Hall, he refused to conform to the reformed Church, was dispossessed, and sought exile at Louvain in modern Belgium, the headquarters of English Catholic exiles. In 1562, on

View of the west front of Stonyhurst from the drive. This picture clearly demonstrates how the buildings added as the school expanded harmonise with the older structures. Those to the left of the Gatehouse Tower blend with those dating from the first building period. The gabled building on the extreme left is an estate office added by Sir Nicholas Shireburne c.1690. On the right can be seen the 'Shirk', the first addition made by the Jesuits in 1799.

PHOTOGRAPH, AUTHOR

the pretext of ill-health, he returned to Rossall and then made a series of visits to relatives and friends who represented the most influential Lancashire Catholic families. With the information thus gained he returned to Europe and began a campaign of agitation which persuaded the Papal authorities to include discussions on the state of the Catholics in England on the agenda of the Council of Trent. It was this discussion that was ultimately to result in Vaux's mission. Allen founded the English College at Rome, to train young men as missionary priests, and became associated with the most powerful of the new religious orders which were spawned by the Counter Reformation.

Founded in 1540 by the Basque aristocrat Ignatius Loyola, the Society of Jesus (or as they were better known, the Jesuits) became the cutting edge of the late sixteenth-century Catholic revival. Their service was to be as obedient soldiers of the Pope: the initial concept had been for militant missionaries to convert the heathen lands. However, the Pope saw in the Order great potential for the fight against the reformed religion in Europe. The Jesuits were recruited from the devout and determined sons of upper-class and aristocratic families. They were selected for their intelligence and education, sophistication, zeal and determination. The reformers had emphasised the importance of education and scholarship and the aim of the Jesuits was to fight them on their own ground. The provision of education had a secondary benefit, in that the schools of the Order gained a reputation as some of the finest educational institutions in Europe, and many a wavering Catholic family was redeemed through the influence of its members who had been educated at a Jesuit school. It was in these schools that the system of 'marks' is thought to

have been introduced – an innovation that has proved to be one of their longest-lasting contributions to education.

The success of this policy of recruitment and training did much to give the Order its reputation for devious, cunning and underhand dealing. The Jesuits were hated and feared by the laity and clergy of the reformed churches and, it is also true to say, by many within the Church of Rome. In the case of England a special urgency was given to the government's fears of Jesuit activity by their close links with the Papacy and indirectly with the king of Spain.

In June of 1581 the first Jesuit missioners, Edmund Campion and Robert Persons (or Parsons, as it is alternatively spelled), arrived in England. Both had a high reputation for scholarship and zeal in the cause. While Persons worked mainly in London and the south, Campion made a journey throughout the most Catholic areas of the Country and by August 1581 was in Lancashire. He is reputed to have spent some time with Richard Hoghton at Park Hall and also to have visited the Southworths, Bartholomew Hesketh of Aughton and the Talbots of Salesbury. It also seems likely that he visited the Worthingtons of Blainscough, where according to legend a quick-witted maid servant pushed him into a duck pond to conceal him on the unexpected arrival of the sheriff's officers. He also made a visit to the Fylde, spending some time at Rossall, at Mowbreck with the Westbys and with the Rigmaidens at Garstang. The impact of Campion's visit on the Catholic community in Lancashire has been disputed, some authors believing it to have been inspirational, while others believe that Campion's purpose was to find a period of quiet and safety while he completed his 'Decem Rationes', a refutation of Protestant theology. One thing is certain: much to the chagrin of the later Jesuits of Stonyhurst, he

The Quadrangle from the north-west. The block on the left of this picture is the Great Hall, still used as a dining room by the school. The location of the Hall on the first floor was something of a local tradition and was a mark of distinction in gentry houses. The ground-floor room provided storage space for foodstuffs, beer and wine, as well as agricultural produce. The half octagonal bay, or compass window as they were locally known, made a place of retirement for the ladies from the boisterous life of the Hall.

did not visit there. The ambiguous attitudes of Sir Richard would have made that far too dangerous.

Within weeks of leaving Lancashire Campion had been betrayed and captured. Though subjected to appalling torture in the Tower, he steadfastly refused to name his protectors and hosts in the country, and went to the scaffold with sealed lips. Robert Persons escaped capture and returned to Europe, filled with zeal to direct the new effort – not only by the Jesuits but also by other orders and secular missionaries – to serve the English mission and return England to the Roman fold. One can imagine the impact that these new, young, virile, well-trained and highly educated priests made on the Catholic community, which had previously been ministered to by aged and often intellectually ill-equipped clergy. A clear picture of the type of recusant priest with whom they were familiar comes down to us in a report of the arrest and interrogation of James Stonnes, a priest aged seventy-two who was 'neither Jesuit or Seminary but is a priest and received that function from Doctor Tunstall, then Bishop of Durham, forty and six years since'. Father Stonnes, or Uncle James as he was affectionately known by his flock, followed the traditional pattern: the old priest declared the legitimacy of the queen's secular power and wished her 'Nestor's years' (Nestor was King of Pylos, reputed to have lived through three generations of man), but denied her spiritual authority.

The south front from the east. This block is described by Nikolaus Pevsner as 'one of the largest single scholastic blocks in England', and he goes on to praise its style as 'free and exuberant English renaissance'. The block was added to the school between 1877 and 1889. The use of cupolas and turrets helps this to blend into and harmonise with a collection of very disparate buildings.

The Gatehouse, Stonyhurst. The building was revolutionary in its introduction of the new 'classical style' to Lancashire. The façade of four paired columns, Doric, Ionic and two Corinthian, are correctly arranged and the rest of the design is carefully based on ancient models. The turrets and the cupolas were added in 1712.

PHOTOGRAPH, AUTHOR

He openly admitted that 'He hath continued for the most part in the Bishopric of Durham, Yorkshire and sometimes Lancashire. He hath said the mass as often as the opportunity of time, place or company have given leave'. Naturally, he could give no names of those who had attended the services or given him shelter. The inventory of his possessions which accompanies the deposition gives the clearest picture of this old, gentle and resolute man; a few scraps of vestments, a fragment of a battered primer, a piece of an ancient sermon book, an old mass book, three pewter bottles in a leather case for oil and chrism and a tin chalice, made up his equipment. Even the authorities viewed him with leniency for despite his obvious and admitted guilt he was kindly treated.

The Courtyard, Stonyhurst. This view shows the courtyard wall of the family wing of Stonyhurst. The windows on the ground floor are of the unusual sets of self-contained apartments provided either for the accommodation of members of the family or upper servants. The larger windows on the first floor are those of the Long Gallery, which extended to form a tribune, or family pew, in the original chapel located in the 'Blind Tower'. The canted bay and doorway were added to the façade by Sir Nicholas Shireburne whose monogram it bears. Originally the topmost floor would have provided chambers for the domestic staff.

PHOTOGRAPH, AUTHOR

The image of the new missionary priest was very different. In 1585 another priest, Holford, was arrested at Nantwich and his appearance is also described in detail: 'A tall, black, fat man, the crown of his head bald, his beard marquezated, his apparel was a black cloak with murrey lace, open at the shoulder; a straw coloured fustian doublet laid on with white lace, the buttons red, cut and laid under with red taffeta, ash coloured hose, laid on with byllicut lace, cut and laid under with black taffeta, a little black hat lined in velvet in the brims, a falling band and yellow knit stock'. Here we have the antithesis of the old priests and in the colourful figure of Holford the new character of recusant Catholicism can be seen.

The Garden Pavillion and Terrace at Stonyhurst. The last man of the Shireburne family, Sir Nicholas, made a number of alterations to the grounds of Stonyhurst, including the excavation of the 'canals' beside the drive, as well as adding the cupolas with their crowning eagles to the gatehouse towers. He was also responsible for the construction in about 1710–12 of the terrace, with its prospects across the Ribble valley, its twisted wooden pinnacles, and two flanking gazebos. The pavilions are a very early expression of the fashion for 'chinoiserie', which is displayed in the shape of the roofs and the use of chinese heads as keystones of the door.

Holcroft represents the face of recusancy which most alarmed Elizabethan England. A man of ability and, to judge from his dress, a man of means, he moved about the country in a secretive and subversive way, pouring who knew what poison into the ears of Her Majesty's subjects. Though the intolerance shown by the government offends our twenty first-century liberal and secular society, and though undoubtedly the vast majority of Elizabethan recusants were loyal both to their Church and to their sovereign we must remember that there were among the Catholics, and especially among the exiled fanatics rather than the indigenous community, a group which seriously contemplated the assassination of the queen and involved themselves in plots with foreign powers to bring this about. This was a real threat to a regime which was becoming increasingly stable, popular and respected. Though many of the plots were marked by inept planning and bungled attempts at execution, and though they were often penetrated by the government's intelligence agents, there was a real danger. Just as Gavrillo Princip, a frightened boy and an inept assassin, was able by a lucky shot to plunge Europe into a cataclysmic war, so a chance could have destroyed Elizabethan England. It is not surprising that the government took increasingly stringent steps to try to eliminate the threat.

In 1581 a new series of statutes was passed by parliament which increased the penalties for recusancy. Anybody who willingly withdrew himself from the established religion or attempted to persuade anybody else to do so, or who acknowledged the authority of Rome was to be considered guilty of treason. Every person who said or sang the Mass was to be fined two hundred marks and to be imprisoned for a year. The penalty for failure to attend Church on Sunday was raised to £20 per month, and a husband was made responsible for the recusancy of his wife. Unlicensed schoolmasters were to be fined at the rate of £10 a month. In an attempt to enforce these laws in Lancashire a new High Commission had been established the previous year. All the indications are that its efforts were as unsuccessful as those of previous Commissions.

If there was little about the new church to win converts the efforts of the authorities at compulsion were ineffectual. It is probably true to say that the majority of Lancashire men and women retained a heartfelt allegiance to the Roman Church and were either prepared to risk the penalties or to think that they could evade them or, in spite of the condemnation of the practice by Vaux and the later missioners, to use the compromise of 'Church Popery'. There was only a minimum risk in choosing the path of recusancy. In the majority of cases the local agencies of enforcement of the laws were, as we have seen, themselves tainted with Catholicism.

Another factor in the success of Lancashire recusancy was the continuous flow of missionary priests into the county. In the early years of Elizabeth's reign the local recusant priests had served the community, but under the influence of men like Vaux, Campion and Allen it attracted many seminary priests from the Continent. Many of these were Lancashire men themselves: one in six of those entering the seminary at Douai in 1584 was from Lancashire. Others came to the county because it was an attractive area in which to work – the gentry could provide hospitality and the generally favourable climate of opinion reduced the risks to the priest. By the end of 1603 452 missionaries had been sent from Douai and of these sixty-six worked in Lancashire. The presence of so many priests ensured the care of their flock, the winning of converts and the prevention of any backsliding by recusants who might seek an easy way out of the penalties. It must also have seemed to many Catholics that the standard of the clergy of the Anglican church fell far short of the character and behaviour of the new missionary priests to whom they were becoming accustomed. The spectacle of the Vicar of Whalley, who was notorious for his ale house tricks, 'When he cannot discern black from blue, dances with a full cup on his head, far passing all the rest', can have done little to impress them with the superiority of the Church of England. However, it is worth mentioning that in the same complaint, brought in 1575, Dobson, the dancing vicar, was also accused of Popish practices. It must be remembered that great difficulty had been encountered in finding men of suitable calibre to replace the dispossessed recusant priests and many unworthy clergy had been appointed.

This, briefly, was the climate of opinion in which that enigmatic figure, Sir Richard Shireburne, lived. Certainly most of his contemporaries were convinced that in his own heart he adhered to Rome. However, Shireburne was a pragmatist whose main preoccupation seems to have been the enhancement and preservation of his estates and the increase of his fortune. In this he was very successful and it cannot be expected that such a man would sacrifice his gains, abandon by a quixotic gesture his position in society, loose his prestige and imperil his new fortune by declaring his religious disloyalty. Shireburne needed his offices and his standing in the county to reinforce his campaign of territorial aggrandisement, while the authorities needed Shireburne because no one else could so effectively represent them in the area. An agent in 1591 reported that Shireburne's wife and children seldom went to Church and never took communion, and that the marriage services of some of his daughters had been carried out by men suspected of being massing priests. He had obviously covered his tracks very carefully, and it is apparent that names and dates by which he might be condemned could not be given. The seventeenth-century antiquary Dodsworth hints that Shireburne was so valued by Queen Elizabeth that he was given permission to practise his religion free from interference. This seems improbable, for though Shireburne's co-operation was valuable it would hardly seem worthy of such a great concession.

Almost as an act of defiance, Sir Richard resolved in about 1590 to use some of his new-found wealth to build a house at Stonyhurst which by its palatial style and the grandeur of its design, would make an arrogant assertion of the power of the Shireburnes. The house is of special interest since it marks a turning point in the architectural development of buildings in Lancashire. In design it is a medieval courtyard house, with the traditional great hall, service wing and family accommodation, and much of its architectural style is derived from earlier Gothic roots – as exemplified by the mullioned and transomed windows and the crenellated parapets. But in the great gatehouse, with its intelligent use of Classical forms and decorations, we have the first large-scale example of Renaissance architecture in Lancashire. We have no explanation of what forces of taste or ostentation made this essentially conservative man decide to order the construction of so revolutionary a piece of work.

It seems that the original house stood on the site now occupied by the west wing of the school. Until the nineteenth century various remnants of this building, of fourteenth and fifteenth-century date, remained, but these were cleared away for the building of the present wing. Sir Richard's house, which was built during the 1590s (the actual dates being uncertain) was to be disposed around a quadrangle some 80 feet by 90 feet (24m × 27m). To the north-east was the wing containing the great hall. This was a two-storey stone-built block with storage rooms on the ground floor and the hall above. Access to the hall was by an external stone staircase, the remains of which are still to be seen in the grounds of the school. The hall is now used by the school as a dining room, and at its lower end has a gallery of timbers recovered from the earlier house and dated 1423. At the upper end of the hall a doorway led to the withdrawing room, which was demolished as part of the Victorian extension of the school building.

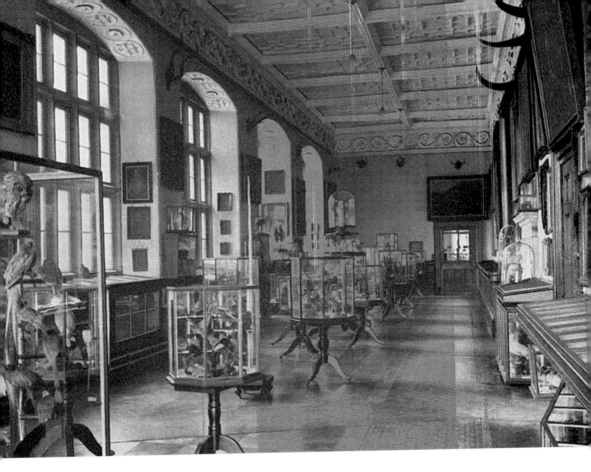

This withdrawing room adjoined the long gallery, which extended the full
length of the east wing and ended in a balcony that served as a family pew in
the chapel. The ground floor of this wing was made up of four smaller rooms,
each with its own entrance to the courtyard. These may have served as
rooms for members of the household. If so, they hark back to an old
arrangement which was typical of the later medieval period and can be seen in
fortified houses such as Wingfield (Derbyshire). The present arrangement of
this wing, and the addition of a staircase in a demi-hexagonal tower, is the
result of the building work of Sir Nicholas, the last of the Shireburnes, in
the early years of the eighteenth century.

The east wing ended in what, from the outside, appeared to be a shallow
square turret, strengthening the impression of a defensible house. This tower
was known as the Blind Tower due to the absence of windows on the south
front. The tower, together with the width of the rooms of the east wing, formed
the chapel, a room which extended through both floors. The windowless design
was to prevent casual observers from being aware of the purpose or the furnishings of the room, which could have betrayed its Catholic intent. The present
large Perpendicular-style window is a much later insertion, and was
brought from Bayley Hall, the original family home, by the Duchess of Norfolk
in about 1750.

A short wing with of Elizabethan transomed windows connects the chapel to the amazing gatehouse. In essence the gatehouse is yet another retrospection to the Middle Ages, since no house built in the purely Classical tradition would have such a feature, but an apparently fortified entrance was de rigeur for the larger Tudor house. Originally the gate towers would have looked more military, as the turrets and cupolas with their lead domes and heraldic eagles were added in 1712 by Sir Nicholas. On the tower are the four classical orders of architecture, arranged correctly according to the principles enunciated by Palladio. The columns of the ground floor are Doric, above this Ionic columns are used, and on the two upper floors those of Corinthian style. For perfection the height of the columns should increase with distance from the ground but at Stonyhurst they tend to telescope. Otherwise, with its round headed arch, coffered ceiling, antique busts in the spandrels and its triglyph frieze, it is a very good effort by a provincial and anonymous mason working in a totally unfamiliar style. It must have created astonishment and envy among the neighbouring gentry by its bold radicalism. We have seen how it formed the pattern for emulation at nearby Browsholme.

At this point in the work construction of the house stopped. Sir Richard died in July 1594 and was succeeded by his son, also Richard. The younger Richard was prepared to make public acknowledgement of his Catholicism and thus incurred heavy recusancy fines. In 1632 he compounded for the two-thirds of his estate liable to confiscation, by an annual payment to the Crown of £48 13s. 4d. This was followed by further drains on the family's financial resources during the Civil War. So it was probably lack of money which forced the abandonment of the ambitious plans of the elder Sir Richard. The entire west wing and parts of the north wing, at the lower end of the hall, remained incomplete or were not even started.

The last two Shireburnes, yet another Richard and Nicholas, made few changes to the house itself, except the additions that we have already noted. However, Sir Nicholas did a great deal to contribute to the splendid setting of the house today. The two canals flanking the drive and the ornamental gate piers are the result of his wholesale landscaping of the grounds. He was also responsible for the terrace with its two gazebos looking out over the Ribble valley. These elegant little structures, with a hint of chinoiserie about them, are reminiscent of the work of Vanbrugh at Castle Howard and his Temple of the Winds.

Following the death of Sir Nicholas in 1717 the inheritance passed to his daughter, the Duchess of Norfolk, his only son having died – reputedly after eating yew berries. The Duchess lived at Stonyhurst occasionally during her husband's lifetime and made it her home during her widowhood after 1732. On her death in 1742 the estates passed to her aunt, Elizabeth, the sister of Nicholas, who was married to William Weld of Lulworth in Dorset. From then until 1794 the house fell into neglect and dereliction. However, the Weld family had many connections with the Jesuit school at St Omer, an establishment which found itself increasingly under threat in the revolutionary Europe of the 1780s and 1790s. A move to Bruges and then on to Liege gave them some temporary respite but, as the hostility of the authorities increased, Thomas Weld, great grandson of Elizabeth Shireburne, offered the Order his disused house in Lancashire as a safe haven. There the school has remained and the building has been added to and enlarged at various periods to form what Pevsner has described as 'the most successful scholastic buildings of their day in England'.

Adjacent to, and virtually incorporated within, the school buildings is the gorgeous and exuberant parish church of St Peter designed by Scoles in 1832. It is one of the first Catholic churches built after the final repeal of the penal laws against Catholicism in 1829. For a short time the triumphalist feelings of the newly-emancipated Catholics were reflected in the architectural forms that they used. It was a time when it was believed that a triumph of the Counter-Reformation was at hand – a mood encouraged by the Oxford Movement within the Church of England and the conversion of several notable Anglicans.

It is fitting that such a monument should remain here at Stonyhurst, where the recusant tradition of Lancashire life was so strong and where it had been

St Peter's Church, Stonyhurst. This building by J.J. Scoles was one of the first Catholic churches to be built and consecrated after the repeal of the legal restrictions on Catholics in 1829. It reflects the triumphal feelings of some English Catholics at this liberation after so many years of constraint. The careful copying of medieval architecture can be seen as an attempt to return to the days when Catholicism had been supreme throughout Britain. There was a religious dimension to the 'Battle of the Styles' in Victorian England which is often overlooked.

PHOTOGRAPH COURTESY OF JOHN W. PRICE LBIPP, LMPA, WESTMINSTER STUDIOS, LANGHO reinforced by the arrival of the Jesuits to create a permanent home for the Order in a county where they had been active since the first days of the Mission. The strong thread of Catholicism has always run through the distinctive fabric of Lancashire life. Stonyhurst is a living reminder of this facet of the history of the county both in its origins and in its second incarnation as one of the foremost Catholic boys' schools. If one cannot truly see Sir Richard Shireburne as a faithful son of the Church, he was an eyewitness to and participant in those conditions of official neglect, negligence and inefficiency, which gave strength to the simple but determined piety of sixteenth-century Lancastrians. To these factors were added the isolation of the county from the main channels of intellectual life and, by a strange irony, the uncertain parochial structure of the county, to make a fertile soil in which the old Church had struck deep roots. Aided by the support of the landowning families this 'sink of Popery', this 'dark corner of the land' was able to set a pattern that was unique to the area and in contradiction to the national trends.

CHAPTER 4

Samlesbury Hall
and Witchcraft

THOMAS POTTS STARTED IT. The story was taken up by Harrison Ainsworth, and continued by Robert Neill. Books both serious and not so serious have been written, plays performed, and even a musical has been based on their activities. Around Pendle the witches have become almost an industry, so that the events of 1612 have been trivialised and distorted. Yet in the early seventeenth century, Lancashire had a country-wide reputation as a haunt of witches. Indeed, so far flung was their fame that the word Demdike, the nickname by which Elizabeth Sowans, leader of the Pendle coven, was known, for a time became almost synonymous with witch. So we find in 1627 William Wilkinson of Skippool, near Poulton le Fylde, calling his awkward and feared neighbour, Dorothy Shawe, 'Witch and Demdike' and fearing that his wife, children and goods were in peril from her malignity.

The Lancaster assize of August 1612 had proved sensational. A total of nineteen people including ten women and two men from the Pendle area, were arraigned on charges of witchcraft and all but two were found guilty and executed on the new gibbet on Lancaster Moor. The Clerk of the Court, Thomas Potts, saw his opportunity and wrote and published his account of the trial, held before the judges Sir Edward Bromley and Sir James Altham. His *Wonderful Discoverie of Witchcraft in the Countie of Lancaster* seems to have become a bestseller for a time. The stars of Potts' book were the Pendle witches and it is on them that subsequent attention has been focused. Much less interest was aroused by what is in many ways a more significant case, which took place on the morning of the third day of the assize, Wednesday 19 August 1612. It was heard in the time between the trial of the first batch of the Pendle witches, who had been tried the previous day and that of the second group. On that Wednesday afternoon the case against Anne Redfern, Alice Nutter, Katherine Hewitt ('Mouldheels' to her intimates), John and Jane Bulcock, Alizon Device and Margaret Pearson was heard. Of these only the Bulcocks were acquitted: the rest were condemned to death. Also that afternoon another indictment for witchcraft was heard, against Isobel Roby of Windle near St Helens: she was also found guilty – a remarkable example of the speed at which seventeenth-century justice could move!

The case heard on this Wednesday morning concerned a group of women who lived in the village of Samlesbury and the case had been brought on the testimony of the granddaughter of one of the defendants. Grace Sowerbutts was fourteen and she accused her grandmother Jennet Bierley, and Ellen Bierley her aunt, together with Mistress Jane Southworth of Samlesbury Lower Hall of 'wasting' her body by the practice of witchcraft. The appearance of child witnesses, often relatives, was a feature of witchcraft trials. In the Pendle case the most damning testimony against the women came from the nine-year-old Jennet Device; and in the famous American Salem witches case the evidence of children was the basis for the prosecution.

The Sowerbutts family were farmers at Yew Tree Farm in Samlesbury, the father, Thomas, being described as a husbandman. The distinction between husbandman and yeoman was a fine and variable one, but it would seem that Thomas Sowerbutts was one of the lesser farmers of the area, a man of some substance and not one of the landless labourers and cottagers on the margins of poverty who so often feature in witch cases.

The story that Grace revealed to the court was a strange and fantastic one, in which all the elements of contemporary demonology appeared. The first incident took place some two years before when the accused women, together with an unnamed old 'Doewife' of Samlesbury, was said to have lifted Grace by the hair of her head to the top of a hay mow in Henry Bierley's barn. Henry was the husband of the accused Ellen Bierley. Shortly afterwards, when on an errand to her aunt's in Osbaldeston, Grace had met her grandmother in a field. At that time Jennet Bierley was in her own shape, but soon afterwards she reappeared in the form of a black dog, which pushed Grace off a stile – though neither the fall nor the apparition did her any harm. On the return journey, when she was accompanied by her father, Grace told him the story of that day's adventure and other attacks that she had suffered. When asked by the court why she had delayed telling her father or anybody else she claimed that the evil women would not allow her to speak. An unanswerable riposte!

A few days later, on a Saturday, Grace was walking towards Samlesbury Boat (a ferry across the Ribble), when she met her grandmother who repeated her metamorphosis. The black dog walked beside her, on the left hand side. One is reminded of Gilbert's 'Corroborative detail ... to give verisimilitude to an otherwise bald and unconvincing narrative'. Of course, the left was always the Devil's side and regarded as unlucky and 'sinister'. On reaching a water-filled pit the dog invited Grace to drown herself, assuring her it was an easy death. Grace, a model of moral rectitude, declined the invitation. At this point a 'Being', wrapped in a white sheet appeared, and took her to safety, the black dog disappearing on the arrival of this apparition.

A few fields further on the black dog appeared again and transported her to the barn of a neighbour, Hugh Walshman. There the dog laid her on the straw, covered her with more straw and then lay upon her until she lost consciousness. She recovered to find herself lying in a bed at Walshman's house. By this time it was Monday night. She learned that she had been found by some friends and brought to the house. As she was taken home the following day her grandmother and Ellen Bierley met them on the road, whereupon Grace fell down and was not able to speak until the Friday. She now claimed that 'a good while before this' she had been told by Jennet Bierley to go with her to the house of Thomas Walshman; they were joined by Ellen, and on arrival her grandmother had opened the doors by magic. Jennet Bierley had then gone to the Walshmans' chamber and taken their baby from between the sleeping mother and father. She had thrust a nail into the child's navel and sucked the blood, using a quill as a straw. The child was then returned to its unconscious parents and the witches returned to their homes. Shortly afterwards the baby sickened and died.

The night after the child was buried the two women, taking Grace with them, went to the church yard and dug up the body and took it to Jennet's house. There they dismembered the corpse; some portions were boiled in a pot and some were roasted on the coals. The cooked flesh was eaten by Jennet and Ellen, who urged Grace Sowerbutts and Ellen's daughter Grace to join them. They steadfastly refused. The grisly meal having finished, the remaining bones were seethed in a pot. The witches told her that with the grease thus obtained they would anoint their bodies and thus be able to change their shape. They also assured her that after they had finished the bones would be returned to the grave.

Some six months before the assize Grace went to meet her grandmother at a place called Red Bank on the side of the Ribble. Ellen was there and also Jane Southworth. Jane Southworth was an illegitimate daughter of Sir Richard Shireburne, and the wife of John Southworth of Lower Hall at Samlesbury. Southworth had died shortly before, and so it was as a recent widow that Jane stood accused.

When the trio and Grace reached the waterside

There came unto them, as they went thither, four black things, going upright, and yet not like men in the face; which four did carry the said three women and the examinate [Grace] over the water, and when they came to Red Bank they found something there which they did eat. But Witness saith she never saw such meat; and therefore she durst not eat thereof, although her grandmother did bid her eat. And after they had eaten, the said women and the witness danced every one of them and after their dancing the said three black things did pull down the said three Women and did abuse their bodies, as this examinate thinketh, for she saith the black thing that was with her, did abuse her body.

Further similar incidents, with more fainting fits and mysterious trances and transportations, followed these events. On two occasions Mistress Southworth had rendered Grace unconscious and carried her, the first time to the top of a hay stack three or four yards high and at the second meeting had thrown her in a ditch. The previous Tuesday Jane had come to her father's house, and taken Grace and carried her to a barn and had thrust her head between the planks that were in a pile there.

Just to round off her testimony Grace recollected that during the riverside orgy various other women, who she did not know, but thought lived north of the Ribble, came and looked on but did not participate.

Further evidence was called. Thomas Walshman gave evidence about the unexpected death of his child some twelve months before, although even he did not speculate about the cause of death or make any allegation of witchcraft. He also testified to having found the apparently unconscious Grace Sowerbutts in his barn. A further witness was John Singleton, yeoman of Samlesbury who testified that he had heard that old Sir John Southworth, grandfather of Jane's husband, had accused her of being a witch and refused to pass the house where she lived. This evidence was corroborated by Thomas Alker, another Samlesbury farmer, who said that he had heard 'Sir John Southworth say that he liked her not and that he doubted she would bewitch him'. This evidence, though sounding convincing, was weakened by the fact that old Sir John had died in 1595, seventeen years before the trial and that at the time his grandson was about fourteen and unmarried – not that this was pointed out at the time! This evidence concluded the case for the prosecution. The Judges then asked the prisoners to make a statement: they begged him 'humbly upon their knees with weeping tears … for God's cause to examine Grace Sowerbutts who set her on, or by whose names this accusation came against them'. It must be remembered that at this time the prisoners in a capital case were not allowed counsel or to examine witnesses.

On hearing this request the prosecution witnesses were thrown into confusion and quarrelling broke out. The judge then interrogated Grace and her father. Thomas Sowerbutts denied any knowledge of a conspiracy but eventually Grace broke down and confessed that she had 'gone to learn with one Thompson, a seminary priest who had instructed and taught her this accusation, because they were once obstinate Papists and now came to Church [had been converted to Protestantism]'. On examination Jane Southworth said that some six weeks or a month before she had met 'Master Thompson alias Southworth, a priest and had conference with him in a place called Barn Hey Lane, where and when she challenged him for slandering her to be a witch'. He replied that he was only repeating family gossip which he had been told by her mother and her aunt. However, Jane put it down to the fact that she had been converted to the Church of England and would not be persuaded from it. Master Thompson was Christopher Southworth, a well known Catholic priest. He had been one of the original students at the English College in Rome and had signed a petition to retain the Jesuit administration of the college. In 1587 he was arrested and imprisoned in the Compter in London and at Wisbech. Later, he had served as missioner in the Ribble valley area. This was his family's district and it is likely that their houses provided a base for him. He was the son of old Sir John Southworth and therefore uncle to Jane's late husband.

Whether or not this new story was any more likely than Grace's farrago may be wondered at, but in the intellectual climate of the times anything associated with Popery was hated and feared almost as much as witchcraft. It was then widely believed that a seminary priest and a Jesuit was capable of any mischief, and the case against the three accused women was dismissed. No action was taken against the witnesses, except that Grace was sent to the charge of Mr Leigh, a sound Protestant preacher from Standish, and Mr Chisnall of Chisnall Hall, both justices of the peace. On examination by them she confirmed that the whole story was a lie prompted by the urgings of Christopher Southworth.

Something of a mystery surrounds those accused in this case. Our sole source for the story of both the Pendle and the Samlesbury witches is Potts' *Wonderful Discoverie*: no other record of the trial or the depositions survives. At the beginning of the book he lists 'The names of the witches committed to the Castle of Lancaster' and under a sub-heading 'The Witches of Samlesbury' gives, in addition to the Bierleys and Jane Southworth, John Ramesden, Elizabeth Astley, Alice Gray (who was, in fact, implicated in the Pendle trial), Isabel Sidegraves and Lawrence Hay. Nothing more is heard of them until the end of the assize when Sir Edward Bromley was discharging those found not guilty. His reported address to them implies that although the jury had acquitted them their innocence was far from proved; 'Yet without question there are among you, that are as deep in this Action as any of them that are condemned to die for their offences: the time is now for you to forsake the Devil'. If they were as guilty as those condemned to die, what were they guilty of? The Samlesbury case had collapsed in ruins, and the other three accused were discharged utterly and not bound over to appear at the next assize as were these five mysterious prisoners. As far as we know, no one was condemned to die for the Samlesbury case, which had been accepted as a tissue of Papist-inspired lies, and at no stage in the evidence given by Grace Sowerbutts or the other witnesses are these people mentioned. Did Potts get his first list wrong and include names of those involved in Pendle? But then, with the exception of Alice Gray, none of these names is mentioned in either the depositions prepared by Nowell before the trial or the evidence given in court. This mystery will now never be resolved.

It was well known that the Southworth family were stubborn recusants and that members of the family were serving in the English mission. In strongly recusant Lancashire they could be regarded as some of the most stalwart upholders of the Roman Catholic religion, and thus are recorded on Lord Burghley's map of the county of 1590. This map had been prepared for Lord Burghley at a time when it was widely feared by the government that subversive Catholic elements in Lancashire were involved in plotting against the Crown. On the map are marked the houses of the principal gentry families and those whose adherence to recusancy was well known were branded with a red cross. The Southworths were obviously still under suspicion, although Sir John – after imprisonment and being forced to live in London – had paid a fine of

£400 and received a royal pardon after his attendance at church. The family had long had a violent reputation in Lancashire. Sometimes their violence was directed towards the enemies of their king. Sir Thomas Southworth (c. 1360–1415) had served as an esquire in the retinue of the Duke of Lancaster for a yearly wage of £10, and then in the French Wars, when he provided a company of fifty archers. These seem to have served in the body guard of the king and Southworth was paid £113 15s. 0d. for their services. The Knight died ingloriously of dysentery during the siege of Harfleur. His great-grandson, Christopher, was knighted in 1482 while fighting in Scotland and his son, Sir John (whose reputed funerary helm and sword hang in St Leonard's Church, near the Samlesbury Lower Hall) was at Flodden Field. Sir John's son, Thomas, was knighted for his service in the Scots wars of the 1540s. His grandson, John, also served in Scotland and was rewarded with a knighthood in 1547 when he commanded first 100 and then 200 men. This was the Sir John who was alleged to have accused his granddaughter-in-law of witchcraft.

Sometimes the aggression of the Southworths was directed at other and less worthy targets. In 1450 Richard Southworth was accused by the widow of a kinsman, William Southworth of Southworth, near Warrington, of being responsible for the death of her husband. William had been waylayed on Duxbury Moor and robbed of £17 and at the same time goods and money at Culcheth were stolen. Richard paid £20 to settle the matter. In 1513 Sir John, the hero of Flodden, was accused of inciting two of his servants to kill William Banastre of Lostock and again compensation had to be paid to the widow. In

the following year he was present at a cockfight at Winwick which ended in a riot, in which he was involved. In 1521 his son Sir Thomas, was given safe keeping of a casket of money by a friend. On its return it was found that a bladder containing 100 marks (more than £66) was missing and Southworth was sued for its return.

In Samlesbury the Southworths had two houses – the Lower Hall located in the bend of the river, north of Samlesbury village, and the Upper Hall, now adjacent to the A677 and enclosed by the airfield of BAE Systems. The remains of the Lower Hall lie among the buildings of a farm of that name. It was thought that the riverside site was the original home of the D'Ewyas family and that it was destroyed in the Scots raid led by Robert the Bruce in 1322. At this time the whole of the northern part of Lancashire as far south as Chorley, was devastated and houses and villages burned. Samlesbury was a particular target as half the manor was held by King Edward II, having been confiscated from Robert de Holland. There now are thought to be indications that the lands in this lower area of Samlesbury belonged to the de Holland portion of the manor while the house of the D'Ewyas family was on the higher, drier lands, possibly on the site of the Upper Hall. At about the time of the Scots raid Alice D'Ewyas married Gilbert de Southworth from Warrington, and her father settled his moiety of the manor on her and her husband. It seems likely that it was after this that the decision to build a new home on this sheltered site was made. The Lower Hall was acquired and rebuilt as a subsidiary family home, possibly intended for a dower house. All that remains today is half of the façade, with a central door and a gabled projection that can hardly be called a porch, but is designed to give consequence to the entrance door. The building material is a greyish stone with the mullions and transoms of the 'cross windows' of a

The courtyard, Samlesbury Hall. The oldest part of the house, the attenuated remains of the Great Hall, face the camera; above the oriel window is a solar or oratory. The extended family wing of Sir Thomas Southworth fills the rest of the frame to the left. The proportion of timber to plasterwork is remarkable, even for an area noted for its lavish use of oak.

PHOTOGRAPH, AUTHOR

yellowish sandstone. The masonry of the projection is rusticated and the door has something of the air of a 'Gibbs Door', being decorated with a heavily emphasised architraves and lintel. The façade would seem to date from the late seventeenth century, while the door might be somewhat later. The right hand, or eastern, portion of the façade has been virtually rebuilt into a farm outhouse at some time in the past. Nothing of what lay behind the façade is visible to the casual visitor. This house was settled by Sir Thomas Southworth on his son John and his wife Jane in 1605. Their son, Thomas, sold the hall to the Walmesley family of Dunkenhalgh in 1632. (Please note that permission to view the remains should be sought at the adjacent farm/nursery.)

The Upper Hall, or Old Hall as it is sometimes known, has become a popular attraction, partly due to its picturesque appearance. It must be said that this owes a great deal to its restoration in the 1830s and to its very active development by a vigorous Friends' Trust in more recent years. The hall as it stands today is only a partial survivor of the house of the Southworth family from about 1330 to 1679. Originally the site was moated, though any traces of the defences are difficult to perceive now. The plan of this house was typical of its period. The central feature was a great hall of timber construction with an extension at the eastern end for service rooms and a family portion at the western end. It is thought that when originally built the three portions of the house were in alignment. As might be expected, cruck construction was used in the hall and a portion of one of the original cruck blades can now be seen through a glass panel inserted into the end wall of the hall wing, adjacent to the teashop entrance. Most of the great hall as it survives today dates from the fifteenth century, when there seems to have been a programme of rebuilding.

As part of this building project, in about 1420 Thomas Southworth was granted a licence to maintain a private chapel. A detached chapel was built south of the family wing. In the first half of the sixteenth century another Thomas Southworth undertook an extensive building scheme by which a new and extended family wing was built to the south west to link the chapel to the hall block. The south-west wall was rebuilt in brick with diaper patterns in blue brick, and two stone traceried windows were inserted into the Chapel. The story goes that these were originally in Whalley Abbey but were bought by Sir Thomas at the time of the Dissolution. The other walls of this wing are in the extravagant timber-framed style of the area, and here the fashion is carried to such extremes that the wall is almost solid timber. One suspects that the scattered grotesque carvings are the result of the Victorian restoration of the hall, which did so much to give it its present air of quaintness. In the new family wing the upper floor was taken up by two chambers or private bed-sitting rooms, one heated by an elaborate stone fireplace. The ceilings were originally carved and painted, but were lost when they collapsed in the eighteenth century. These rooms are now opened up to form what is incorrectly known as the long gallery. At the west end there is a small room which, according to repute, was the priest's room, and may have originated as an oratory or as a family solar in the early house.

The ground floor of the west wing is made up of the chapel, the entrance hall that was created in the nineteenth century, and a fine parlour which contains a stone fireplace carved with the name of Thomas Southworth. From here a door leads to the great hall. As we have said, this still makes use of the original timber framing but little else in the hall is original. It has suffered from the decision of its nineteenth-century owners to demolish the north end of the hall. Originally the high table was located in a recess on the south wall and flanked by doors to the family wing of the house: these can still be seen. At the north end of the room was the entrance passage, separated from the hall by a screen. Portions of the screen survive, and these show that it was decorated with fantastic convoluted columns, similar to those at Rufford Old Hall (see chapter 9). With the demolition of the north end of the hall the screen was moved to the other end of the hall, where it occupies a ludicrous position. Fragments of the screen, dated 1532, and other seventeenth-century fragments were re-used to make the absurd minstrels' gallery. The fireplace arch is huge and of sixteenth-century date, but it occupies the site of the original fire and has a massive external chimney. The hall, as at Rufford and Speke, has an oriel or compass window, which, though restored on its exterior walls, is original on the interior. The stained glass of 1932 represents the changing arms of the dukes of Lancaster. The hall has been furnished with examples of the skill of local craftsmen. Though these are excellent in themselves, and symbolic of Samlesbury Hall's reputation as a centre of modern craftsmanship and art in the area, the wisdom of their inclusion in the great hall might be questioned.

Commercialism is not new to the hall. It remained the Southworth home until 10 March 1678, when it was sold by Edward Southworth – impoverished

Built about 1545, Samlesbury is one of the earliest uses of brick in the area. They are of a soft, pinkish hue, decorated with blue brick, and are very narrow and uneven, thick mortar being used to achieve a level course. The traceried chapel window is reputed to have been brought from Whalley Abbey at the Dissolution.

PHOTOGRAPH, AUTHOR

by recusancy fines and the payment of a composition fine of £359 during the Commonwealth – to Thomas Braddyll of Portfield and Conishead. Braddyll seems to have had no intention of living there. The house was plundered of its treasures and was subsequently let as accommodation for handloom weavers and as tenements. Little attention was paid to its upkeep and the house became steadily more dilapidated. In 1830 the turnpike road between Preston and Blackburn was under construction and parts of the house, including the great hall, became the Braddyll Arms serving first the navvies and then the travellers on the road until 1846. It then became a girl's school until 1862, when it was bought by Joseph Harrison, a self-made business man from Blackburn who was then living at Galligreaves Hall.

Harrison began a programme of wholesale restoration and building, which included the construction of a billiard room attached to the lower end of the hall by a conservatory. Today Samlesbury Hall reflects in many of its rooms the ideas and tastes of a wealthy Victorian caught up in nostalgia for medieval England. However, Harrison ensured the continuance of the house though he himself enjoyed it for but a brief period; overcome by debts incurred in the rebuilding and by his lavish life style, he took his own life. The house was again occupied by a local worthy who perhaps lacked the resources for its proper upkeep and by the 1920s it was again scheduled for demolition. Fortunately at this point the Friends' Trust was formed and the long, slow process of bringing Samlesbury back to life was begun.

These then were the homes of the family of Jane Southworth, though it seems that she and her husband as a cadet branch of the family, had lived at the Lower Hall. So we can return to the story of Grace Sowerbutts and the Samlesbury witches.

The whole case of the Samlesbury witches raises a number of points concerning the apparently sudden prevalence of witchcraft in England. Between the first trial at Chelmsford in 1556 and the last witch execution at Exeter in 1686, there were numerous trials and many more accusations of devilish practice. Perhaps between 500 and 1,000 people were sent to their deaths. However, by the end of the seventeenth century, except at a very vulgar level, the belief in witches seems almost totally to have disappeared, so that in 1736 the Act of 1604 – which had introduced the death penalty for witchcraft – was repealed and by the new law it became an offence to make accusations against witches or to pretend to practise the black arts. It is a remarkable transformation in public perception that a belief which received such wide credence should apparently have disappeared of its own volition. We must ask why the belief in such patently improbable activities should have been so widespread in the first place – it is important to remember that this conviction was not confined to the poorer and less educated classes, but that it was accepted by even the most educated and intellectual groups. We must also consider how this particular case at Samlesbury conforms to the norm of the witchcraft trials of the period. There are several important differences between this, and the case of the Pendle witches, as well as the generality of prosecutions brought

throughout the country. Also, we must ask to what extent is the explanation which was accepted at the time – that it was all a Popish plot – a reasonable answer to the accusations that were made.

Belief in witchcraft is probably as old as man. In almost every primitive society we find that there are those who, by claiming magical powers, an ability to communicate with the spirits of the dead, or to act as an intermediary between the people and their gods, have achieved a status of power, veneration and often fear. Certainly in early medieval Europe there was a widespread acceptance that there were in every community people, men or women, who could wield magical powers. By applied psychology, by the use of herbs, and by mysterious rituals, spells and amulets these people could cure illness or conversely cause misfortune or sickness, could create love philtres or induce loathing. These 'Wise Men or Women' could be found in most villages and hamlets and we can see in them some parallels with the witchdoctors of Africa or shamans of the native Americans. Official attitudes to these conjurors, as they were sometimes known from their claim that they could raise the spirits of the dead to reveal truth to the living, was somewhat ambiguous. The church could not approve of their activities but it was in general prepared to ignore them, secure in the belief that God would protect men from the inept attacks of the demons that these necromancers might raise. As for their more earthly activities, if harm (*maleficium*) could be shown to have been done by magical powers, action could be taken in the Church courts.

However, after about 1100 a gradual change is perceptible and a whole new element is introduced into the equation. This had its origins in a growing emphasis in theological thinking, on the actual existence of evil in the shape of Satan, the angel expelled from heaven who, though ultimately under the control

The south wall of the family wing shows an interesting contrast in style of brickwork in which it was originally built and the nineteenth-century reconstructions. The older bricks – visible in the chimney breast and which were hand-made – are thin and of irregular shape and size. The corners are reinforced with stone quoins. The later work is hard and of much greater regularity and makes use of machine-made bricks.

PHOTOGRAPH, AUTHOR

of God as the omnipotent force in the universe, was allowed to act as the instrument for the punishment of men's evil behaviour. Over the chancel arch of every medieval church was a painting of the 'Doom': Christ in majesty sits in the centre, while the living and the dead are judged and sent either to heaven or reprobated to hell where they are tortured by demons. A temporary but potent development of these ideas was the Manachean heresy of the Cathars, who accepted a duality between God who ruled the spiritual world and the devil who ruled the earth.

As Satan loomed ever larger in the minds of the Church, a new belief became accepted – that witches were the agents of the Devil and that they had rejected their Christianity in his favour. In return for their souls the Devil would reward them with wealth, power and whatever they desired on earth. The Faust legend is the best known expression of this belief. On this basis there began to accrue a corpus of knowledge, based on legend, rumour, superstitions, prurient imaginings and fantasies and this became the received picture of witchcraft. It was in the middle of the thirteenth century that the writings of St Thomas Aquinas put all these beliefs into a coherent structure and clearly defined the nature of the evil. From the time of Aquinas to the middle of the fifteenth century the movement gathered force and from 1326 witchcraft was, by papal decree, made a matter for the Inquisition. The years following saw an ever-increasing awareness of the evil of the witches and a growing acceptance of their responsibility for most of the evils and misfortunes of mankind.

In 1486 two German Dominican Inquisitors, Heinrich Kramer and Jacob Sprenger, published their *Malleus Maleficarum, The Hammer of Evil Doing*. This work proved, by the best scholastic methods, the absolute existence of witchcraft, citing biblical, classical and patristic evidence. It went on to become a text book on the detection, trial and execution of witches. Its influence was widespread, partly through the coincidence of its appearance with the popularisation of printing, and it became the recognised authority on *maleficium*, the doing of evil. In its pages details are given of the ways in which the Devil snared his worshippers by obtaining the disposal of the victim's soul in exchange for their desires. The argument raised by sceptics, that the witches were often drawn from the ranks of the poorest in society, was easily deflected by the riposte that this merely demonstrated how Satan cheated his adherents. The book relates the details of the Sabbath, the witches' ceremony that was a perversion of the Mass, of the feasting on the flesh of dead children, of copulation with demons, of the witches' ability to fly (often using an ointment made from the fat of their victims), of the ability of witches to use the familiar spirit that had been given to them by the Devil to inflict harm or death on their enemies, and the use of the destruction of images to bring about death and disease. Most of the ideas which are now popularly associated with the practice of witchcraft are to be found in the *Malleus*.

Another theme running through the book is a virulent misogyny: this was a feature of much medieval thought but it is especially marked in the writings of the two Germans, in which women are depicted as the root and centre of all the evils of the world, they are blamed for the temptation and the fall of man. They are depicted as crazed with insatiable lust, and as people who to satisfy their desires, are much more prone than men to accept the prospects offered by Satan, whose worship involved physical gratification. There can be no doubt that the *Malleus* was at least partially responsible for the fact that the majority of the conservatively estimated 50,000 to 100,000 people destroyed in the great witch persecutions were women.

By the beginning of the sixteenth century the witch cult was seen as established throughout most of continental Europe, and as an ever-growing threat to the Christian church. The Roman church responded by an increasing use of the Inquisitions established in most states to root out and destroy the peril. In an age when the pillars of the accepted world began to show signs of crumbling as feudalism declined, the Protestant reformers challenged the universality of the Church, and the effects of the philosophies of the classical world were influencing thought and politics, some explanation had to be found: the malignancy of the witches and the manipulations of the Devil offered an easily acceptable rationale. In this changing world the attempts to extirpate witchcraft went on, with an ever-gathering momentum. 'The years 1550–1600 were worse than the years 1500–1550 and the years 1600–1650 were worse still … it was forwarded by the cultivated Popes of the Renaissance, by the great protestant Reformers, by the saints of the Counter Reformation, by the scholars, lawyers and churchmen of the age of Scaliger and Lipsius, Bacon and Grotius, Berulle and Pascal'.

As in so many other things, the persecution was slow in reaching England and was diluted to some extent on the way. In England there was no Inquisition and allegations of witchcraft were usually dealt with by the ecclesiastical courts of the bishops, who might treat it as a lapse towards heresy. In other cases, such as the accusations of William Wilkinson against Dorothy Shaw, it was seen and dealt with as a breach of the peace. Throughout most of the period of the Tudors this reasonable tolerance persisted, partly (one suspects) because in English minds the practice of witchcraft was seen as based on Catholic heresies and attitudes and as a product of the repressive influence of the Roman Church and the Inquisitions. Writing in the second half of the seventeenth century John Webster of Clitheroe, scholar and sceptic, virtually puts the onus for the witch persecution on the inventions of the Inquisition. However, England was not immune to the intellectual climate of Europe and as the sixteenth century progressed there was a gathering body of belief in the existence of witch covens in the country. As the Reformation had cast doubt on the rituals of exorcism, witchcraft came to be regarded as a matter for the law and the judiciary. The first legislation specifically directed against witches was an Act of 1542. Even in this it can be seen that the English and the Continental views of the matter were different, since the Act says nothing of covenants with the Devil. The Act was repealed in 1547, perhaps because it was regarded as a relic of Popery, and it was not until 1563 that the Convocation of the Church of England asked parliament for a renewal of legislation. This

resulted in an Act of the same year which was virtually a revival of the 1542 Act, and included the death penalty for causing death by witchcraft and for a second conviction of causing bodily harm by magical means.

The arrival of the new king, James I, brought about a reappraisal of the law as it stood. The Scots king was a firm believer in the witch cult and during his reign in Scotland a number of sensational cases had been brought before the courts. The most celebrated was the trial of the North Berwick witches whose ill-will had extended to an attempt to drown both James and his bride by raising a great storm as he brought Anne from her native Denmark. James, the scholar prince, had made an exhaustive study of the witch cult and had written his *Daemonologie* in 1597. It was reissued shortly after his arrival in England. One consequence of this was the Act of Parliament of 1604 which, in response to the fears of the monarch, strengthened the law against witches to give a death sentence for killing, for causing injury, and for conjuring spirits. It was under this law that the Lancashire witches of 1612 were arraigned.

The evidence given in the trial of the Samlesbury witches exhibits many of the commonly accepted beliefs and superstitions of the period. The innocent Grace Sowerbutts is tempted to give the Devil power over her soul – not in this case by the promise of earthly rewards but by her suicide in the flooded pit – since suicide as the ultimate sin would automatically give her into the control of the Devil. The witches conform, except in one respect, to the conventional pattern: they are women, they are elderly (Potts refers to their

wrinkled faces as being almost tantamount to guilt in the eyes of the public) and they are closely associated by blood and family ties. They are capable of assuming the shapes of animals, they possess familiars and the familiar commits evil at their orders, even if in this case it is only pushing Grace off a stile. The killing of babies is practised, and their blood and flesh are used as part of the rituals. True to form, the meat consumed in their parody of the eucharist is unrecognisable and tasteless. The coven associate carnally with mysterious 'Black Things' and they are capable of flight and of the supernatural transportation of others. It is virtually a page from the *Malleus* transmuted to a Lancashire setting.

The case against the Pendle witches is much more mundane, being mainly based around neighbourly jealousy, antagonism and the malignity of several poor families. The trimmings of the witch cult are almost peripheral and one suspects are the result of leading questions put to the women by someone versed in the writings of King James. The main offences are the casting of spells and the killing of local rivals or attempts to bring about their death. This is the traditional *maleficium*, the evil doing by magic without the Satanic overtones. The mention of sabbaths and covens is superficial, and at their evil feast at Malkin Tower on Good Friday it was stolen mutton and not child flesh that they ate. Demdike, Chattox and their crew may have thought they were witches, and the people of the surrounding countryside may have believed that they were, but knowledge of the literature of witchcraft is largely absent from the evidence in their cases. On the other hand the author of the mischief at Samlesbury was well acquainted with the writings of the Exorcists.

In one particular there is a parallel between the two cases heard at Lancaster in August of 1612, and that is that they both involved a woman who was not of the station and status of those who were usually made to face such accusations. In the main, the English witches came from the lowest and poorest ranks of society and almost without exception they were elderly and socially unacceptable. In the case against the Pendle witches, however, grounds were found to involve the mysterious Alice Nutter, about whom little is known but whose family were certainly of local gentry rank. The size and quality of her house at Roughlee, although it is now subdivided, is clear evidence of this. At Samlesbury none of the accused belonged to the poorest classes and both Jane Southworth's father and husband belonged to families of high rank and importance in the area. On the Continent, during the great witch persecutions, this concentration on the lowest ranks of society, and even the almost exclusive concentration on women, was not so noticeable. An account of the great witch hunt at Wurzburg in 1629 makes this clear: 'Ah the woes and the misery of it – there are still four hundred in the City, high and low, of every rank and sex, nay even the clerics, so strongly accused that they may be arrested at any hour,' and it goes on to relate that a third part of the city is involved and that the 'richest, most attractive, most prominent of the clergy are already executed'. The other victims included a girl of modesty and purity, while children as young as three and four had been put to death in their hundreds.

A study of the witch trials of the seventeenth century in this country clearly shows that certain factors are to be found in the great majority of occurrences and that the women – and the overwhelming majority of cases did involve women – have a great deal in common. These characteristics go some way to explain how normal people could bring themselves to make the accusations against persons who were their neighbours.

One cannot do better than use the words of Reginald Scot, writing his *Discoverie of Witchcraft* in 1584, to describe the situation that we find repeated time after time. Scot was one of the sceptics in the period and his work was intended to show the fallacies and absurdities of the current views of witches and witchcraft. He was careful not to deny that witches existed, but to stress that they did not exist as they were usually depicted. Instead he offered this scene to explain how the accusations came to be made:

> One sort commonly said to be witches are women which are old, lame, blear eyed, foul and full of wrinkles. Poor sullen superstitious creatures in whose drowsy minds the Devil has a fine seat! So as whatever mischief is brought to pass they are easily persuaded the same is done by themselves. These witches are so odious to their neighbours and so feared that few dare offend them or deny them anything they ask. From this they come to think that they can do such things as are beyond the ability of human nature. They go from door to door for a potful of milk or potage, without which they could barely live. It happens sometimes that their expectations go unanswered as in the course of time the witch becomes tedious to her neighbours. So sometimes she curses one, then the other until all displease her, she curses master, wife, children and cattle. In time some of her neighbours fall sick or their cattle die and they suppose it to be the vengeance of witches. The witch on the other hand, seeing one in every hundred of her curses take effect is convinced that she has brought misfortune to pass and confesses it. So she, her accusers and the Justices are all deceived.

Thus, in one paragraph, Scot sums up the evidence of the several hundred witch trials of which we have records. In the last section he touches on one of the points which at the time was regarded as the most salient and to us one of the most mysterious – that in many, if not most, cases the accused confessed to the charge. He deals with this in another passage:

> The poor old witch is commonly unlearned, unwarned and unprovided of counsel and friendship ... void of judgement and discretion. She is daunted by authority, circumvented with guile, compelled by fear, deceived by ignorance and so brought to these absurd confessions.

Scot might perhaps have added another possible motive – pride. These social misfits, despised and loathed by their community, had been able to take some pleasure in the sense of power and the fear that they could engender among their neighbours. As we have seen, Scot considers that they often believed themselves capable of the powers popularly associated with them. The scholars attributed to the witches the power of life and death, of raising storms, of causing sexual impotence, of mysterious flight and control over the weather. The claims of the majority of witches and the matter of most allegations were usually much less important: the sickness of farm stock, the failure of cows to milk, for brewing to go sour, the failure of a crop. Occasionally, as in the Samlesbury and the Pendle charges, the witches were blamed for a mysterious death, often of a child – in an age when many children died in unexplained circumstances – or for other everyday misfortunes and tragedies.

Another feature common to most of the cases of witchcraft is the 'trigger' event or events: the moment when someone decides that an old woman is not just socially undesirable, but an actual threat who can be tolerated no longer. In the Pendle witch trial it is obvious that the women, especially the leaders Chattox and Demdike, had been locally regarded as witches for many years. Yet nothing was done about it until the incident in March 1612 when the pedlar John Law was lamed at Colne, allegedly by the evil actions of Alizon Device, after his refusal to give her pins. Time and time again a case starts with threats made after the refusal of a small charity or gift. In most cases the primary accuser has in some way acted uncharitably towards the accused – a guilty conscience is a fundamental part of the accusation. In some cases the situation was as Scot describes it, and a small gift of food or the loan of an item of household equipment had been refused. Sometimes the accused or a member of her family had been subjected to violence by the complainant. Another frequent occurrence was that the accusations sprang from a failure to allow the alleged witch to join a community festival or a family celebration. Harvest homes, weddings, funerals and christenings were regarded as public events, and not to invite an individual was a serious slight. Remember that, in the realms of the fairy story, it was the failure of the king to invite the bad fairy to the christening which began the story of the 'Sleeping Beauty'.

It seems paradoxical that a sense of guilt on the part of the accuser was an essential element in so many cases of witchcraft, but it reflects a change in

society and of the concepts of neighbourliness and community. The period of the great explosion of witchcraft trials coincides with a time when the sense of private property was becoming much keener in the public mind. Ideas of community were breaking down as a result of population increase, and an economic revolution was taking place. It was also a time when attitudes to the relief of the poor, and to charity and community responsibility, were undergoing major adjustments. The breakdown of the feudal community, the growth of unemployment, and the problem of the bands of beggars wandering the country combined with the developing skill and strength of a central government bureaucracy to create a new situation. Whereas formerly the relief of the local poor had been a Christian duty and a voluntary activity, the shift to a centrally organised system, with a poor house and the collection of a poor rate, produced a new attitude. In most cases the situation was that the very poor had to beg from the not-quite-so-poor. Those from whom alms were sought felt that they had made their contribution to the relief of poverty by paying their rate, and were reluctant to make any further donations. At the same time the traditional values of generosity to the poor, of helping a neighbour, of making sure an old widow did not go hungry or cold were still there and, once charity had been refused, the refuser was tortured by guilt. He or she felt that the refusal must be justified or excused by showing that the beggar was unworthy of help.

The next stage, after the initial refusal of charity, was for some inexplicable misfortune to befall the family or the property of the refuser. This would not take long to occur: a fire, the failure of butter to come, a hen ceasing to lay, the death of an animal or a member, however distant, of the family was all that was required. To this was often added the pungently expressed ill-will of the alleged witch and the threats that she might have made. If a complaint was made to the parish constable or to a local justice, the whole process was set in inexorable motion. In view of Scot's description of the typical witch and her behaviour one can see that there would then be no shortage of 'witnesses'.

In England, at least, the witch had two advantages over her continental or Scottish sisters. First, they were not (officially, anyway) subjected to torture to extract a confession, although the rough handling of a mob and the stripping and searching for the 'witch mark', that allegedly insensitive spot which was the teat from which her familiar was fed, might come close to torture. So might the swimming of a suspect when, with hands and feet tied, she was cast into water. If she floated it was a sign that even the water rejected her and was taken as an affirmation of guilt; if she sank and drowned before she could be recovered then her soul was in no further danger. There are no recorded occasions of this practice in Lancashire. The second advantage enjoyed by an English witch, dubious though it may seem, was that the mandatory death penalty was carried out by hanging and not by burning as in the rest of Europe.

The Samlesbury case is one which does not conform to this pattern, and it is unusually interesting because it was one of the comparatively rare cases which were dismissed by the courts. We know little about the age or the economic circumstances of the participants, although it seems that the Sowerbutts were, even if not affluent, certainly not on the fringes of poverty. Nor is there any suggestion that the Bierley family were in any particular need. There is no occasion when some request for help is refused or some other injustice perpetrated. We hardly get the picture of a happy, normal family, since presumably Grace was brought to accuse her grandmother without any particular difficulty. On the other hand we do see illustrated the web of contacts and relationships within the family as Grace goes to visit her various relatives at Osbaldeston, walks home with her father, and goes to meet her mother returning from a shopping expedition to Preston. No particular incident is singled out, and no cause for the malignity is described, other than the hint of religious conflict, a point that we will return to. Another distinction about the two trials, of the Samlesbury and the Pendle witches, which has been touched on is the involvement of persons of very much higher rank. It was very rare for this to occur, as there was no social contact and hence no opportunity for friction between the accused and the accuser. It will be remembered that in most cases the allegations were made between people of very much the same class. The reason for the involvement of Alice Nutter in the Pendle trial is a mystery. There is no evidence to support legends of a boundary dispute between the Nutters and the Nowells. An ingenious suggestion is that Alice Nutter happened on the Good Friday feast while going to consult the Demdike in her capacity as a herbalist. Some explanation is offered for the attack made on Jane Southworth – her rejection of Catholicism and adherence to the Church of England. In this, too, there is the added element of a degree of family disagreement. If it is true that Christopher

The chimney piece in the parlour. The whole of the family wing of the house was drastically re-ordered in the nineteenth century and interior walls altered. The parlour, or family room, suffered the same fate. The remarkable chimney piece contains a stone naming Thomas Southworth and carrying the date 1545. However, it is, at least in part, a nineteenth-century assemblage of material, though the lintel with the name and date are original.

PHOTOGRAPH COURTESY OF SAMLESBURY HALL

Southworth was the instigator of the plot, then here we have an uncle revenging himself on his niece-by-marriage.

On the very scanty evidence which we have at our disposal (it is only in Potts' book that we find any reference to this case) it is impossible to make an accurate assessment of the truth of the matter. The idea of it all being a plot by the local Catholics to punish three apostates at first sight seems as wild and extraordinary as any of the other tales. Though Grace Sowerbutts may have been an hysterical teenager, possibly subject to epilepsy and certainly possessed of a broad streak of both malice and exhibitionism, it would seem impossible that she would have the detailed knowledge of witch lore displayed in her testimony. On the other hand, the stories and reports of witch activities were so widespread and so much part of the folk culture that this can not be ruled out. John Webster, the schoolmaster who had personal experience both of witch trials and of the area, and whose cabalistic memorial is in the church of St Mary in Clitheroe wrote: 'They suck in with their mother's milk the gross and erroneous opinions of the vulgar people, and confidently believe that they see and do and suffer many strange, odd and wonderful things which indeed have no existence outside their depraved fancies'. It is certain that a man like Southworth, a trained missionary priest, would have had a scholarly knowledge

The Oriel window of the Great Hall. Compass windows, were popular Tudor additions to the Great Hall. Their semi-enclosed nature and their extensive glazing made them a cosy retreat from the bustle of the Great Hall. Additionally, the expanse of glass gave an opportunity for the display of armorial windows which could be used to emphasise the antiquity of one's lineage. In this case the glass only dates from the twentieth century. The name oriel is derived from the French l'oreille, the ear, in reference to its projection from a wall.

PHOTOGRAPH COURTESY OF SAMLESBURY HALL

of the writings of the Church authorities and of the rituals of exorcism. There is something indefinably academic about the evidence that Grace gives as, point by point, she confirms the conventional view of witch ritual. There is little emotion or expression of horror or disgust, though it may simply be that the report of the evidence, regurgitated by Potts, eliminates this. However, the impression is of a child standing up straight, her hands behind her back, and reciting her party piece. It is interesting, and significant of the different attitudes towards the two major cases at the summer assize, that Potts takes the trouble to insert a reasoned attack on the testimony of Grace Sowerbutts but leaves unquestioned the words of Jennet Device, which are equally fantastic.

Even if we accept that Grace had been coached in her part, there is no proof that the coaching had come from the Catholic side as a way of disparaging the

Protestants and obtaining revenge on backsliders. It might almost equally well have been a concerted Protestant attempt to discredit the Catholic mission, by implicating them in demonic practices or complicity in an unsavoury plot against honest God-fearing Protestants. This can only be postulated if one assumes that the instigators of this plot could be assured of the breakdown of the case and the acquittal of the three women they had 'set up'. Perhaps they were prepared to risk the death of their three 'stool pigeons'. This endless speculation is reminiscent of the tortuous espionage novels of cross and double cross.

To the modern mind one of the most startling pieces of evidence given in a witchcraft trial was the testimony of Sir Thomas Browne, a man of science and letters, famous for his cool rationalism, expressing his support for a prosecution at Bury St Edmunds in 1664. There could be no better indication of the way in which the pernicious belief in witchcraft penetrated all ranks of society. While the accusations were usually made against the lowliest members of society by those who were little above them in social and economic status, and that wilder stories represent the superstitions, which John Webster declared 'were sucked in with their mother's milk', there is no evidence that the accusations were disbelieved by those justices and even judges who dealt with the cases.

Today, a knowledge of scientific principles and of the necessity for objective proof is engrained in the majority of the population. The spread of disease is explained, the conditions in which epidemics or natural disasters are created are known or can be ascertained by everybody. But the world looked very different at the time of the witchcraft trials. Science was still the pursuit of a few and their views and conclusions were confined within a tiny and exclusive minority. Those 'facts' which seem so self-evident to us today, the planetary system, the existence of bacteria and viruses, the climatic system, the conservation of matter, which we no longer question were inconceivable in early modern Europe. Nothing in the cosmography or scientific literature of that period contradicted the existence of witchcraft. Nor did the scriptures deny the reality of witchcraft: references to the visit of Saul to the 'Witch of Endor' or the injunction in *Exodus* that 'Thou shalt not suffer a witch to live' could be seen as confirmation. In the New Testament the description of Christ's temptations by the Devil seemed to be the final assertion of the existence of the 'Prince of Darkness'. Nor were these views contradicted by the best scientific knowledge of the period. Much scientific speculation at the time was based on the fundamental inter-relationship and activating forces in the universe that could be, at least partially, detected by the adept after prolonged study. The search for these motivating forces was the true object of the alchemist rather than the vulgar search for the 'Philosopher's Stone' or the 'Elixir of Life'. Others believed that the interlinking of all life and the environment was exhibited by 'signatures': the superficial resemblance of varied objects which was thought to indicate a complex web of inter-relationships. This could lead the doctor to treat afflictions of the head with walnuts because they resembled a brain, or to the attribution of pre-eminence to the sun, the lion and the

Samlesbury Hall, Oriel Window and Oratory exterior. The oriel at Samlesbury is unusual in that its upper stage, instead of being polygonal, is replaced by a rectangular structure with a gabled roof. Its purpose is unknown but the most likely explanation is that it was an oratory for the family and their chaplain. The small, porched entrance in the foreground is a nineteenth-century addition and would have no place in the original structure.

PHOTOGRAPH COURTESY OF SAMLESBURY HALL

sunflower in the three 'kingdoms' on the grounds of their shared colour. Yet others might seek the great motivating force of the universe in the movements of the stars and planets and to attribute to them a control and influence over the affairs of man. In the early seventeenth century the astrologer and the astronomer were not divided by a gulf of academic respectability.

Therefore, the intellectual climate and popular superstition combined to give credence to a belief that by exploiting the hidden motivating powers of the universe the successful student might acquire power over people and the natural world. It seemed not unreasonable that Satan, a fallen angel, had supernatural knowledge which he and his devotees could exploit to perform acts such as flying or sailing in a sieve which though impossible to the ordinary person, might be possible if one could exploit some hitherto unknown magical power. If the Devil was seen as a supreme magical adept, then these things might be within his capability. The question of why an omnipotent God could allow evil to flourish in this way, in a world where his direct intervention in the daily affairs of man was widely accepted, could easily be answered by the argument that God allowed the Devil to exist in order to punish the wicked and to tempt the frailty of man. In Lancashire at the time of the witch trials there must have been a clear recollection of the scandal some years earlier, when Edward Kelly, a disreputable 'conjuror' and necromancer was accused of practising his black arts in the churchyard of Walton-le-Dale. It is indicative of the shadowy division between magic and science that Kelly was later the henchman of Dr John Dee, Warden of Manchester Collegiate Church and mathematician of a European reputation. If a man of Dee's distinction could accept such beliefs and activities how could it be questioned by a country justice of the peace or yeoman juryman?

One must also remember that it was possible for outside pressures on belief to impinge on the judgement of the men of the time. For example, the second edition of King James' *Daemonologie* had appeared in 1603. Here was a clear endorsement of popular belief from the highest authority in the land. The work's publication had been quickly followed by the harsh witchcraft statute of 1604, and the publication of the new legislation had probably brought the king's book to the attention of many country magistrates. Indeed, it seems evident from the form of the depositions taken by Nowell that he was not unfamiliar with the contemporary literature concerning witchcraft. Knowing of the king's sentiments he may also have seen the prosecution of the witches and his diligence in pursuing them as a way to stand well with authority. In his introduction to his account Thomas Potts describes Nowell as 'a very honest, religious gentleman, painful [painstaking, diligent] in the service of his Country: whose fame for his great service to his Country, shall live after him'. Whether Potts was using the word 'Country' in its present sense or in the contemporary usage to indicate his home area or county is immaterial; by his action Nowell had gained in prestige. It is perhaps significant that no such comment is made about the examining justice in the Samlesbury case, Robert Holden, but then his case had collapsed and perhaps cast doubt on the reality of witchcraft. It is worth mentioning that Holden was the son-in-law of Nicholas Bannister, who with Nowell, had examined the Pendle witches. While one would not suggest that these two cases were in any way a plan to obtain credit for the Justices involved, it is likely that information was circulated, and that they were made aware of the peril and danger of witches in the county; consequently they were observant of the slightest sign of diabolic activity in their district.

Though the acceptance of the belief in the power of witches in the early part of the seventeenth century seemed to be buttressed by tradition, scripture and science, by the end of that century all these props to credibility had been removed. John Aubrey (1625–1697), historian, antiquarian, scientific amateur and entertaining gossip writes of his Wiltshire childhood:

When I was a child (and so before the Civill Warres), the fashion was for old women and mayds to tell fabulous stories nightimes, of Sprights and walking of Ghosts &c. This was derived down from mother to daughter, from the Monkish Ballance which upheld Holy Church, for the Divines say, Deny spirits and you are an Aetheist. When the warres came and with them Liberty of Conscience and liberty of inquisition, the phantoms vanished. Now children feare no such thing, having not heard of them and are not checked with such feares.

While Aubrey is correct in his assertion that belief in the supernatural declined in England after the Civil War he probably over-estimates the speed of that decline, certainly at a popular level and is over simplistic in his reasoning.

After the Restoration the character of the king and the Court, lazy, tolerant and sceptical, permeated the attitudes of the country. The new generation of scientists and the work of the universities and the Royal Society propagated a new cosmology in which the supernatural or the mystical had no place. The universe, it was thought, could be subjected to a mechanistic explanation, a huge clock that ran to a predetermined plan. Aubrey is probably right in his

This illustration for an Italian work on witchcraft of 1626 shows how clearly the story told by Grace Sowerbutts reflects the continental narratives of the activities of the witches. The idea of sabbats and the exhumation and consumption of human flesh first appear in England in the Lancaster trials of 1612. This arouses many questions about the sources from which the local prosecutors gained their knowledge. In the woodcut it is also noticeable that, though in England witch trials usually involved women, in Europe the participation of men was regarded as commonplace.

view that religious orthodoxy had less influence: not that men and women were any less religious in themselves but the heat had gone from religious controversy. The chaos of the mid century had engendered a deep suspicion of, and repugnance towards, religious fanaticism. At first these attitudes were only apparent in the upper echelons of society and government, but this was where it was important. The decline in the number of witch trials and their virtual cessation before the end of the century reflect not a change in attitude among the ordinary people of the village and town – they still believed – but among those to whom they brought their complaints. There can be no doubt that for a period there were many of intelligence and education who found themselves uncertain and unable to reject outright a belief in witchcraft *per se* but they were increasingly convinced that the feeble dotards who appeared in the courts were not actual practitioners of the Black Arts. Again the writings of Aubrey illustrate this period of confusion. Having explained away ghosts and sprites, he also reports a case at Salisbury; 'I think there were 7 or 8 old women hanged. There were odd things sworne against them, as the strange manner of the dyeing of H. Dennys horse: of flying in the Air on a staffe etc. These examinations &c Sr James hath fairly written in a Book which He promised to give to the Royall Society'. Here the ancient and the modern world meet and it seems that the modern world is not prepared to dismiss the stories out of hand but to examine the evidence dispassionately before reaching a conclusion. Gradually the balance swung inexorably in favour of the new realities of science, until the old beliefs were vanquished.

Belief in witchcraft did not die for any one cause or in a brief moment: its decline was a process of attrition which occurred among different people at different times and for widely different reasons. In the first place it was destroyed among the intellectual minority who wielded both religious and secular power. In this new climate there was no longer any credit for the zealous Justice who brought such troublesome activities before the courts. Among ordinary people the belief in witches took much longer to die, but it must have remained at a level of popular superstition which could no longer expect to be carried into the great court room of Lancaster Castle.

The assize of 1612 was a spectacular exhibition and one which has ensured for the county, and for Pendle in particular, a reputation that is now unlikely ever to be lost. Thomas Potts has immortalised the Lancashire witches and visitors crowd to Pendle to see what physical traces of the world of the witches can still be discerned. The majority of the sightseers are totally unaware of the events at Samlesbury and that at the two halls there one can literally walk in the footsteps of an alleged witch.

CHAPTER 5

Turton Tower and the Career of Humphrey Chetham

H
UMPHREY CHETHAM'S NAME has associations which make it well known far outside the boundaries of his native county. The school or hospital he founded in Manchester is a recognised centre of excellence in musical education. The library he endowed, this country's first free public library, is well known to scholars for its ancient books and collections of manuscripts. It was very appropriate that when, over 150 years ago, a learned society was set up to publish historical documents and research into the counties of Lancashire and Cheshire it should have been given his name. As a result the works of the Chetham Society are to be found in places of learning throughout the world. What is not so widely known and is not sufficiently publicised is his ownership of a delightful house, Turton Tower, situated well off the beaten tourist track and surrounded by the lovely moorland that stretches between Bolton and Blackburn.

In the Middle Ages Lancashire had a reputation as a wild and lawless place whose people were much given to violence, and where even the priests rode armed. Within the county there existed blood feuds of an almost Sicilian virulence. It was not uncommon for bands of friends and retainers to fight what were almost pitched battles against their opponents. Even as late as the reign of Queen Elizabeth, when we are told the rule of law ran throughout the country, serious fracas could break out between the bands of rival families. In 1589 at Lea Hall near Preston the fight between the followers of Richard Hoghton and Thomas Langton left Hoghton and another man dead, while Langton and several others were severely wounded. This deadly affair arose from a dispute about the ownership of some strayed cattle, but was the culmination of a long standing enmity. It is indicative of the attitudes of the county that, even after a serious affray of this nature, no prosecutions followed because no one could be found willing to give evidence on either side. Violence could also come from outside the county and the area had been subjected to raids by the Scots; one of the most serious was in 1322 when they had struck as far as the Ribble and possibly burned and destroyed south of the river as far as Chorley.

Turton Tower in 1851, oil painting (detail) by Selim Rothwell. When this painting was made the house had been in the hands of the Kay family for some fifteen years. The lower stages of the tower are plastered and whitewashed. The central section of the building presents a completely different appearance to today as it has not yet acquired its fantastic roof-line or bogus timbering. The north wing has had the dutch gable built on, but the alterations are not complete. The painting illustrates a mid-stage in the refurbishment of the tower and makes an interesting comparison with later views.

In these circumstances it was not unusual for the wealthier families to build fortified houses for themselves. Unfortunately, none of these pele towers survives in its original form as a single, stone-built tower, the bottom storey of which gave a safe refuge for cattle and livestock and the upper floors provided accommodation for the owner, his family and his household. They offered a low standard of comfort and may not have been permanently occupied. It is probable that additional accommodation for everyday use was provided by adjacent, expendable wooden buildings. The pele towers were not castles designed to withstand prolonged attack but simply places of temporary refuge which were defensible. To increase the protection they offered, some of the peles were moated. The Ordnance Survey maps of Lancashire, especially for the richer lowland areas, are dotted with moated sites and there has been much discussion of their purpose. Though the possession of a moat may have become little more than a way of providing a cattle fence, or may simply have served as a status symbol, their origins must surely have been as defensive works. A few houses still retain some semblance of the pele tower despite later changes. Gawthorpe Hall is reputed to have an ancient pele at its core and the military origins of Borwick Hall are obvious. However, Turton Tower is perhaps the best survivor, even though here the prominence of the pele is the result of deliberate policy in later rebuildings.

The date of the first house at Turton is unknown. It used to be said that the derivation for the name of the village was from 'Tower Town', but this explanation is now rejected by the most modern authorities, who prefer Thor's Tun as the original name. The earliest parts of the present house were built in about 1400 and comprise the lower stages of the square stone tower. Originally the lowest floor would have been windowless to improve its security and the other two floors would have had nothing more than arrow loops or narrow, easily defensible windows. Internally the three floors were linked by a stone spiral staircase of which one short stretch was preserved in the Victorian refurbishment of the house. This can be seen by visitors but is to some extent concealed by a trap door in the floor outside the 'Chetham Room' on the top floor of the tower.

Since about 1200 the manor of Turton had belonged to the estates of the Torboc family, and it was they who built the present tower to replace whatever buildings preceded it. They were not a local family, but took their surname from their main estates situated at Tarbock in the parish of Huyton on Merseyside. In 1420 the builder of the tower, John de Torboc, died leaving his lands to be divided between his only daughter Elizabeth and her cousins, his brother's children. They retained the Huyton lands while Elizabeth became the heiress to Turton. The Orrell family of Wigan were appointed as her guardians and eventually she married William Orrell: thus the lands at Turton became a part of the estates of her husband's family. It seems that Elizabeth and William actually lived at Turton – they are the first recorded inhabitants (as opposed to owners) – but they did not enjoy it undisturbed as her cousins continued to claim the land and the powerful Latham family also felt that it had some entitlement. Eventually these claims were successfully resisted, and Turton remained a property of the Orrells for more than two hundred years.

During this time the family carried out various building projects designed to make the tower a more comfortable dwelling place. In 1596 the tower itself was raised in height and the storeys rearranged to give increased head room: the original residential floors must have been cramped and oppressive. The new and larger windows which were installed at this time reflect not only

Turton Tower in the Middle Ages. This artist's impression shows the original pele tower built by the Tarboc family. The windowless ground floor and the small windows on the residential floors aided the defence of the building. The spiral staircase was contained in the projection from the wall on the right-hand side of the building. The space between the tower and the cruck-framed building shown on the right was filled in the sixteenth century by the buildings of the Orrell family.

PHOTOGRAPH COURTESY OF LANCASHIRE COUNTY MUSEUMS SERVICE

the changing pattern of life in Elizabethan England, where defensive capability was no longer a prime requirement, but also the increased standards of comfort demanded even by a family who were not particularly affluent. Clear evidence of this later stage of the tower can be seen in the masonry of the upper floor and in the remaining heads of the defunct windows of the previous building, which appear low down in the walls of the Chetham room. At about the same time the Orrells added a cruck-framed building, intended as a service wing, to link the tower to the previously detached cruck-construction building that lay on the north-east side of the tower. This linking building now contains the morning room on the ground floor and the tapestry bedroom on the first floor. The original detached building may, when built, have been intended as residential accommodation for the family and household during peaceful times, when the tower was not in use, or it may have been a kitchen and service wing. Remains of the cruck, and of wattle and daub walls, can be seen, but the whole appearance of this wing was radically altered in the nineteenth century when the crucks were beheaded and a second floor added. This building is represented today by the entrance area and the teashop wing of the tower with the Victorian bedrooms above.

By the reign of James I the Orrell family found themselves in financial difficulties. In part these may have stemmed from the expensive building work they had undertaken, but there was a more deep seated cause. Like many Lancashire gentry families the Orrells had remained true to the Roman Church. Unlike many of their peers, though, they were not prepared to accept the new state of affairs and avoid drawing attention to themselves. For example, the family had presented to Turton Chapel various items of furniture and equipment including the bell and the chalice. Unsuccessfully John Orrell claimed that these were family heirlooms loaned to the chapel and that he had

no wish to see them used for the new rites. John was known as an irascible man and he was obviously well able to operate in the climate of barely controlled violence that we have already described as existing in the county. In 1560, for instance, he was brought before the courts charged that he 'of his great might and power, with force of arms, entered upon Turton Moor and enclosed certain parcels of ground to the utter disinheritance of Christopher Horrocks'. Horrocks was no injured innocent and the account goes on to relate how he '... and about twenty others, armed with long pikes, staves, bows and arrows, swords, spades and short daggers, did assemble at the enclosure and cast down and destroy the same'.

As a determined and vocal recusant Orrell was forced to pay the swingeing fines of £20 a month that were imposed after 1583 for non-attendance at the Anglican church. An additional burden for the recusant squires was that they were debarred on account of their religion from those local, national and public offices and professions by which their Protestant peers were able to supplement their income. To meet the demands of the fines and to maintain their way of life the squires borrowed heavily, often at exorbitant rates of interest.

John Orrell had done this, and at his death in 1627 his brother and heir William was advised to try to repay the family's debts by taking a mortgage of £1000 on the security of the Turton estates. William Orrell approached a man who was rapidly acquiring a reputation in the county as a likely source for loans, the wealthy Manchester clothier, Humphrey Cheetham.

Cheetham agreed to Orrell's proposal and a deed was drawn up, but for

Turton Tower, lithograph by James. This early nineteenth-century view shows the Tower at the time when it was in the occupation of tenant farmers and before any of the renovation and rebuilding undertaken by the Kay family. The house at the time of Humphrey Chetham would have looked very much like this.

some unknown reason it was not put into effect. Instead some fifteen months later the whole estate was sold to the clothier. The transfer was not undisputed; Richard Orrell, the uncle of William, made claim that Turton by right should have passed to him. He was unsuccessful and the courts rejected his case, but the row rumbled on well into the 1630s. The deed of sale of the manor and Lordship of Turton shows that it was a major property transfer involving the 'Capital Messuage' of Turton Tower (this was the term always used for a manor house). The demesne lands, the water corn mill which still exists in the grounds of the house, all William Orrell's land and the private chapel and aisle situated on the north side of Bolton Church were all conveyed to Cheetham in consideration of the sum of £4000. It was calculated that the tower, the demesne and 700 acres of land were worth £190 *per annum*, and the woodlands would be expected to provide an income. To put these sums in perspective, it is calculated that in the early seventeenth century a labouring man, his wife and four children living in the south of England where prices and wages were higher might expect on an income of about £11–£14 a year to maintain a decent standard and meet their expenses. A change of ownership did not simply affect the families directly involved: the Turton estates included some sixty tenants who would now have to accustom themselves to a new landlord. They must have viewed his arrival with a degree of trepidation and concern.

We must ask ourselves how it was possible for an old established and reputable family such as the Orrells to become unable to retain their place in society. After the sale of Turton they disappear into obscurity, but a parvenu

such as Cheetham could afford to buy them out lock, stock and barrel. Cheetham represented new money and he is one of the earliest examples in the county of a breed which was to play a vital part in its history – the self-made man, whose fortune was derived from trade and whose ambition it was to establish himself and his heirs as members of the county's elite.

Though related to a family which could claim gentry status, the Cheethams of Nuthurst, Humphrey's immediate antecedents were on a lower social plane. In 1903 Canon Raines wrote a biography of Cheetham in which he went to elaborate lengths to prove the antiquity and gentility of the family to which his subject belonged. This reflects the interest in genealogy and landed families of the early local historians but today it only gives the impression that the author 'doth protest too much', and in a cause of little interest. Humphrey Cheetham, as they spelled the name at the time, was born in July 1580 at Crumpsall near Manchester in what was little more than a farm house. His family belonged to a class numerous in sixteenth-century Lancashire, of yeoman farmers who were to some extent engaged in the textile industry. As early as 1541 there is a reference to a Cheetham of Crumpsall who was a cloth merchant. His son, Humphrey's grandfather, continued the business and made a fortune sufficient to buy land at Kersal and elsewhere. His son Henry, the father of Humphrey, was another prosperous merchant and his marriage to Jane Wroe, the daughter of a gentry family of Prestwich, indicated that the Cheethams were making considerable social progress.

It is necessary to try to define what was meant by 'gentry status' in early

Turton Tower: the Staircase Tower. Part of the development programme of the Orrells in the 1590s was the construction of a newel staircase in a new timber-framed structure located between the pele tower and the other wing of the house. By the time of the Kays at Turton this staircase was much decayed and the stairs as we see them now are heavily restored and the exterior refaced; only some of the original work survives.

Crumpsall Hall, lithograph by James. This early nineteenth-century view of the original house of the Cheetham family shows it to have been little more than an enlarged farmhouse with a central hall and two cross wings. The addition of these wings, set at right angles to the body of the house in the position which seems to have symbolised 'gentility', reflects the increasing prosperity of the family through their enterprises in farming and trade.

modern Lancashire, although this is an almost impossible task as even at the time there were no hard and fast rules. In theory there were definitions which were accepted by the Heralds on their visitations, but in fact the status of a gentleman could be claimed by any, provided they had the means to sustain their claim and that they could have their aspirations confirmed by the acceptance of their neighbours. Gentility was a complex mixture of lineage, wealth and status.

An early social commentator, William Harrison, wrote:

> Whoever can live without manual labour and thereto is able and will bear the port, charge and countenance ... he shall for money have a coat of arms bestowed upon him by the Heralds and be reputed a gentleman for ever after.

This view of the situation shows an almost cynical sense of reality, and recognises the fact that though the College of Heralds might have a supposed set of definitions what was in fact important was a combination of wealth and social acceptance. Ancient lineage and blood ties might be an advantage to the would-be gentleman, but they were by no means essential provided he had sufficient money and that at least a proportion of his income was derived from the freehold ownership of land.

Land was the touchstone of gentility, and without the possession of an estate any claim to the highly prized status of 'gentleman' was likely to be dismissed as bogus by one's contemporaries. Cheetham is a good example of the process at work. Having acquired by inheritance and shrewd purchase extensive estates, including Turton, no one would dispute his claim to style himself Gentleman or even to claim the higher grade of Esquire. His status was such that when he was 'pricked' as sheriff* for the year 1635 he was able to purchase a grant of arms based on the coat armour of the Nuthurst branch of the family, though this was not done without dispute. At the same time it was suggested by Sir Henry St George, the Herald, that his name should be spelled with one E, this being considered more ancient and distinguished. However, the name continued, and still continues, to be pronounced 'Cheetham'.

Humphrey Chetham, 1580–1653, owner of Turton Tower, 1628–53. This painting, now in Chetham's Library, shows the shrewd Manchester businessman at the height of his powers and gives an impression of the man. He was able to make a fortune in his trade as a clothier and also to make the transition to an esteemed place in the ranks of the gentry.

Like many Lancashire arrivist families of the period the Cheethams had based their rise to fortune on the textile trade of the county. Although cloth had been made in Lancashire for many years – rough, homespun woollens for everyday domestic use – the early part of the sixteenth century saw the growth of commercial production. In the Middle Ages Lancashire was underpopulated and was regarded as one of the poorest and most backward parts of the country. Industry and commerce were absent and the farming, due to infertile soils and a harsh climate, remained at subsistence level. Large areas of land were unavailable for agriculture, being marshes, meres, mosses and moorland, or incorporated within the extensive Forest lands. At the beginning of the sixteenth century two things occurred that were to change this picture. First there was, for reasons that remain to be satisfactorily explained, a general growth of population throughout the country. This expansion of population was particularly marked in the North West, where the increase is considered to have been greater than in any other area. It is calculated that Lancashire's population doubled in the hundred years subsequent to 1500. In part this increase can be explained by the second factor: the decision by the Crown to abandon the

---

* The term 'pricking for sheriff' originated from the method that had been used for choosing the sheriff: a list of suitable names was presented to the king and he selected one by jabbing a bodkin into the list. By this time the method had fallen into desuetude and only one name was presented for ceremonial selection, but the term continued to be used.

Forest status of the lands in Lancashire and to open them to copyhold occupancy, which amounted to a perpetual lease of the lands at a fixed rent. In a land-hungry society the prospect of obtaining one of these tenancies was so attractive that they were quickly snapped up. In part the new occupants were members of local families, who saw the opportunity to acquire a farm or even an estate at very little cost. However, there is also evidence that the prospect attracted settlers to the new farming areas from more distant places. While it would be absurd to think of post-1507 Lancashire as resembling the American West in the nineteenth century there is a certain parallel, as settlers moved in to occupy the cheap land made available to them by the State.

These new settlers found that life on a farm on the Lancashire moors involved hard work for little reward, and consequently they looked for a way to supplement the returns from their lands. As the countryside they were farming was good land for sheep it was natural that their thoughts should turn to the making of textiles, for which they had the raw material to hand. In addition knowledge of the process was readily available and the equipment required easily obtained at low cost.

Cloth manufacture had other advantages – an assured market and work itself that was easily fitted into domestic and farming routine. A further advantage was that the Yorkshire woollen industry was enjoying a boom period and was ready to expand into new areas in order to increase production. As this incentive spilled over the Pennines the areas of east Lancashire began to respond and a manufactory of coarse, cheap, low-grade cloth developed in the areas centred on Colne and Trawden, on Rochdale, and in Rossendale, where Haslingden became the most important centre. This southern zone looked towards Manchester as its commercial capital. Soon the industry had a flourishing market both at home and overseas. From Manchester cloth was taken to Liverpool for export to Ireland and the Isle of Man. Some was carried southward by the Kendal packmen to Southampton, some went eastward to Hull for export to the Baltic, Scandinavia and Russia or to its other important market on the Biscay coast of France and Spain. At home the first consignment of cloth which we know was sold outside the county went to Lawnaford Priory in Herefordshire in 1535. Lancashire cloth was soon on sale at Blackwell Hall in London and in the markets of towns in the Cotswolds and East Anglia. The product of the Lancashire industry consisted of a variety of cloths which were usually described as friezes, rugs and kerseys, all variants of a thick, rough-napped cloth used for heavy outdoor clothing.

During this early period the cloths were produced in small quantities by self-employed artisans working on their own machines in their own farms and cottages. When the pieces of cloth were complete they would carry them to their local market and sell them by bargaining for the best possible price. The raw materials for the cloth were either from the backs of their own or their neighbour's sheep or were bought in small quantities from itinerant vendors known as broggers. Some wool usually had to be bought in from elsewhere as Lancashire wool was considered to be of the poorest quality and an admixture of some better material was necessary. The finished cloth was bought by clothiers or drapers – the terms seem to have been almost interchangeable – who would collect a consignment and then be responsible for its transportation to the market and its eventual sale to the consumer. Until the seventeenth century the clothiers were not usually responsible for commissioning work or for the supply of raw materials. It is obvious that this was a possible development which could change the whole commercial relationship between the weaver and the clothier from one of independent tradesmen to one of master and employee.

It was as clothiers that the Cheethams had begun their rise to fortune and it was in this trade that Humphrey was to prove himself the most successful of his family. It seems that his early life and training were designed to fit him for a commercial career rather than for the life of a country gentleman. He was educated at Manchester Grammar School, and the fact that he remained a student there until he was seventeen is an indication that not only could his father afford the fees, but must also argue for a certain academic ability on the part of the pupil. Humphrey's later life was to show that he fully recognised the advantages of a sound education and that he valued learning. In 1597 he was bound apprentice to Samuel Tipping of Manchester, linen draper. There were close links between the two families. James, Humphrey's eldest brother, had been an apprentice to Samuel Tipping and had later married the widow of John Tipping, Samuel's brother. George, the second son of Henry Cheetham, had been apprenticed to George Tipping, Samuel's younger brother. Having completed his seven-year apprenticeship, Humphrey seems to have continued to work for Tipping until 1605 when he moved to London in partnership with his brother George. George remained in the capital and eventually became a freeman of the City and a member of the Merchant Taylors' Company, but Humphrey returned to their native town. This was a common arrangement among the cloth merchants: one member of the partnership remained in London and saw to the sale of the cloth, while another was responsible for the collection and dispatch of the goods from Manchester. In the Cheetham partnership this became Humphrey's role.

The establishment of this arrangement coincided with a change in the fortunes of the Lancashire industry. Until this time the products had been of a low value and there had been little success in establishing the manufacture of the finer grades of lighter woollen cloth, then referred to as 'the new draperies'. However, it seems that about 1601 a new manufacture was introduced. Fustian was later to be regarded as a cheap and perhaps rather shoddy cloth, useful for the clothing of working men. Yet originally it was an expensive imitation velvet made from a mixture of linen and cotton. There was an existing and prosperous linen industry on the plains of South West Lancashire, using locally grown flax supplemented by imports from Ireland, but cotton was unknown (although confusingly a woollen cloth known as Manchester Cottons had long been made around that town). The source of supply of raw cotton was the eastern Mediterranean and the Levant and it reached England by the ships of the Levant Company which docked in London.

For reasons that are obscure the new trade of fustian manufacture rapidly established itself in the area around Bolton. Fustian making had to overcome the obvious problem of obtaining the supplies of cotton. Nothing could be more simple than that the clothiers who sent their cloth to London, should order their carriers to bring back supplies of the precious material. On this basis the fustian trade flourished and expanded rapidly, but this arrangement laid the foundations for a complete change of relationship between the textile producers and the clothiers. It was no longer an equitable arrangement where the craftsman got the best price for his goods in a free exchange. He now became dependent on the clothier for his materials, which were sold to him on credit, and he was in a position where his marketing outlet and the price he obtained could only be negotiated through one channel. The first steps towards a putting-out system, a master and servant relationship, had been laid and the way opened for capitalist domination of the textile trade.

The new Cheetham partnership was in an excellent position to exploit the potential of this situation, for while Humphrey was responsible for the procurement of fustian and other cloth in Manchester, George was acting as both a wholesaler and a retailer at his Cheapside mercer's and grocer's shop. Although originally cloth retailers, mercers at this time seem to have sold a wide variety of goods. The contemporary inventory of Matthew Markland, a mercer of Wigan, includes not only a wide variety of cloths, some of them very expensive imported fabrics valued at ten and twelve shillings a yard, but also more mundane locally produced materials. An obvious extension of the mercer's basic trade was the provision of haberdashery, buttons, laces, tapes and ribbons, needles and pins. Less obvious were the items such as spices, sugar comfits, lute strings, books, spectacles and senna pods which found their way on to Markland's shelves. It would seem that the Cheetham's shop might have been very similar in its content.

The partnership proved successful and continued until the death of George in 1626, by which time the Cheethams enjoyed a fair degree of wealth and prosperity. However, they faced a difficulty in knowing how to re-invest their profits. The textile industry, with its home-made machines knocked up by the village carpenter and blacksmith, offered no potential for investment. Increased stocks of wool and linen and cotton could be bought but only in small quantities due to problems of storage and deterioration. At the best these would offer small returns on the investment. For some families who had social ambitions the target for spending was on their advancement in society: we can see this in action in the rise of the Mosley family, whose origins were very similar to the Cheethams. Humphrey seems to have had no interest in advancement in society and he had no wife or family to provide for and to establish in the world. For him investment had to be in that which would increase his income rather than his prestige.

In the mid-1950s and early 1960s the academic world of the historians was rent by a bitter controversy between the followers of Professor Tawney and the disciples of Hugh Trevor Roper over the economic fortunes of the gentry in this period. Were all the revolutionary fervours of the seventeenth century due to the decline of the fortunes of the old gentry and their replacement by newly-made men like Chetham, as Tawney believed: or was the opposite true, as Roper postulated, and that the leaders of opposition to the Crown were men from old-established families trying to conserve a vanishing world? Though eventually it was conceded that neither view was wholly true or wholly untrue and that while some gentry were declining others were gaining in prosperity, the followers of Tawney would have found ample evidence for their case in the career of Chetham. The Orrells of Turton were by no means the only Lancashire family to find themselves in financial straits in the early decades of the century.

The basis of their problem was the underlying sharp inflation that had occurred throughout the sixteenth century. This was especially severe for those families whose income was based on revenue from land. The increase in rents lagged well behind the rise in prices because most lands of an estate were either on lease or copyhold and so were fixed for some period, whether it was long or short. Gentlemen had a position to maintain in the world and the mark of gentility was a life of lavish, conspicuous consumption. The maintenance of these standards became increasingly difficult as income declined and alternative sources of revenue had to be sought. Some families were able to overcome their difficulties by finding employment, in the law, in royal service, in other professions, in investment in trade and commerce or in the development of industry on their estates by the exploitation of coal or other mineral reserves. Others lacked the initiative or the resources, or in some cases were barred by their religion from being able to seek these alternatives. For them the only options were to borrow money on the security of their estates or, catastrophic as it might seem, to sell land. There was no organised system of credit or borrowing, other than by a direct approach to an individual. We have already seen how William Orrell negotiated a mortgage with Humphrey Chetham, even though it was never executed, presumably because a rapid deterioration in the situation made it inadequate.

The negotiations with the Orrells were not Humphrey's first venture into this sort of activity; among the local families in straits were the Byrons of Clayton Hall, near Manchester and Newstead Abbey, Nottinghamshire. As early as 1608 they had begun to sell off their extensive lands and farms in Butterworth and Rochdale. The Cheetham brothers bought heavily, but these sales were only a palliative in the Byrons' case and in 1620 more desperate measures became necessary. They decided to abandon the bulk of their Lancashire estates and concentrate their resources at Newstead. George and Humphrey between them bought Clayton Hall and all its attendant estates in Failsworth, Ashton, Droylsden and Manchester, together with 340 acres of land, and a pew in Manchester Church, for £4,700. Clayton Hall was a large

and spacious house, surrounded by a moat and those necessary adjuncts to a gentleman's residence: a deer park, a chapel, a gate tower and ancient woods. After its purchase the two brothers both used the house, Humphrey as his main residence and George and his family when they visited Lancashire. Six years after its purchase George died and Humphrey became the sole owner of this imposing residence. It was only a few months after the death of George that the purchase of Turton took place and Humphrey Chetham was established as one of the major landowners of south-east Lancashire.

As the years progressed Chetham found many other opportunities to lend money and to acquire further properties. The period of the Civil War and its aftermath saw many North-Western landed families in financial difficulties. To the problems already outlined were added the costs of their part in the war which even for the non-combatants brought a sharp increase in taxation. In an area in which support for the king was strong many families, after the defeat of the royalist cause, found themselves facing the threat of sequestration of their estates or were forced to compound to save them from confiscation. In the case of the numerous Catholic families the fines imposed were automatically doubled. Financial hardship was not however confined to Cavaliers. Among the families that turned to Chetham for help were the Breretons and the Booths of Dunham Massey both of which had parliamentary sympathies. The Greenhalghs of Brandlesholme were forced to hand over their house to Chetham as security, but did eventually recover it – unlike the Radclyffes of Ordsall Hall, much of whose land was sold to Chetham, but whose support for the king lost them their fortune and their house.

It would be easy to see Chetham as a Stuart loan shark or asset stripper but this would be unfair to him. The rate of interest that he charged on his loans was moderate, some 7 or 8 per cent, which was the legal limit until it was reduced to 6 per cent in 1660. Though he charged to the limit he did not, as many others did, exceed it. Nor does he seem either to have neglected his properties or treated his tenants harshly. At Turton he allowed Mrs Orrell, the widow of John, to remain in the house, possibly as a rent-paying tenant. His treatment of her was unusually generous as she was a Catholic and, had he wished, she could have been treated much more harshly. When he acquired an estate he seems to have been anxious to fulfill the traditional role of the lord of the manor. At Turton he began a restoration programme for the chapel, whose foundation and maintenance had originally been a responsibility of the Orrells. It had been much neglected in the last fifty years, understandably in view of that family's overt recusancy. Now Chetham ordered his steward, Walmesley, to spend £38 2s. 3d. on repairing the chapel. Shortly afterwards a further £9 12s. 4d. was spent on unspecified work and Walmesley was ordered to make a payment of 4s. to the poor of the village. A further 4s. 6d. was spent on 'Mossing the Chapel at Bolton' – that is pointing the walls of the former Orrell chapel and pew in Bolton parish church. At this time joints between the stones were usually filled with rammed clay and moss. In 1627 a chaplain, Richard Denton, was appointed to Turton Chapel and Protestant worship was once more possible for the inhabitants.

It was not only Bolton Church and Turton Chapel that were of interest to Chetham, for he was deeply concerned with the ecclesiastical affairs of his native town. For several years he had been 'Farmer of the Manchester Tithes'. All householders within a parish were expected to make an annual contribution to provide the salary of the local priest. Originally, as the name 'tithe' indicates, this was supposed to be one-tenth of the parishioner's income from certain selected sources. In earlier days the payment had been made in kind but by the seventeenth century a sum in cash had often been substituted. As can be imagined, the parish incumbents often found difficulty in collecting this payment and in the large parishes had resorted to 'farming': that is selling the right to collect the tax to an individual who could recompense himself by the stringency of his tax gathering. This was a common practice at the time and most government taxes were collected in this way, the authorities being willing to accept a lower yield to avoid the expense and trouble of collection. Humphrey's success with the Manchester tithes caused him to be regarded as the Collegiate Church's man of business. He was appointed bursar of the College and in this capacity was deeply involved in the conflicts between the various factions among the canons in 1634–35 over the appointment of a new warden, a dispute that was finally settled only after Archbishop Laud had issued a new charter to the College.

Wealth, estates and a position in society brought obligations as well as privileges, and Chetham could now expect that his debt to society might be called in. At the coronation of King Charles I Chetham paid a £40 fine rather than accept a knighthood, but he could not avoid local office. In 1634 he found that he had been pricked for sheriff of the county and although he tried to have the appointment nullified he was forced to serve. His objections on the grounds of incapacity and expense were brushed aside.

The selection of Chetham was unexpected. He was not a man who had held any local or county office nor was he a justice of the Peace. However, his recommendation by Lord Newbrugh, Chancellor of the Duchy, may have been the result of his wealth and trade connections which gave him a widespread acquaintance with all levels of society in the County. There may have been a lack of suitable candidates, at a time when the first collection of Ship Money was in contemplation many more likely men for the post may have avoided nomination. Whatever the reasons for his selection Chetham was sworn in and faced his obligations.

The honour of acting as the king's personal representative in the Shire was an expensive undertaking. The sheriff was expected to put on a show and to provide lavish entertainment for the assize judges and a retinue of hangers-on. Chetham's accounts show that he was reluctantly forced to follow tradition. Items shown include the purchase of gold lace, a best velvet suit, a lace collar, rosettes for his shoes and a hat with a feather. Not only did he have to dress himself in smart clothing but it was also necessary to provide clothes and livery for his gentlemen attendants and his servants. Two years later, when he was appointed as high sheriff, William Farrington of Worden listed no fewer than fifty-six servants and household officers and seventy-six gentlemen who had to be provided with livery. Chetham dressed his servants and attendants, including his two trumpeters, in scarfs and ribbons. It was also expected that doles to the poor would be distributed. As we have seen, it was this appointment that persuaded Chetham to have the College of Heralds set their seal on his gentility by a grant of arms.

All this was mere frippery compared to the main obligation of the sheriff, which was the collection of the king's arbitrarily demanded 'Ship Money'. Lancashire had been assessed for £3,500. It was the sheriff's responsibility to allocate the amounts to be raised by the various divisions of the county and to ensure its collection and safe dispatch to the treasury. Though in later years this tax was to be cited as one of the principal causes of the Civil War, and John Hampden's refusal to pay was to be regarded as the act of a patriotic hero, no such reluctance was to be found in Lancashire. Chetham had not only collected the £3,500 well before the time limit – for which he was commended by the king – but acting on sound business principles, he had raised an additional £96 to cover the expenses of collection. He was eventually forced to refund this quite illegal additional contribution. The willingness of Lancastrians to pay probably sprang from two causes. As a coastal county they were accustomed to paying this levy; it had not been collected for some time but it was a familiar payment. Secondly, there seems to be evidence that the county community was not nearly so poverty-stricken as the government thought it to be. Estimates of the county's wealth were well out of date and failed to take into account the economic progress made in Lancashire in the past hundred years. It was assessed as one of the poorest counties in England, only slightly superior in wealth to Cumberland and Westmorland. The gentlemen of the county had no wish to provoke a more rigorous assessment of their wealth, such as might be caused by showing a reluctance to pay a very moderate tax assessment.

Chetham's diligence over Ship Money might lead one to suppose that he would have taken the king's part on the outbreak of the Civil War. This was not the case: in general the business community of Manchester were fervent parliamentarians and the town became the centre of roundhead activity in the county. In part this may have been due to the strength of Puritan sentiment in the town as much as to the burdens of taxation imposed by the king during his period of personal rule. Opposition to the pervasive influence of Lord Derby, both in the town and the county, may also have played a part, and his autocratic attitudes were another alienating influence. Chetham played a leading role in organising the financing of the county's parliamentary war effort, as he was appointed treasurer of the county committee.

This was an *ad hoc* body set up to collect levies on the areas under parliamentary control and to execute the sequestration of royalist estates and property. It was also responsible for the payment of wages and expenses to maintain the troops of the county and for the payment of a contribution to towards the the costs of the main armies to the parliamentary treasury in London. Chetham proved as diligent and punctilious over these duties as he had been in the collection of Ship Money, but he was not so occupied as to forget his own interests.

There is a legend at Turton that the house adjacent to the tower and now known as 'The Barn' was built by Chetham as a barracks for Roundhead soldiers. This would seem unlikely, as at this time barracks were unknown and it was usual for soldiers to sleep in private houses, taverns or in sheds and outbuildings if nothing better was available. In Chetham's accounts dating from 1643–44 there is an item which suggests how this legend originated, as he put in a claim for reimbursement of expenses incurred.

> In free quarters at Turton to majors and captains by 2 or 3 at a time for divers times and to troops sometimes 12, sometimes 16, sometimes 20, sometimes more. And likewise in footsoldiers sometimes 60 or 70 a night and daily relieving of horse and foot especially at that time when Preston was regained from us to the enemy [20 March 1642/43] at which time my servants were forced to brew and bake almost every day for relief of the said soldiers that came to my house of which it is impossible for me to give a perfect account; but I think it will amount to above £80 00s. 00d.

Obviously Turton was regarded as a safe and good billet where food and drink could be relied on and it may well have seemed to the locals that Mr Chetham's newly-built barn was continuously occupied by soldiers. Indeed, it is likely that some small garrison was maintained there.

Chetham remained in office as Treasurer until 1648 when, at the age of sixty-nine, he resigned, no doubt hoping for a well earned rest. But within a few

An eighteenth-century view of Chetham's Hospital and Library. Bequeathed by Lord de la Ware to house the canons of his church, these buildings may stand on even older foundations. At the dissolution of the College in 1549, they became the property of Lord Derby, but were recovered by the Church on its re-establishment by Queen Mary. The buildings were purchased by Chetham when the College was once more dissolved by the Commonwealth government. They now form an excellent example of medieval collegiate planning. The facing building comprises the hall and library and the right-hand wing contained the service rooms.

weeks he was horrified to learn that he had once more been selected as sheriff. One of the problems faced by the parliamentarians in Lancashire was the small number of men from the ruling elite of the county who supported their cause and were prepared to assist in the shire's administration. Chetham's appointment as sheriff may have been partially intended as a recognition of his zeal in parliament's cause but was, more probably, actuated by the problem of finding an adequate alternative.

Whatever the reasons for his appointment, Chetham was horrified and made despairing efforts to have it withdrawn. It may be that he was exaggerating his infirmities but there is the ring of truth when he wrote

> My case is this, I am almost seventy years of age, of a very weak constitution; I am not able to get on horseback or light but I am helped by another, nor being on horseback to ride two miles but with extreme pain and grief for my particular infirmity increaseth so upon me that it will shortly bring me to my grave, which being sensible of I have for this half year and more confined myself for the most part to mine own house and mine own chamber.

Eventually his plight was recognised and the shrievalty was withdrawn from him. He spent the last few years of his life in quietness and - charitable works and died at Clayton Hall on 20 September 1653. He was buried at midnight on 11 October in the church he had attended and served for so long in Manchester. The long delay is reflected in an item in the funeral expenses of £23 for 'The spices and odours for the Embalming of Mr Cheetham [sic]'.

His will showed that he posthumously intended to continue the charitable work which had occupied so much of his attention in his latter years. We know that he had devoted resources to maintain twenty-two poor boys from Manchester, Salford and Droylsden but the details of this are lost. In 1648 he conceived the idea of the establishment of a school or hospital for poor boys and approached Lord Derby to try to purchase the former college building as a home for this project. Not surprisingly he could get no response from this arch-royalist who would have no truck with such an avowed enemy of the king. In his will this scheme was revived and he ordained that the number of boys should be increased to forty. They were to be between the ages of six and ten and were to come from the townships of Manchester, Salford, Droylsden, Crumpsall, and Bolton: five places were to be reserved for children from Turton. It was laid down that all those admitted were to be the sons of honest, industrious parents and that they were neither to be bastards or diseased. Their education was to continue until the age of fourteen and was to be designed to 'fit them for learning or for labour in the towns of Manchester and Salford'. At the time they left school they were to be bound as apprentices in one of these two townships.

Lord Derby had been executed at Bolton in 1651 and his properties confiscated, so it was now possible to buy the college buildings and a sum of £500 was included in the endowment for this purpose. To provide for the maintenance and running of the school an annual endowment of £180 was to be made from the rent of various lands, including some of Humphrey Chetham's estates in Turton. The first overseer or master of the Hospital was

Ordsall Hall (*left and above*). This fine house had its origins in the hall of David de Hulton, as recorded in 1251, and subsequently came into the possession of the Radclyffe family. The present house dates from the rebuilding of the Great Hall in the 1520s. The west wing was added by Sir Alexander Radclyffe in 1639. Funds for this may have been provided by the sale of much of the Ordsall estates to Chetham in 1634. Twelve years later Chetham had the Great Barn, mentioned in his inventory, built nearby. For more details of Ordsall Hall see Chapter 11.

CITY OF SALFORD MUSEUMS AND ART GALLERY

Richard Dutton, who served in the post until he was dismissed, probably for his nonconformist tendencies, in 1671.

Humphrey's interest in providing education for the peoples of his townships did not end with the establishment of his Hospital. In his will the sum of £200 was dedicated to the purchase of 'Godly English Books' which his Executors were to see 'chained upon desks or to be fixed to pillars or in other convenient places in the Parish Church of Bolton in the Moors and Manchester and in the chapels of Turton, Walmesley, and Gorton'. The Chetham bequest of books remained in Turton Chapel for many years and a special cupboard, or press, inscribed with the origin of the bequest was made to contain them. This cupboard is now to be seen in the room known as the 'Chapel' at the Tower. In 1855 the library at Turton Chapel comprised fifty-six volumes, though how many had been lost during the two centuries it had existed is not known. A catalogue of the books is given by G. J. French in the Chetham Society's *Bibliograhical Notices of the Church Libraries at Turton and Gorton* (volume xxxviii, old series) and shows the Turton library to have contained many of the familiar books of the Puritans, commentaries, sermons and biblical histories.

This donation of books was in addition to the £1,000 set aside for the creation of the library in the town of Manchester, 'for the use of scholars and others

Chetham's Library, Manchester. In 1653 the redundant buildings of the former college of priests serving Manchester Church were bought by Humphrey Chetham to provide the accommodation for his two most cherished charitable works – the Hospital which was to provide education for poor boys, and the Library which was to be available to all as England's first free public library. Today the library contains about 100,000 volumes, of which about one third date from before 1850. The library was used by Marx and Engels, who frequently sat and worked there together.

well affected to resort to'. The will clearly laid down that no book was to be taken from the library at any time, which would have been difficult as he also specified that they were to be 'chained or fixed as well as may be within the said Library for the better preservation thereof'.

Chetham's generous bequests show the extent of the fortune that he had made. The inventory accompanying the will is a parchment scroll ten feet long, and it includes the contents of Tower of Turton, valued, at £23 2s. 2d. It does not include the value of his real estate, but lists only his 'Goods and Chattels'. Even so the sums shown are enormous in seventeenth-century terms. The property in his various houses totals £1,459 18s. 10d. to which is added £6,748 3s. 5d. in ready cash. Mortgages and debts 'whereof some are doubtful and some desperate' totalled £5,688 18s. 11d. This gives a total inventory value of £13,897 1s. 2d. which makes Chetham in his period the equivalent of a multi-millionaire.

In many ways Chetham seems to be an almost Victorian figure, an

The Dining Room, Turton Tower. Originally the base of the pele tower, this room would have been intended as a place of storage and a refuge for cattle in times of emergency. Brought into daily use during the period when the Orrells modernised the house, its present appearance owes a great deal to the work of James Kay, who brought the late seventeenth-century panelling from the demolished Middleton Hall and collected contemporary furnishings.

epitome of the Northern business man, who is sharp, vigilant and ruthless in his pursuit of trade but, either for personal motives or to gain the esteem of his community, can prove himself generous in a 'utilitarian' way. His charitable donations are for hard-headed projects. Whereas a hundred years earlier a man of his wealth might have left legacies for religious endowments, Chetham is concerned to provide practical benefits that will enable others to make their way in the world, and to follow the path he had so successfully trodden himself. The poor are not to be encouraged by easy doles of food or clothing or money; nothing is done, as it had been previously, to inspire prayers for the soul of the departed, or to show gratitude by the beautification of the church, or to repair roads or bridges. Instead the less fortunate are to be given the opportunity for self improvement: all the principles that would have been extolled by Samuel Smiles.

Although he was its owner, Chetham seems to have spent little time at Turton Tower and for the most part it was in the occupation of tenants. At his

Turton Tower, showing the Masonry Tower. The differences in the masonry of the original tower and the stage added by the Orrells in 1596 are clearly perceptible, as are the changes in fenestration. The timber-framed porch and three-storey structure were also added to the original house to link it to the detached residential building which, re-faced and with an upper floor added, faces the camera. Much of the superficial appearance of these structures is a result of Kay's restoration. This photograph may be compared with the view *c*.1800.

death it, like most of his estates, passed to his nephew, George. George did live at the Tower and fitted it with modern and luxurious furniture but, although he was a wealthy man, George was not a happy one. His son Humphrey died at Turton at the age of twenty-three, making one of those 'good' deaths that were so much admired at the time. We are told he had his coffin by him and 'Oh! how pleasantly would he discourse of death and of his bed [coffin] in his study'. After the death of George in 1664 the house passed down the family line. It was seldom used as a residence and, like many of these older, smaller houses, went through a period of neglect and decay, having become unfashionable and too lacking in comfort for the standards of the later seventeenth and the eighteenth centuries.

The salvation of Turton Tower came with its purchase in 1835 by James Kay, a local wealthy flax spinner. By this time the fashion had changed once more and the English had begun that long love affair with the Tudors which still results in modern houses having laths tacked to their external walls. The romantic revival and the novels of Walter Scott created a new interest in timbered buildings, crumbling towers and mullioned windows. So it was that over the next sixty years the Kays spent a great deal of time and money in restoring and enlarging the house. The timber frontages were refaced and restored, and the north-east wing had a second storey added and a Jacobean, dutch-gabled frontage built. In the old pele tower itself the rooms were restored and brought into use as a dining room on the ground floor, and a parlour on the first floor, the top floor being divided into a bedroom and a billiard room. To make the rooms in the tower more accessible a new staircase was added, though a portion of its spiral predecessor was retained as a curiosity. The present decor of these rooms reflects the taste of the Kays. To create the right atmosphere they bought panelling from Middleton Hall, then being demolished. A late seventeenth-century example was used in the dining room, while an oak wainscotting of the early part of that century was used in the drawing room. In this room a new plaster ceiling in the Elizabethan style was added. It may be that the design for this was based on that of its predecessor, installed at the time of the Orrells.

In the Orrell wing, linking the tower to the former service building, evidence can be seen both of the original cruck construction and of the Kays' refurbishment, the most striking example being the Courtney bed in the Tapestry Room, a vast Victorian construction making use of original Elizabethan carved oak. This taste can also be seen in the late Victorian second floor of the north-east wing which displays the influence of William Morris and the Arts and Crafts movement.

In 1890 the Kays put the tower on the market but it did not sell, and instead passed through several tenancies before it was bought by Sir Lees Knowles. Sir Lees gave the tower to Turton Urban District Council in 1930 as their headquarters and town hall. On the extinction of that authority in 1974 the house came under the control of trustees and was administered by Blackburn Museum Service until 1987, when Lancashire County Council took over.

Turton Tower is an interesting house in many ways. Architecturally it displays a variety of styles that clearly show the changing taste and requirements of the different periods – from the grim functionalism of the Middle Ages to the romantic 'Gothick' of the Victorians. Its furnishings reflect the changing expectations of comfort and privacy that were demanded. Today it is an interesting house in itself, and one that deserves to be better known. Perhaps its greatest interest is that it was once owned by a man whose career was to reflect a new pattern in the life of Lancashire as commerce began to impinge on what had essentially been a landed and feudal society. It is true that Chetham used his money to buy his way into the landed gentry, but that was an acknowledgement that the basis of the economy and society of the county was changing. If Chetham seems in many ways a Victorian figure it is because his fortune had been made in shaping and developing the industry that was so to dominate the economy not only of Lancashire but the world during the nineteenth century.

CHAPTER 6

Towneley Hall and the Lancashire Renaissance

W HEN I VISITED Towneley recently, the lake in front of the house was surrounded by a class of primary school children, many of them of Asian origin, all with strong Burnley accents. They were busy on a pond-dipping exercise and were getting very excited as they took their nets to the teacher to have their finds identified. I was struck with the thought that earlier generations of the Towneley family would have been delighted to see that their old home was still providing inspiration for budding scientists. Through almost the whole of the seventeenth century the house was the place of resort, encouragement and patronage for a remarkable group of young scientists and mathematicians, whose work is still of importance in the development of science. It is all the more remarkable that this *coterie* was to be found in a county that was considered a primitive backwater, whose educational provision lagged far behind that of other more sophisticated parts of the country.

The Towneley family had been established in the Burnley area ever since the marriage in 1200 of Geoffrey, the secular Dean of Whalley, to a daughter of Roger de Lacy, the Lord of Clitheroe. As a part of the marriage settlement de Lacy granted Geoffrey two bovates of land (a bovate being the amount of land that could be worked using a single ox-team – about 15 acres). This formed the nucleus of estates which were steadily increased, partly by careful marriages and partly by military service to the Crown. A Towneley was at Agincourt, and another was knighted for his service at Hutton Field in 1482. In the reign of Edward VI, Richard Towneley gained his knighthood for his bravery at the siege of Leith. However, this period marked the end of the family's prosperity and acceptance by the Court. Sir Richard's heir, John Towneley, steadfastly refused to conform to the Church of England and as a result was frequently imprisoned and forced to pay swingeing recusancy fines. The tale of his sufferings for his Church is proudly recorded on the family pedigree portrait that he had painted and which is now on display in the house. At his death in 1607 the estates passed to his sons, first Richard, then Charles. They continued to maintain the Catholic religion and also suffered fines and periodic imprisonment. In these times of trouble, they relied to a considerable extent on his younger

Pedigree portrait of John Towneley, artist unknown. This painting shows John Towneley, 1528–1607, and his wife May Wimbyshe, together with their seven sons and seven daughters. The inscription relates John's sufferings as a recusant: 'This John about the sixth or seventh year of her Majesty that now is, for professing the Apostolic Catholic Roman faith, was imprisoned first in Chester Castle, then sent to the Marshelsea, then to York Castle, then to the Blockhouse in Hull, then to the Gatehouse in Westminster, then to Manchester, then to Broughton, Oxfordshire, then twice to Ely in Cambridgeshire, and so now seventy-three years old, and blind, is bound to appear and keep within five miles of Towneley, his house, who hath since the statute of '83 paid unto the Exchequer £20 the month and doth still; that there is paid already about £5000 ... 1601.'

PA/OIL 117 'JOHN TOWNELEY & FAMILY' c.1600; ARTIST UNKNOWN (PHOTOGRAPH COURTESY OF BURNLEY BOROUGH COUNCIL)

son, Christopher, who was to be the founder of the illustrious Towneley scientific circle.

The house at Towneley reflects the varying fortunes of the family. It began in the Middle Ages as a single free-standing building, of which the present south-east wing is the remainder. This has only recently been proved by the discovery of diagonal buttresses at each corner. These had become buried in the masonry of the subsequent building which turned the house into a courtyard dwelling with the great hall in the southern range. The northern range was composed of the gatehouse and chapel, and possibly some other rooms for servants and guests. This wing was demolished in the eighteenth century to

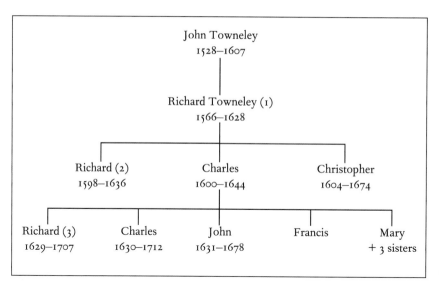

John Towneley
1528–1607

Richard Towneley (1)
1566–1628

Richard (2)
1598–1636

Charles
1600–1644

Christopher
1604–1674

Richard (3)
1629–1707

Charles
1630–1712

John
1631–1678

Francis

Mary
+ 3 sisters

Genealogical table of the Towneley family in the seventeenth century.

give the present E-shaped plan. The two other wings would have been made up of family rooms, with the long gallery in the south-eastern wing which, with its six-foot-thick walls is now the only part of the house that contains medieval masonry. The north wing contained the kitchen, store rooms and work rooms on the ground floor and some servant's accommodation, and possibly some family rooms, on the upper floor. Much of this original layout has been obscured by three major periods of rebuilding and refurbishment, the first of these carried out by Richard Towneley between 1607 and 1628. His aim seems to have been to provide more private family accommodation. This was the period when the communal life of the great hall was no longer in fashionable favour and there was an increasing tendency for the family to eat apart, in their parlour. In his plan Towneley provided just such a parlour, or family dining room, on the first floor of the north-west wing. Access was by a new oak newel staircase of generous design and the room was graced by remarkable diagonal panelling. Only two other examples of this are known: one is at Norbury Hall, in Derbyshire, the other is now in the library of Browsholme Hall, though it was originally made for Parkhead in Whalley and taken to its present location in the early nineteenth century. The three examples are so similar that they must be the work of one man. Usefully, the panelling at Towneley is dated 1628. The aspect of the room has been radically altered by the eighteenth-century addition of a parlour alongside the dining room, which blocked the window on the north side and caused it to be converted into a display alcove. After 1628 the Towneleys were preoccupied with things other than domestic improvement. They continued to be fined as recusants but, like the majority of Catholics, were prepared to support the king on the outbreak of the Civil War. By this time the estates had passed to Charles Towneley, who played a prominent part in royalist affairs in the county before he was killed fighting at Marston Moor. His wife travelled to York to seek his body

Towneley Hall, by George Barrett, 1777. An idealised picture of the house set amid a partly imagined landscape of the type created by Claude.

and was found wandering the battlefield in search of it by a senior parliamentary officer. He treated her with much gentleness and consideration, she was led away, and troopers were sent to continue the grisly search. They eventually found and buried her husband's body. On enquiring of the identity of the officer who had been so kind, she learned that it was Colonel Cromwell. The family estates were heavily sequestrated by parliament, the usual penalties imposed being automatically doubled in view of the Towneleys' professed Catholicism, but it did little to shake their loyalty to the house of Stuart. Richard, the son of Charles, recovered his estates at the Restoration but was still forced by poverty to sell much of the land – notably the family's extensive estates in Lincolnshire.

He later became involved in the various Jacobite plots of the 1690s and was one of the Lancashire squires accused of complicity in a plot to assassinate William III. The alleged conspirators were put on trial at Manchester where – to the amazement of all, in view of the character of a treason trial of the period – they were acquitted. Richard Towneley, who was to continue the tradition of scientific enquiry set by his uncle Christopher, died in 1707. In 1715 his grandson, Richard, was one of the few Lancashire gentlemen to join the Jacobite army of Tom Foster. Towneley was taken prisoner after the Battle of Preston and put on trial for treason but he, too, was acquitted, perhaps because the inevitable penalty of hanging, drawing and quartering was too horrible for a local jury to contemplate.

In 1745 his younger brother, Francis, joined the army of the Young Pretender and was given command of the so-called Manchester Regiment, the only considerable body of troops the Prince was able to recruit in England. As the Jacobites retreated, Towneley volunteered to take command of the garrison

The family dining room, Towneley Hall. This room is documented as having been part of the work carried out by Richard Towneley in the 1620s. The fireplace wall represents the medieval exterior of the wing, but the inner wall was built when the room was re-constructed. The panelling is of an unusual and interesting pattern only found here at Browsholme and at Norbury in Derbyshire. The Barrett painting of Towneley Hall, visible on the right-hand wall, has now been re-hung in another part of the house.

PHOTOGRAPH, AUTHOR

of Carlisle Castle and to fight a delaying action. After a brief siege the castle surrendered and Towneley was taken prisoner. The government was in no mood to be merciful, and he was beheaded in London in 1746. His severed head was brought back to Towneley for burial after being displayed on Temple Bar. Another member of the family was also involved with the '45: Sir John Towneley (the knighthood was a Jacobite one) served as an officer with the French contingent supplied by Louis XV. This Sir John has the doubtful distinction of having been the first translator into French of Samuel Butler's poem *Hudibras*. This satirical work relies for its humour on pun, word-play and double meanings – indeed it was considered to be an impossible subject for translation and Towneley undertook it as a wager.

In spite of the dangerous political involvement with the Jacobite cause, Richard, the owner of Towneley between 1725 and 1730, decided on a major refurbishment of the house. The days of the great hall had long gone and the term 'hall' had begun to assume its modern meaning of the entrance area. It was fashionable to make the entrance hall as impressive as possible, to overwhelm the visitor with the grandeur and importance of the house. The new domestic arrangements coincided with a revolution in taste which drew its inspiration from the classical world of antiquity. Both these features can be seen in the new hall of Towneley. It is not clear whether the old great hall had run through the entire height of the house, or if it had had a ceiling inserted and a storey of rooms above it. Whichever may have been the case, it was now opened to the roof, a new back wall with windows in a rather crude Gibbs style was inserted and the whole was redecorated in the new taste.

Towneley employed the Swiss-Italian stucco artist Francesco Vassali and his assistant Martino Quadri, and they produced a *tour de force* of plasterwork in

Portrait of Christopher Towneley (1604–74), by an unknown artist. This is one of a number of the family portraits which formerly lined the Long Gallery and were sold on the death of Lady O'Hagan. The portraits can be seen in the drawing by John Weld of the Gallery in 1825 and the painted identifications are still on the panelling. Six of these paintings were rediscovered in the 1990s and returned to the Hall.

PA/OIL 314
CHRISTOPHER TOWNELEY
(1604–1674) ARTIST
UNKNOWN (PHOTOGRAPH
COURTESY OF BURNLEY
BOROUGH COUNCIL)

the great hall. The walls were divided by coupled Ionic pilasters supporting a full cornice which, in turn, is pierced by small windows. The spaces between the pilasters are filled with stucco medallions decorated with Roman busts and ribbon mouldings. At both ends of the hall splendid marble chimney pieces support antique marble statuary, the satyr frustratingly separated by the length of the hall from the nymph. The ceiling, too, is rich in stucco and supports lavish crystal chandeliers. The simple marble chequerboard floor makes a remarkable contrast with the splendour that surrounds it. Recently the plain white decor that had existed for years has been improved by the painting of the walls in a rich terracotta shade, with the pilasters and mouldings in white. The whole makes a room of striking beauty and elegance.

Also dating from this period of work is the beautiful cantilever staircase added at the south end of the hall and leading to the long gallery. The stairs ascend apparently unsupported, and each step is a superbly cut and proportioned piece of masonry. The elaborate iron balustrade is the work of John Ashbourne of Derby, and its extravagant scrolls complement the severity of the steps.

The third major period of works at Towneley came in 1817, when Peregrine Towneley employed the fashionable architect Jeffry Wyatt to create two state rooms on the ground floor of the south wing. Wyatt carried out several important commissions in Lancashire in this period, including his work on Liverpool Town Hall and at Browsholme. His work at Towneley was confined to a general updating of the exterior of the house and the construction of what are now known as the two Regency rooms. These rooms run through two floors and on the third floor are a number of small chambers linked by the long gallery. The panelled rooms are now furnished in a variety of seventeenth- and eighteenth-century styles. The long gallery, with its oak panelling still bearing the ascriptions of the family portraits that used to hang there, is similarly furnished. Also on this floor, through a door which once led to the servants' quarters, is the one survivor of the eight hiding places originally built into the house. These were, no doubt, used by fugitive priests and possibly by fleeing Jacobites.

Today Towneley contains the art gallery and museum of Burnley Borough Council, but its two most interesting and important treasures are relics of its days as a family house. For many years the Towneleys were closely associated with Whalley Abbey, which they served in a secular role, and Whalley is thought to be the place of origin of the Towneley vestments. These are a dalmatic and chasuble which date from long before the dissolution of the monasteries. The vestments are made of Italian cloth of gold, woven with a pattern of strawberries and leaves running in diagonal bands, and sewn with orphreys or embroidered bands. The workmanship of the vestments suggests that they were made in the period from 1390 to 1420: by this time the great period of English embroidery – the world famous *opus anglicanum* – had passed but, nevertheless, the work on these vestments is superb. The orphreys are stitched with a series of scenes illustrating the Nativity story. The work is so delicate that even the facial expressions are accurately rendered in fine silks. The other great artistic treasure of Towneley is the remarkable early sixteenth-century Flemish carved altarpiece in the chapel. This is the chapel that was adopted in the eighteenth century, after the demolition of the original chapel in the vanished gatehouse wing. This altarpiece was acquired and installed by Charles Towneley, the connoisseur, in the late eighteenth century. The main carving shows the Passion story, but it is surrounded by scenes about whose significance there is no agreement by the experts. Originally the carved panels could have been concealed behind painted doors.

However, perhaps the most important and remarkable legacy left by the Towneley family is neither in the house nor in its artistic content, but in the development of scientific thought in England. By the early seventeenth century the intellectual developments of the Renaissance were beginning to have an effect on the thinking and outlook of more than just a small number of international scholars. Men in many places and at all levels in society were challenging established ideas and principles. This was especially true in the field of scientific and natural philosophic speculation. New ideas about the cosmos, the sun, the planets and the place of the earth in the universe were rife. The fact that in Lancashire there should emerge a group of able and important scientists, centred around Towneley Hall, who were to make a vital contribution to the advancement of learning is both a remarkable phenomenon and an indication of how widespread scientific speculation and experimentation were at this time. It is important to examine the achievements of this 'Towneley Group' and the possible reasons why they emerged in such an unlikely environment.

The first Richard Towneley (1566–1628) was succeeded as squire of

The Nativity as shown on the Whalley Abbey vestments at Towneley. The orphrey or band of embroidered decoration extending vertically on the back of the chasuble illustrates the story of the nativity of Christ in a series of scenes. In this depiction of the stable scene the buildings of Bethlehem are those of a medieval European city, Mary reclines, while Joseph stands on guard. The stable animals look on. The fine work is remarkable and the skill used to depict expressions is a tribute to the talent of the English embroiderers.

The Chasuble. This picture shows the back of the chasuble and allows the quality of the embroidery of the orphreys to be appreciated. In this sequence the nativity story is related. The scenes depicted include the Annunciation, the Nativity, the Virgin and Child, the Annunciation to the shepherds and the visit of the Magi. Though there is no documentary proof to link the vestments to Whalley Abbey the circumstantial evidence is compelling.

Towneley by his eldest son, also Richard, who died childless in 1636. The properties were inherited by his younger brother, Charles, who was killed at the battle of Marston Moor and was succeeded by his son, the third Richard, born in 1629. During the years of young Richard's minority the management of the Towneley estates was in the hands of his uncle Christopher, third son of the first Richard. It was Christopher and his nephew who were to be the leaders of the scientific and academic group.

Biographical information about Christopher is sparse. He was born in 1604 and lived at Carr Hall, and later at a house called Moor Isles in Pendle Forest. It seems probable that, like many members of the family, he was educated abroad, although one source suggests that he had spent some time at Gray's Inn acquiring some legal training. As a Catholic he would have been unable to practise as an attorney but many sons of the gentry spent some time at one of the London Inns of Court at which they acquired – it was hoped – a degree of cosmopolitan sophistication and also a knowledge of law, which would be useful in the management of their estates and in the constant disputes with their neighbours that were such a feature of seventeenth-century estate management. Christopher Towneley seems to have put his knowledge to good effect, and to have developed something of a career in estate management. He had also acquired something else – a deep interest in a wide field of knowledge and a determination to be involved in and encourage academic activity. He became known as a collector of books and manuscripts, and laid the foundations for a library that was of considerable significance. Most of this collection was lost in a fire in the hall later in the century, and those parts that survived were dispersed when the Towneley library was sold in the nineteenth century.

Christopher was particularly interested in two fields of intellectual activity. He was closely involved in antiquarian research into the history of the area, and he and the celebrated Dr Kuerden co-operated in the projected history of Lancashire; a design that never reached fruition. Towneley found and transcribed many medieval documents of considerable significance. Some of his papers in this field were preserved and were eventually bought by William Farrer: they are now housed in the Manchester City Archives Office. As an antiquarian Christopher built up a network of important contacts, including Sir John Gascoigne, Richard Gascoigne and Roger Dodsworth, the Yorkshire collectors of manuscripts. This was a period during which the fascination of historical and archival research gripped many men. It could even have practical and political importance: in the period before the Civil War both the king and parliament made constant reference to ancient documents in their justification

The Great Hall of
Towneley Hall. It was
the decision of Richard
Towneley in the 1720s
to reconstruct the Great
Hall. In the past it had
been the communal
living room of the
house, but this was no
longer the fashion and
he ordered its
conversion into an
impressive entrance
room. It is possible that
an intervening floor
was removed to carry
the hall to the full
height of the house. It
has been suggested that
the architect was James
Gibbs (1682–1754) but
it is more probable that
his style was copied by
a provincial designer.
In 1728 the Italian
Swiss Francesco Vassali
and his assistant
Martino Quadrigi
carried out the
spectacular stucco
decoration making
extensive use of a wide
variety of classical
motifs.

or criticism of policies. The king's revival of ancient extra-parliamentary taxation was based on the discovery of archaic precedents. In fact, he established a special department to search the archives for useful material. In its turn parliament cited the charters and acts of the medieval kings to bolster the legality of their claims. Perhaps the most famous case was their revival of the long-forgotten and unimportant *Magna Carta* of King John.

The other subject that Christopher found of great interest was the study of natural philosophy, particularly astronomy. At this period there was a special enthusiasm for the study of the stars and planets: partly due to the revolutionary theories of planetary movement which had been propounded by Copernicus, Kepler and Galileo; partly because of the development of the telescope, which allowed so much more accurate and detailed examination of the skies; and partly because of the all-consuming interest in astrology. At the time the latter was inextricably entwined with the scientific study of the stars and it was accepted as a genuine and authentic science. Many of the famous natural philosophers of the day made no distinction between the two, and there was widespread public demand for astrological predictions. Both Queen Elizabeth and Oliver Cromwell consulted their astrologers about propitious dates for major actions. This was also a time when many men were able to combine an interest in scientific and historical research. In his prison in the Tower, Walter Raleigh occupied his time with chemical and alchemical study and wrote his *History of the World*. The corpus of knowledge in all fields was small enough for there to be no necessity for the specialisation in one discipline with which we are familiar.

In astronomical and other scientific thinking there was a growing realisation of the necessity for accurate and careful observation and experiment to justify hypotheses. Men such as Francis Bacon and Sir Thomas Browne were laying

The Red Drawing Room, Townley Hall. Drawings by Jeffry Wyatt, later Sir Jeffry Wyatville, made in 1817 exist for both the Red Drawing Room and the ajoining Green Dining Room. The colours used in the recent restoration were determined by 'scrape' tests which revealed fragments of the original paints. The fireplace in this room is probably by Richard Heyward and is a relic of the former dining room built by John Carr of York in 1766. The appearance and decoration of this room is strongly reminiscent of the Wyatt rooms at Browsholme. (See p.26)

PHOTOGRAPH, AUTHOR

the foundations of modern scientific method. Previously, even the most important scientists whose ideas were revolutionising thought – men like Copernicus and Kepler – had given a great deal of time to philosophical speculation on metaphysical questions. The new generation, led by Galileo, abandoned theoretical speculation in favour of careful experimentation and minute observation. Christopher Towneley seems to have undertaken no significant research into astronomy himself, but saw his role as that of a collector of information, the creator of a library of scientific literature, and as patron and encourager of the scientists he found around him in the North West. It might be thought that an area so remote from the centres of learning would have contained few people interested or occupied in astronomical studies, but Towneley was able to contact, and establish a correspondence with, a circle of young men whose work was to be of great importance. They were largely self-taught and had no contacts with the academic world or – as far as we know – with each other until Towneley brought them together.

Perhaps the most celebrated of this group was Jeremiah Horrocks. He was born in about 1617 in a farm house at Toxteth Park: the house has now disappeared and the site is that of Otterspool railway station. Almost nothing is known of his early years or education, but in 1632 he was admitted as a sizar to Emmanuel College, Cambridge. Sizars were young men from poor backgrounds, but of academic ability, who were admitted to the colleges on condition that they repaid the costs of their tuition by acting as servants to the wealthier undergraduates. It seems that even at Cambridge Horrocks did not find the scientific education that he craved, and he left without taking a degree and returned to Toxteth. He devoted his time to astronomical observation and recording of tidal data. In some way that is not recorded he became acquainted with Christopher Towneley, who in turn introduced him to William Crabtree. Crabtree was a few years older than Horrocks, having been born in 1610 at Broughton, and educated at Manchester Grammar School. He had gone into business as a clothier and chapman but his consuming passion was astronomy.

During his time at Cambridge Horrocks had become acquainted with the ideas and work of Johannes Kepler (1571–1630), and it was he who introduced Crabtree to Kepler's writings. Crabtree was fascinated by the new ideas of planetary motion and began a close study of the tables of the movements prepared by Kepler and published as the *Rudolphine Tables*. Meanwhile Horrocks was faced with the problem of earning a living, and eventually he chose to be ordained and became the curate of the new church at Much Hoole. According to legend he lived in Carr House, the home of the Stones family, at Bretherton. Horrocks had been giving particular attention to the movements of the planets and his research had led him to predict that at a certain time the planet Venus would pass between the earth and the sun. He decided that this would occur at 3.15 p.m. on 24 November 1639. It is said that the predicted date was a Sunday and the time that of the service in the church. Undeterred, Horrocks set up his 2s. 6d. telescope in such a way that the image of the sun's disc would be projected on a white sheet. As the time of the transit approached he rushed from the church, leaving a stunned congregation, and was in time to watch the small shadowy disc of Venus cross the surface of the sun. He had made his prediction known to Crabtree, who was also able to watch the passage of the planet, and to his brother Jonas Horrocks, but the cloudy sky in Liverpool prevented the latter from witnessing the phenomenon.

The importance of this observation was that it not only confirmed the predicted motions of the planets but, because the diameter of the sun was known, it was for the first time possible to calculate the speed at which the planets (or at least Venus) moved. Shortly after this Horrocks left Hoole and returned to his home. Whether his departure was of his own choice, or because the congregation objected to his combining astronomy with his clerical duties, we shall never know. Back at Toxteth he wrote an account of his observations which was given to Christopher Towneley, and also completed a most thorough study of the tidal movements. Unfortunately Horrocks died in 1641

St Michael's Church, Much Hoole. Originally a chapel of ease to Croston, Hoole became a parish in its own right in the early seventeenth century. The church is of great interest for a number of architectural reasons – the early use of brick in an anachronistic 'gothic' style, the strange composite tower built in 1722 with gothic detail on three sides but with the west front supported by Tuscan columns, and a Roman arch enclosing an oculus window. Historically the interest of the church is in its association with Jeremiah Horrocks.

at the age of thirty-one and left much uncompleted work. Apart from his significant discovery he was important to the Towneley Group as the only one who had attended university and who was able to contribute a knowledge of the scientific ideas of the outside world.

Christopher Towneley had also established links with other young men who were studying science and mathematics in the North West, whom he was able to put in contact with each other. Particularly important in improving the accuracy of astronomical observation was the work of William Gascoigne. He was a member of a Yorkshire landed family of which other members were Towneley's colleagues in antiquarian research. William was passionately interested in astronomy and in the development of improved instruments for observation. Like Horrocks he had found the conventional paths of education unsatisfactory and had abandoned them. He is thought to have taught himself mathematics using the most famous textbook of the period, Oughtred's *Clavis Mathematicae*. During his work on improving the telescope he devised a new and more accurate method of grinding lenses, but his most important invention

The Long Gallery, Towneley Hall, John Weld, 1835. Architecturally the Long Gallery of Towneley is unusual in that a number of small rooms, probably used as accommodation for the bachelors of the household, open off it. The room, with its early seventeenth-century panelling, is little changed today except for the lowering of the ceiling and the loss of the family portraits which were sold and dispersed when the house was purchased from Lady O'Hagan by Burnley Corporation in 1901. Recently six of these paintings – including a portrait of Christopher Towneley – have been returned to the Hall.

was the astronomical micrometer which, when fitted to a telescope, allowed for the accurate measurement of stars and the creation of categories of magnitude. Horrocks and Crabtree both used instruments made by Gascoigne and were in frequent correspondence with him. In this intercourse Christopher Towneley acted as the clearing house and intermediary.

Another member of the group was Jeremiah Shackerley, born in Halifax, and a refugee from the rebellion in Ireland, but about whose life very little is known. It is possible that he spent some time as a guest of Christopher Towneley and was involved in his work. He became acquainted with the researches of Horrocks and Crabtree, and made himself a reputation by his investigations as an astronomer and as the writer of *An Anatomy of Urania Practica*. He was also the first person to publish the work of Horrocks and Crabtree, which appeared in his *Tabulae Britannicae* in 1653. In 1651 he was in India, where he observed the phenomenon of the transit of Mercury. His observatory, using cheap and primitive equipment, was established at Surat. There he made some significant observations and found great interest in the astronomical and astrological knowledge of the Brahmins. He soon became ill, and died before making any other significant observations.

Another member of the circle which Christopher gathered around himself was Jonas (later Sir Jonas) Moore, who features in that marvellous gallery of seventeenth-century pen portraits, John Aubrey's *Brief Lives*. Aubrey tells us that 'Moore was born at Whitelee in Lancashire, towards the Bishoprick of Durham' – Aubrey was an amateur of many disciplines but geography does not seem to have been amongst them – 'He was inclined to Mathematiques when a boy which some kind friends putt him upon and instructed him in it; and afterwards Mr Oughtred more fully enformed him and then he taught gentlemen in London, which was his livelihood'. Among his London pupils was the young Duke of York, the future James II. It would seem very likely that the 'kind friends' who ensured Moore's education included Christopher Towneley. Aubrey then goes on to give an account of Moore's life and service as surveyor, royalist officer, expert on fortifications, reclaimer of fenland and Surveyor of the Royal Ordnance. The account includes two of those gems of personal information and anecdote which are such a feature of Aubrey's writing: in the middle of his account of Moore's plans for fortifying London we find: 'Sciatica – he cured it by boyling his buttock'. Aubrey then goes on to tell of a remarkable event which involves Gascoigne, and shows that the experiments of the Towneley Group were not always as practical or as rooted in scientific principle as one might hope.

> I remember that Sir Jonas told us that a Jesuit (I think it was Grenbergerus of the Roman College) found out a way of flying, and that he made a youth performe it. Mr Gascoigne taught an Irish boy the way, and he flew over a river in Lancashire or thereabouts, but when he was up in the ayre the people gave a shoute, whereat the boy being frighted, he fell down on the other side of the river, and broke both his legges, and when he came to himself, he say'd that he thought the people had seen some strange apparition, which fancy amazed him. This was anno 1635.

The days of aviational experiments were drawing to a close and the Civil War took a heavy toll of the Towneley group. Both Christopher and Charles Towneley joined the Lancashire royalist army. Charles was killed and Christopher wounded and captured at Marston Moor; Gascoigne, a captain in Langdale's Northern Horse, was killed at Melton Mowbray in 1645; Horroocks had died before the outbreak of the war and Crabtree had died in 1644. Shackerley survived the war after serving in the king's army but his fatal voyage to India meant that only Christopher Towneley and Jonas Moore survived these turbulent times. On his release from imprisonment Towneley was occupied in acting as estate manager for his young nephew, Richard, during the dark days of sequestration of royalist estates by parliament.

So it was Jonas Moore who was to carry the spirit of the Towneley Group into the new age: an age when the practice of scientific investigation became evermore popular and began to distance itself from the association with hermetic speculation and practices. It was to be the age of Newton, of Wren, of Descartes, of Boyle and Hooke, and of the Royal Society. If a new age was beginning there were writers who recognised the importance that the Group had in the development of natural philosophy. Sir Edward Shireburne had been involved peripherally with the Towneley Group and in 1675 he wrote his *Sphere of Marcus Manillius*, in which he gives details of the work and lives of many of these Northern scientists.

> These four [Horrocks, Crabtree, Gascoigne and Moore] were lights of the first magnitude in the northern Hemisphere who were happily brought to acquaintance by means of Christopher Towneley of Carr in Lancashire, Esquire, who stuck not for any cost or labour to promote as well astronomical as other mathematical studies by a diligent correspondence kept and maintained with learned professors in these sciences; upon which Account he was very dear to All the Four and for which reason, as for the particular respect I owe him, he merits to be named in this catalogue.

However, the tradition at Towneley did not come to an end. Christopher lived until 1674 and he had succeeded in imbuing the new squire of Towneley, Richard, with his own interests and determination to continue the tradition. In this Richard was to be encouraged and assisted by his younger brothers, Charles, John and Francis during the period from about 1657 to 1704, when Towneley Hall remained a centre for the northern scientists. Of his brothers the most active in research was Charles, but that he was not immune to the current chimeras of scientific thinking is proved by a note in the writings of Henry Power of Halifax, who wrote of Charles' experiment 'by which he would deduce perpetual motion'.

Richard Towneley continued to establish contacts with other researchers both in the North and further afield. He enlarged the scientific library at Towneley and maintained a lively and vigorous correspondence with many. One of his closest associates was Dr Henry Power, who became one of the first members of the Royal Society and was able to put Towneley in touch with some of its most prominent members. Richard Towneley was interested in the current subjects of speculation, which mainly concerned the properties of gases, atmospheric pressure and temperature, capillary action, and the vacuum. In this work he was particularly influenced by the philosophy of Descartes and his belief in the existence of aether. The Towneleys carried out numerous experiments in their locality, taking barometers up Pendle and Beacon Hill at Halifax and down local lead mines, recording the readings with scrupulous accuracy. It seems that Richard employed a servant, George Kemp, who acted as laboratory assistant and took part in these expeditions.

It was this work on atmospheric pressure that brought Towneley into contact with Robert Boyle. In 1661, while visiting London, Towneley had been charged

Altar Piece in the Chapel of Towneley Hall. The first record indicate that there was a chapel at Towneley a early as the thirteenth century. The position of this chapel i uncertain but it was replaced, about 1515 by a new building ordered by Sir John Towneley Subsequently, as the house grew, this chapel became incorporated into the fourth wing which was demolished in the early eighteenth century. Wood and stone work was preserved and used to build the present chapel by Charles Towneley, the diletante. This altar piece, made in the Low Countries, is of early sixteenth century date and was part of his collection of medieval woodwork.

by Power with delivering a packet of papers to William Croone, register, or secretary, of the new Royal Society. Croone invited him to attend a meeting, where he met Boyle, who had reached a crucial stage in his experiments on the pressure of gases. The two men discussed their respective findings. During the conversation a remark of Towneley's suggested a possible hypothesis to Boyle who, when he followed it up, was able to formulate his famous law which states that there is an inverse relationship between the pressure and the volume of gases at a constant temperature. In his account of his work Boyle generously acknowledged the debt he owed and wrote of the importance of Mr Towneley's hypothesis to his own work. The two men remained friends and communicated over the next ten years.

By the intervention of Sir Jonas Moore, Towneley became acquainted with the new generation of scientists. Among them was one of the most distinguished astronomers, Richard Flamsteed of Derby, another largely self-educated man, who at Moore's recommendation was appointed as King's Astronomer in 1674. In the following year he was given the responsibility of setting up the new observatory at Greenwich. One of the preoccupations of science at the time was the accurate measurement of time. This was not only a mechanical challenge but it was appreciated that it was essential for the determination of longitude. A successful and practical method of which was essential to navigation and the commercial success of England. The invention of the spring driven watch was a vital step and such pocket watches were first developed by the Dutchman Huuygens and by Robert Hooke (1635-1703). Towneley co-operated with Hooke and the famous clockmaker Thomas Tompion in creating the dead-beat anchor escapement and clocks of this pattern were installed in the Royal Observatory. It was Sir Jonas who arranged for Flamsteed to have the opportunity to examine the then largely unknown manuscripts of Horrocks and Crabtree. Flamsteed visited Towneley in 1671 and returned the following year to make copies of the manuscripts. He rated Crabtree's explanation of certain phenomena as superior to that of Descartes, and for the first time became aware of the use of Gascoigne's micrometer. It is probable that Richard Towneley and Flamsteed continued to correspond and exchange views but few papers of this later period survive. One account of the activities at Towneley comes from Ralph Thoresby, the Leeds antiquary and scientist, who visited Towneley to see the experiments and to make use of the splendid library that Richard had built up.

Meteorological observations made by Richard Towneley.

A Prospect of the Weather, Winds, and Height of the Mercury in the Barometer, on the first day of the Month; and of the whole Rain in every Month in the Year 1703, and the beginning of 1704: Observed at Towneley in Lancashire, by Ri. Towneley, Esq;, and at Upminster in Essex. By the Reverend Mr W. Derham, F. R. S.

Month.	Weather at Towneley.	Weather at Upminster.	Winds at Towneley.	Winds at Upminster.	Barometer at Towneley.	Barometer at Upminster.	Rain at Towneley.	Rain at Upminster.
			SE 5	SE 1	29 04	29 39		
January.	Overcast.	Overcast.			28 91	35	15 17	8 89
					80	22		
February.	Overcast.	Frost and Fair.	SSE 3	E 1 Clouds. S.	29 29 37	62	15 88	6 41
					47	68		
March.	Chequer'd.	Frost, and Fair. Snow.	WSW NE	NW 1	64 67 73	82 83 9.	10 .02	4 75
April.	Chequer'd and Cloudy.	Fair. Cloudy. Fair.	W	WSW 1 W 4	59 5y 5.	93 91 91	17 63	12 49
May.	Cloudy.	Cloudy. Thunder, with Hail & Rain.	NNE	Ni W 3 NWbN 3	66 co 60	66 76	10 17 64	20 77
June.	Cloudy.	Cloudy. Clear.	S	S o S 1	38 4y 63	61 62 88	75 24 06	14 55
July.	Cloudy.	Fair.	SSE. SE E 1	E 1 NbE 2	84 80 77	99 96 90	3 65	14 90
August.	Cloudy.	Thunder and Rain. Fairer.	SE 1 4 4	N 2 N1yW2 Clouds SE	57 55 58	72 72 6y	14 21	3 36
Septemb.	Clear Chequer'd.	Cloudy. Fairer.	E	NW 1 WNW 1	co co 18	3c 4c 4:	32 40	.14 86
October.	Chequer'd.	Fair.	N	NNW 4	28 -6 83 86	8y	7 04	9 55
Novemb.	Overcast.	Cloudy.	E	NbE 1	29 56 5i. 52.	29 72 69	28 56	7 27
Decemb.	Overcast Cloudy.	Overcast. Rain.	W	3	36 45 48 80 82 85	30 c8 07 10 10	10 24 iyb 31 39	3 14 119 94 4 06
January.	Overcast.	Overcast.	SSE SE 2	E o SEbEi	5o 0: 0:	31 2 20	23 3 .93	2 19
February.	Overcast.	Milling. Cloudy.	W	NWbN 1		2		
March.	Overcast.	Overcast.	S	iEbE o SE 1	29 11 45	29 58	20 78	16 04

Charles Towneley and his friends, by John Zoffany, 1733–1810. This portrait shows Towneley seated among the choicest pieces of his collection in his gallery at Park Street in Westminster. He gazes at the statue of 'Clytie'. Of the two standing figures, that on the left is Sir Charles Greville, a politician and connoisseur. With Greville is Thomas Astle, a member of the Society of Dilettanti and trustee of the British Museum. The man seated by the table is the French antiquary Pierre Hughes or, as he was better known, d'Hancarville.

Thoresby describes Richard as 'that famous mathematician and eminent virtuoso' and goes on to mention how he was shown the rain gauge invented by Towneley; a brass quadrant made by Adams, the most famous instrument maker; a carriage designed to pass smoothly over the roughest roads; a method of propagating the cuttings of coniferous trees; and a sundial. The variety of these experiments gives us some idea of the breadth of vision of Richard Towneley and his associates. One of the more extraordinary aspects of the diversity of interest amongst this group of *savants* is that on one occasion Sir Christopher Wren was called on to suggest a cure for a smoking chimney at Towneley. He responded by designing a prototype of the tin cowl. These subjects show the universality of the interests of the amateur scientists or 'virtuosi' of this period. All the topics mentioned here were things which had

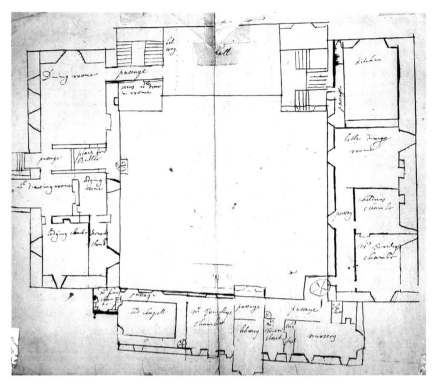

Ground plan of Towneley Hall, c.1700. This plan and its companion for the first floor show that at this time the house was still quadrangular in shape, with the chapel situated above the room to the left of the entrance passage. To the right were the library and nursery. This wing had been demolished by the 1770s when the house was painted by Barrett. These plans provide evidence that prior to the alterations of 1730 the Great Hall and the dining room extended through two floors. It is possible that there were garrets above them which are not shown on the plans.

been preoccupations of the nascent Royal Society and its alumni. It would be interesting to know if Towneley's researches were spontaneous or if he was exploring ideas which he had gleaned from his correspondence with members of that illustrious group.

Among the next generation and following Richard Towneley's death in 1707, scientific activity seems to have come to an end, perhaps because of the political involvements of the family. However, in the following generation, Richard's great-grandson, Charles (1737–1805), was to make himself a reputation, not in science but as a connoisseur and collector of works of art. He inherited the estates in 1742 but it was not until 1772 that he took up long term residence in this country. Although he spent much of his time in London it seems that he retained an interest in Towneley, which he visited, and considered making major alterations to the house. His main project was for the construction of a special rotunda gallery, similar to that built at Ince by his friend Henry Blundell, in which to display his collection of classical sculptures, but this was never put into effect. He had been educated, like so many of the family, at the College of Douai and then spent years in Florence and Rome. While he was in Italy he acquired a comprehensive knowledge of classical art, and in particular sculpture. He made a collection of statuary that was of the highest order. On his return to England he built a special gallery to house the collection at his house at 7 Park Street (now known as Queen Anne's Gate) and his home became the centre of an artistic circle which included among its members, the painters

Reynolds, Zoffany, and Angelica Kaufman; Nollekens the sculptor; and Sir William Hamilton, the collector of Greek pottery and husband of the notorious Emma. A well known painting by Zoffany shows Charles Towneley seated among the best pieces of his collection of statuary and surrounded by his friends. Charles Towneley has a special interest for Lancashire historians as it was to him that T. D. Whittaker dedicated his *History of the Parish of Whalley* with its illustrations by the young Joseph Turner. On Towneley's death his collection of terracotta reliefs and Roman coins alone was valued at £3,000, and the entire collection was sold to the British Museum, which he had helped to found, at the favourable price of £29,000. Included amongst these objects was the world-famous Ribchester helmet and material from the celebrated Cuerdale Hoard of Viking silver. The museum built a special Towneley Gallery to house the collection.

Earlier the question was asked as to why it should have been at Towneley, in a comparatively remote and isolated area, that such a group of able and important scientists should have been gathered. Having summarised their work it is now necessary to try to find an answer. First, it is obvious that the particular interest, genius or inclination of certain individuals, notably Christopher and Richard, was very important. Had their taste been different then so would the story of the Towneley Group. They were in the fortunate position that they had the money to indulge their whims and interests: they could afford to employ a scientific helper, to buy books and manuscripts and to obtain instruments of the finest quality. Their place in society enabled them to know and make contact with the people who mattered and to bring themselves to the notice of the scientific community. These factors perhaps applied to many other landed families, yet few others made a similar contribution.

There were also some special factors which, it can be suggested, made the Towneleys more effective in their chosen role as the patrons of learning. Their determined Roman Catholic stance may have been relevant to this in three ways. Firstly, because of the prohibition on Catholic schooling in this country they had been, as far as we can tell, educated abroad at the Jesuit College of Douai. The Society of Jesus had always used the high quality of their schools and the education they provided as one of their main weapons in the fight against the Protestant religion. The Order had always tended to attract men of the highest intellectual ability and education, and the quality of their teaching was unsurpassed. In addition, the continental location of the school brought more cosmopolitan and wide-ranging influences to bear on the boys than if they had remained in Lancashire. They acquired a fluency in foreign languages and an awareness of intellectual development on a European scale. They thus avoided the insular and almost xenophobic attitudes of many Englishmen of their time and class. The Towneleys, therefore, had a sound basic education and had acquired a love of learning and intellectual speculation. Secondly, after their return opportunity was added to education. Men of their position in society who were non-Catholic would have found themselves caught up in the round and commitments of local and national administration. In this period

most of the work of government, whether local or national, was carried out by unpaid local officials supervised by the squirearchy. The Towneleys, had they been a Protestant family, would have been in the forefront of this work. Instead they were excluded from office and had abundant free time to devote to their special interests. The same prohibition excluded them from most other avenues of employment. They could not attend university, they could not practise medicine or the law, and they were excluded from any employment under the Crown either in the civil or military service. They could follow their inclinations undisturbed, and a man like Christopher – a younger son who, in other circumstances, would have had to make his way in the world – remained at home absorbed in his hobbies. It can therefore be suggested that the Towneley's allegiance to Rome benefitted them in this way and created an ambience in which they could could pursue their inclinations towards scientific research.

The third advantage derived from their Catholic commitment is more speculative. One of the features of the scientific development of this period is the emphasis placed on corporate groups working in mutual support to investigate phenomena. There were a number of these groups, both informal (like the Towneley circle) and formal (like the Royal Society) throughout the

Towneley Hall, the main front. The central block of the house, to the right in this picture, is the Great Hall as re-modelled in *c*.1730, with the nineteenth-century addition of the porch and steps. To the left is the oldest part of the house which contains the Long Gallery and the Regency rooms of Wyatt, who was also responsible for the enlarged buttresses, crenellated parapets and corner turrets which actually contain and conceal the chimneys.

country. It may be postulated that the recusant community was even more keenly aware of the values of co-operation and the quick and accurate transmission of information. There can be little doubt that a form of recusant underground movement existed and played an important part in preserving its members from the worst effects of persecution. It was quite natural, then, for the Towneleys to be aware of the value of group activity and the benefits of mutual support and contact between like-minded people. This can be little more than an airy speculation, but it might go some way towards explaining the success of the Towneley group. It must, though, be emphasised that it was by no means a group confined to Catholics, or concerned with denominational adherences and indeed Horrocks was an ordained minister of the Church of England. There has been a tendency for historians to link the development of science in the seventeenth century to the rise of Puritanism: in this case, at least, the very opposite is true.

Enough has now been said to give a new perspective to Towneley Hall and its family, in a field which one might not associate with it. One of the fascinating aspects of the story is tracing the interwoven threads of contacts and interactions, and seeing how they have influenced the modern world. Let your imaginations take flight. Horrocks, an intimate at Towneley, discovers the Transit of Venus; his friends Crabtree and Gascoigne extend, expand and publish his discoveries. As a result they help to create a new awareness and interest in astronomy. One consequence of this is the establishment of the Royal Society and the Royal Observatory, with Flamsteed as its guiding light. He, in turn, is influenced by his contacts at Towneley and another member of the circle makes a contribution. In his will Sir Jonas Moore bequeathed to the new observatory a seven-foot sextant and two Tompion clocks. Thus begins the association between Greenwich and time that has become so inextricably entwined in our language. Later, the Royal Society and the Royal Observatory, both organisations with which Towneley had been associated, sent out the first expedition of Captain James Cook, whose destination was the Pacific where he was to observe the Transit of Venus. On that voyage he explored the coastline of parts of Australia – and so the chain of connections goes on.

In 1700 Dr Charles Leigh, another Lancashire scientist who was familiar with Richard Towneley, wrote in his *Natural History of Lancashire and Cheshire*, 'The world owes a great many obligations to the great industry and knowledge of Richard Towneley of Towneley'. Were we to associate with this sentiment the names of Christopher Towneley and the other members of the circle, few would disagree.

CHAPTER 7

Swarthmoor Hall and the Quakers

'As we went I spied a great high hill called Pendle Hill, and I went on the top of it with much ado, it was so steep; but I was moved of the Lord to go atop of it; and when I came atop of it I saw the Lancashire Sea; and there atop of the hill I was moved to sound the day of the Lord; and the Lord let me see atop of the hill in what places he had a great people to be gathered. As I went down on the hill side I found a spring of water and refreshed myself, for I had eaten little and drunk little for several days.' Thus, somewhat repetitively, does George Fox tell of his first vision of the countryside which was to provide the first home and recruiting ground for his life's work, the creation of the Religious Society of Friends. He goes on to relate how later in the day, after seeking food and shelter at an inn, a further vision followed. In this he saw 'a great people in white raiment by a river's side coming to the Lord and the place was near John Blaykling's where Richard Robinson lived'. The river is identified as the Rawthey at its confluence with the Lune; the homes of Blaykling and Robinson being at Briggflats near Sedbergh.

In his time George Fox was not unusual. This was the period in the aftermath of the Civil War and the execution of the king, when England was in a ferment of political, religious and social speculation and discussion. Fox was born in 1624, at Fenny Drayton, or as it was then known Drayton in the Clays, Leicestershire. His father was a weaver, named by his neighbours 'Honest Christer'; a man of known probity and high religious feeling. George's mother, too, was known as an honest and god-fearing woman and she did much to encourage in her son an interest in religious speculation and a deep knowledge of the scriptures. After serving as an apprentice to a shoemaker and cattle dealer, George entered into a period in which he sought religious truth. He found himself increasingly dissatisfied with the teachings offered by the Church, whose ministers and members he saw as hypocritical. He seems to have drifted, like an Indian holy man, through Civil War England almost untouched by the conflict around him: occasionally spending time with soldiers, and engaging in theological debate with them. During this troubled time he sought discussion and instruction from any highly reputed minister who was prepared to give him the benefit of his views. In ways which are not clear and which are not

Swarthmoor Hall, near Ulverston. This late Elizabethan house is very typical of both its age and its area. Originally built of stone, the exterior has been roughcast for protection from the weather. This portion was originally the family wing and contains the rooms most closely associated with Fox and the Fell family. The house, as it stands today, is only part of the original structure, which may have been of an H-plan with a central hall and two wings set at right angles. If this was the case, it makes some of the present nomenclature of the rooms speculative.

PHOTOGRAPH, AUTHOR

explained by Fox in his writings, he obtained an extensive knowledge of the more controversial ideas that were circulating in England and in Europe. He also accumulated an extensive and intimate knowledge of the Bible. It was said that if all the Bibles in the world were to be destroyed in some cataclysm it could have been re-written, word for word, from Fox's memory.

As he made these journeys through the Midlands he encountered other men and women who were also in quest of a satisfactory religious code. In some cases they were persuaded by Fox to his way of thinking and he began to acquire a number of disciples, notably James Naylor and Richard Farnsworth. However, his increasingly radical views led him into conflict with the civil authorities. At Derby, in 1650, the name Quaker was first coined. Fox was brought before the magistrates on a charge of blasphemy, and stung by the taunts of Mr Justice Bennet, bid him 'tremble at the name of the Lord'.

It was after one of his wanderings through south Yorkshire and the West Riding that Fox was moved to climb to the summit of Pendle. Either divine providence or information that he had acquired in Yorkshire had brought him, as he foresaw, to an area ripe for the message he had to give. There existed in the northern areas of Lancashire and in adjacent parts of Cumberland,

Westmorland and Yorkshire, a loosely organised but co-ordinated religious group known as the Seekers. They, like Fox, rejected the established church, and emphasised the ministry of all believers. In addition, they rejected the Calvinist doctrine of predestination, and taught that salvation was open to all men who accepted God's mercy. It is obvious that Fox was acquainted both with the existence of the group and possibly with leading members of the Seekers, two of whom are named in his vision of the river Rawthey. Also, he was aware of a great Seeker meeting to be held on Firbank Fell, at Sedbergh, on Sunday 13 June 1652. On his journey to this meeting Fox met and talked with Mr Gervase Benson, an important local justice of the peace, who was to play an active part in the early days of the Quaker movement. Fox addressed the Firbank meeting and his words were well received. Over the next few days he continued to wander the area before making his way to Swarthmoor Hall, near Ulverston, the home of Judge Thomas Fell and his wife Margaret.

The Fell family had emerged from obscurity by the route used by so many Tudor gentry families; that is, by making money from a career in the law and by acquiring land during the period of the sale of former monastic property. In the first two decades of the seventeenth century George Fell had used part of his new fortune to build a house worthy of the family's position in the world. The site chosen was on the 'Blackmoor' (Swarthmoor) a mile south of Ulverston and set between the sea-shore and the fells. The new house was of stone but, like many in the area, it was subsequently rendered to weather-proof the walls. The windows are typical of their time, being stone-mullioned with square dripstones set over them. The roof and the floors of the ground floor were made of local slate. The house as it stands today is only a portion of a much larger structure, parts of which were demolished during the period of decay suffered in the eighteenth and nineteenth centuries. The building was redeemed and restored in the early years of this century by Miss Emma Clarke Abraham, a direct descendent of Thomas and Margaret Fell, who purchased the virtual ruin of the house and devoted her fortune and energies to its restoration. On her death the house was willed to the Society of Friends, who maintain the building as a conference and study centre for the organisation.

Six rooms within the hall may be visited. The first, leading off the entrance passage, is known as the Great Hall. This spacious, stone-flagged room is lit at its southern end by a well-proportioned bay window of four lights, and by three mullioned windows in the west wall. The floor is flagged with its original slates and the beams of the ceiling have been enclosed in rather rough, plain plasterwork. The walls are panelled in oak and on the frieze are mounted lively dragons carved in the same wood. This panelling is not original and dates from the restoration by Emma Clarke Abraham, who carved the dragon figures herself. The room is furnished with an interesting collection of seventeenth-century furnishings which, though correct in period, have no connection with the house. The most interesting relic is the document chest of Thomas Fell, not the owner of the house, but a namesake who served as steward to the estate. It was in this box that the original *Journal* of George Fox, as taken down by his stepson-in-law Thomas Lower, was discovered.

A door in the panelling of the hall leads to the Judge's Chamber. Here are kept a number of relics and books, of which the most interesting is the edition of the 'Treacle Bible' which belonged to George Fox and was given by him to the Swarthmoor Meeting House. The pilasters of the fireplace in this room are the amputated bed posts from Judge Fell's bed, placed in their present position by Miss Abraham.

The visitor returns to the entrance passage and ascends the very unusual four newel staircase. The central support for the stairs, instead of being the customary single post, is made up of a box girder structure composed of four vertical posts linked at intervals by tie beams. The ties are joined by small, turned spindles. The remarkable strength of this structure is demonstrated by the fact that it is free-standing, the top not being attached to the roof timbers.

The first flight of stairs carries the visitor to the main bedrooms. The principal chamber, known as Judge Fell's room, retains its original panelling, and contains a bed so massive that it must have been built in the room as it is too large and heavy to have been brought in. The original crewelwork hangings and bed cover are still in place. The room was heated by a stone-built fireplace surrounded by a carved overmantel which is so similar in detail and concept to the screens in the Priory Church of Cartmel that one feels the same craftsman must have been responsible for both works.

Adjoining Fell's room is another chamber, also panelled, which is described as having been his wife's room. It contains a contemporary bed and various other items of furniture, including a seventeenth-century cradle. The short passage way linking these two rooms gives access to the wooden balcony from which Fox is recorded as having addressed the assembled crowds. On the same landing is the smaller room which is reputed to have been used by Fox during his visits to the house. It is now furnished with his travelling bed – a robust structure that would have required a pack horse to carry it – his travelling chest, covered in hide and decorated with elaborate patterns of brass nails, and his sea chest. The latter is pierced on every side with a row of holes, through which rope was threaded to form a net in which bottles could be stowed and safely transported. The last flight of the stairs carries the visitor, provided the trip-step has been safely negotiated, to the garrets which contain further furniture and Quaker relics. These rooms would originally have been used as accommodation for the household staff.

In 1652 the house was the home of one of the most eminent men in Furness. Thomas Fell was the son of George, for whom the house had been built. Thomas had been trained as a barrister at Gray's Inn and on his return to his home county had been made a Justice of the Quorum – those among the local magistrates who had a superior knowledge of the law were so designated – and was appointed to various high legal offices in the Duchy of Lancaster administration. He served as Chancellor of the Duchy Court at Westminster and as Vice Chancellor of the Palatine Court at Preston. During the Civil War he was a supporter of parliament and was selected to sit as one of the members of parliament for Lancaster when the royalist sympathies of the sitting members caused them to be ejected from the seats that they held. The execution of the king and the growing arbitrary power of Cromwell caused Fell to retire from politics. However, the Lord Protector valued Fell's advice and ability to the extent that he was appointed as a judge on the Chester and North Wales circuit. In the events that followed the arrival of Fox at Swarthmoor, Fell is something of a shadowy figure but, in his less demonstrative way, he was important to the early nurturing of the Society of Friends. In her *Brief Relation* of her life Margaret Fell paid him a just tribute:

> He was much esteem'd in his Country [county] and value'd and honour'd in his day by all sorts of People, for his Justice, Wisdom, Moderation and Mercy: being a Terror to Evil-doers, and an Encourager of such as did well, and his many and great Services made his Death much lamented. We liv'd together Twenty six Years, in which time we had nine Children. He was a

tender loving Husband to me, and a tender Father to his Children and one that sought after God in the best way that was made known to him.

This evidently happy marriage had taken place in 1632. Margaret Askew was the daughter of a neighbouring gentry family who lived at Marsh Grange on the slopes above the Duddon valley. It has been claimed that her family was related to Anne Askew, the Protestant martyr of 1546 but the evidence for this connection is inadequate and a firm conclusion cannot be drawn. At the time of her marriage Margaret was 'between seventeen & eighteen years of Age', while Thomas, who had recently concluded his legal studies was in his early thirties. Both the bride and the groom had a shared interest in their pursuit of religious truth. Both were dissatisfied with the existing churches and both went out of their way to encourage visits to their home by itinerant preachers. Margaret tells us how 'I … was Inquiring after the way of the Lord, and went often to hear the best Ministers that came into our Parts, whom we frequently entertain'd at our House; many of those that were accounted the most Serious and Godly Men, some of which were then called "Lecturing Ministers", and had often Prayers and Religious Exercises in our Family'. Their reputation for hospitality to preachers had reached the ears of Fox and led him to the door of the house.

On his arrival he found that neither the master (who was on circuit in Wales) nor the mistress of the house (who had travelled to Lancaster) was at home. He was received by the son and six daughters of the family, whose ages ranged from nineteen to two years, and by the curate of Ulverston, William Lampitt or 'Priest Lampitt' as Fox always contemptuously referred to him. Lampitt probably knew of Fox's reputation and the two men took an instant dislike to each other. Shortly before the return of Margaret Fell, Lampitt left the house in a rage following a bitter argument with Fox. Fox's account of the return of the mistress of the house is full of his usual self-confidence and self-righteousness but it still gives some hint of the mutual suspicion and antagonism that lay between them at their first meeting. He writes: 'And so Margaret Fell had been abroad and at night when she came home her children told her that Priest Lampitt and I disagreed'. This was a somewhat euphemistic term, as during their dispute Fox had told Lampitt among other things, that, 'He was full of filth … and that the way was not prepared in him for the Lord'.

Fox continues 'It struck some thing at her because she was in profession with him, though he hid his dirty actions from them. So at night we had a great reasoning and I declared the truth to her and her family'. A few days later the battle between Fox and Lampitt was renewed. A 'Lecture Day' was to be held in Ulverston Church. These were occasions when visiting preachers and the resident clergyman would preach sermons and instruct the congregation on some theme or biblical text. At these meetings participation by the auditory was expected and encouraged. Margaret invited Fox to go with her to the 'steeple house' and hear the speakers. Perhaps at this stage she hoped that Fox, in whom she was showing increasing confidence and acceptance, could be reconciled with her former spiritual guide. At first, Fox refused to go, but then 'the word of the Lord came to me go to the steeplehouse after them and when I came in the priest Lampitt was singing with his people. His spirit and his stuff was so foul that I was moved of the Lord to speak to him, and the people'. He spoke to such effect that the hostility of the congregation was aroused and it was only the intervention of Margaret Fell and – to his credit – William Lampitt that prevented them attacking Fox.

Shortly after this, George Fox went on another preaching tour through Furness, visiting Rampside Chapel, where the minister, Thomas Lawson, was won over, though Fox's reception at other places was much less welcoming. Fox returned to Swarthmoor just before the arrival of Judge Fell from London. By this time most of the family and the household at Swarthmoor had been converted to the views of Fox. This conversion was viewed with alarm by the local clergy and the civil authorities, who saw the most prominent family of the district enmeshed in a sect which was apparently subversive of normal everyday values. So strange did it seem that it was suspected witchcraft had been used by the man they regarded as a disreputable hedge preacher. They must have viewed the apparent seduction of the Swarthmoor family with dismay in much the same way that today membership of the more extreme sects is regarded by the more conventionally minded.

News of Judge Fell's return led the local worthies to take action, and a group set out to carry advance warning of events at Swarthmoor to the Judge. The party included Lampitt and Justice Sawrey. Margaret Fell later told of the homecoming.

> Some envious People of our Neighbours, went and met him upon the sands as he was coming home [at this time the route across the sands of the Kent and Leven estuaries was regularly used in order to save the very long land route via Lancaster, Levens Hall and Newby Bridge] and Inform'd him, that we had entertain'd such Men as had taken us off from going to Church, which he was very much concern'd at; so when he came Home, he seemed much troubled.

This, one feels, is probably an understatement of Fell's mood as tired, saddle sore and hungry, and concerned by the always perilous crossing of the sands, he was bombarded by the babble of his excited and indignant neighbours. However, Fell's legal training and experience stood him in good stead and he endeavoured to keep an open mind, not making any judgment until he had heard both sides of the story. On his arrival at Swarthmoor, Margaret used all her feminine experience to deal with the matter. First she helped her husband to remove his boots, then 'his dinner being ready, he went to it, and I went in and sat me down by him'. So far all was peace and harmony and Fell must have begun to believe that the reports were much exaggerated. However, Margaret could not contain herself 'and while I was sitting the power of the Lord seized upon me; and he was struck with amazement, and knew not what to think; but was quiet and still'. After the meal George Fox had arrived and

Market people crossing Lancaster Sands, Morecambe Bay, 1839. The watercolourist David Cox, 1783–1859 found the expanse of Morecambe Bay, with its swirling clouds and misty sea and sands, a very attractive subject and painted several similar pictures. Prominent in all of them is the Guide, mounted on a light-coloured horse and swathed in his many caped coat, who is here marshalling his charges for the crossing of the River Kent. The guide service ever since the Dissolution of the Monasteries had been a responsibility of the Duchy of Lancaster, as it still remains. The scene when Judge Fell returned to Swarthmoor must have looked very similar.

was given permission to speak to the Judge in his parlour. In this address, so eloquent that 'had all England been there, I thought they could not have denied the truth of those things' (Margaret Fell), Fox was supported by his colleagues, James Naylor and Richard Farnsworth. Whether or not what Fox said could have been denied by all England, it was effective in making Judge Fell realise the deep sincerity and religious feeling that Fox exhibited and dissipated any fears of witchcraft that he might have entertained. Thomas Fell himself never joined the Society and continued to worship at Ulverston, but he showed a notable tolerance of his wife's, his family's, his servants' and his guests' activities, giving permission for the Friends to meet in the great hall of his house. Until his death in 1658, Fell also played a part in mitigating the worst hardships imposed by the law on their activities.

It is now necessary to try to outline the beliefs and practices of the Quakers so that the attitude taken by the authorities and by public opinion can be understood. The essential tenet of Fox's teaching was that there existed in all people a spark of divine awareness and a personal relationship with God. In most people this link was suppressed and buried beneath superstitious beliefs and practices taught by the established churches. To open this direct communion with God it was necessary for every individual to make a personal effort to become aware of his divine links. This could best be done by seeking God in quiet contemplation. Eventually God would speak to the individual in what the Quakers called an 'Opening' and from that moment onward the new 'Convinced' Quaker would direct his life according to the divine guidance he received.

Fox constantly emphasised two features of the life of the Quaker. The first was the equality of all men under God. This was a particularly contentious issue in a hierarchical and ceremonious society such as existed in the seventeenth century. The emphasis on the equality of all men caused the Quakers to refuse those gestures of deference, such as removing their hats, while the use of the 'thee' and 'thou' form of pronouns – 'Quaker speech' – when addressing their superiors was seen as disrespectful and subversive of the social order. The other aspect of this belief in equality and rejection of formal and ceremonious worship was the abuse which they poured on the existing churches, contemptuously dismissing them as 'steeplehouses' with 'hireling priests'. If one accepted that divine inspiration was open to all and that believers were equal before God, the necessity for a priesthood was destroyed. Quaker 'Meetings for Worship' were to be a simple gathering of friends who would wait in silence and tranquillity for one of their number to be moved by God to speak.

The second source of irritation to the authorities was the refusal of Fox and his followers to take an oath. Basing their attitude on the biblical injunction not to swear, and on their principles of honesty and truthfulness, it constantly brought them into conflict with the authorities when both the law and society in general, placed much importance on the use of oaths as tests of loyalty and respectability. It was this point of principle which frequently gave the authorities their excuse for the imprisonment and persecution of the Quakers. If a Friend was brought to court on some minor charge his refusal to take the Oath opened him to a charge of contempt, which in turn allowed indefinite incarceration until the contempt was deemed to have been purged.

Had Fox and his friends been content to practise their beliefs in private they might have remained un-persecuted, but this was not their way. Fox worked without pause, and very publicly, to spread the word. The rest of his life was spent in a series of missionary journeys, preaching at every opportunity – often interrupting conventional services in the local church, to the fury of the ministers and congregation. These tours were interspersed with periods of recovery from the ill-treatment that he received either at the hands of infuriated mobs or during his frequent imprisonments. These usually stemmed from charges of blasphemy, exacerbated by his behaviour in court, when his refusal to be sworn or to remove his hat were seen as contemptuous. Two of his most grievous imprisonments were in the county gaol in Lancaster Castle. There he was kept from May 1660 until September of the same year. In January 1664 he was again arrested at Swarthmoor, tried together with Margaret Fell in March, and kept at Lancaster until April 1665. He was then transferred to Scarborough for a further eighteen months' imprisonment. Margaret remained in the prison at Lancaster until June of 1668, using her time to write at least six Quaker tracts.

During all the times of persecution Swarthmoor remained for Fox the one place at which a welcome was assured and where he could rest and recuperate from his privations. During the long periods when Margaret was absent, either imprisoned or on one of her numerous journeys about the business of the Society, the household was under the direction of one or other of her seven daughters. In October of 1669 George and Margaret were married at Bristol, but this was a minor diversion: after the wedding George continued on a preaching tour through the South and Midlands, followed by a journey to America, while Margaret returned to Swarthmoor. It was not until June of 1675 that the family were reunited at the house and George remained there for the next twenty-one months, the longest time he spent there. In September 1678, after time spent in London and Holland, Fox returned to Swarthmoor for the last time. He remained there until March 1680 when he and Margaret moved to London, but the house remained her property, in spite of the efforts of her son to wrest it from her. After the death of Fox in January 1691, Margaret returned to Swarthmoor and apart from one journey to London remained there until her death in April 1702.

The years between the end of the Civil War (1646) and the restoration of King Charles II (1660) were a time in which most of the established views of social organisation were challenged. The breakdown of society and social systems encouraged libertarian speculation and experiment. In politics, groups such as the Levellers, the Diggers and the Fifth Monarchy Men, propounded a new and egalitarian society. In religious affairs furious argument took place between Presbyterians and Independents, Anabaptists and Ranters, Seekers and Brownists, whilst individuals, like Fox, established their own bizarre groups and sects. The turmoil of the decade caused alarm and anxiety among the established groups in society and following the Restoration there was an almost universal desire to return as quickly as possible to stability and well-defined patterns. As a result most of these newly established religious groups disappeared quickly, either of their own volition or due to their suppression by the authorities to whom such groups appeared a likely breeding ground for further rebellion. One of the outstanding features of the Quaker movement was that it was able to survive and establish itself in the course of two generations as a recognised and recognisable force in society and one which had earned respect and admiration.

Where it differed from other similar sects which emerged from the speculative cauldron of the Commonwealth was the ability the Society showed not only to create a dynamic and vital movement but also to organise and control a movement based on individuality and equality.

Perhaps the main difference between George Fox and the other zealots who tramped the country intent on their varying routes to salvation was the contribution of Margaret Fell and Swarthmoor Hall. If Fox was the sower of the seed of the 'Word' it was Margaret who tended the soil and weeded the ground to allow the plant to grow and flourish. Many historians mention the contribution of Margaret Fell, the Quakers themselves calling her the 'nursing mother of Quakerism'. At times it appears that some are too blinded by the glamour of Fox to appreciate that without the work of Margaret Fell the whole movement would have fragmented and collapsed in ruins. Her gifts to the Society were twofold. Firstly, Swarthmoor gave Fox a base, a headquarters in which he could rest and recuperate and be sustained in the intervals between his exhausting missionary journeys. He had an iron constitution, but it is doubtful if even he could have maintained the effort without a secure place in

Swarthmoor Hall from the garden. Seen from this angle the original configuration of a central great hall with an end wing is more apparent. The bay window on the ground floor is that of the Great Hall. The balcony, which is entered from the short passage between the two main bed chambers, is reputed to have been used by Fox to preach to the gathered locals.

PHOTOGRAPH, AUTHOR

which to recover from his periods of imprisonment and the casual mistreatment he received along the roads. Secondly, and more important than the refuge she provided were Margaret Fell's personal abilities and contribution.

In the early years of the growth of the Society Margaret was inhibited in the contribution that she could make by her domestic circumstances. She was a married woman with a growing family; her youngest daughter, Rachel, was born in 1653, twelve months after the first arrival of Fox at Swarthmoor. Her other six daughters ranged in age from Margaret, born in about 1633, to Susannah, who was two at the time of her family's 'convincement'. These girls all became eager members of the Society and worked tirelessly as their mother's helpers and colleagues on Society business and in maintaining the household while she was away either suffering imprisonment or on a missionary journey. In time they all married prominent members of the Society and helped to establish a Fell dynasty within the movement.

The one unsatisfactory member of this family was Margaret's only son, George, the fourth of her children. George seems to have totally rejected the atmosphere of holy piety and to have deliberately set out to flout the conventions and standards of his parents. While a student at the Inns of Court in London he pursued a life of debauchery and as an adult worked hard but unsuccessfully to try to seize his mother's inheritance at Swarthmoor. The education and upbringing of the Fell family provides an interesting insight into mid-seventeenth-century domestic life. It is obvious that the girls, contrary to the usual expectations of the time, were well educated both in scholastic subjects and in the arts of domestic management. No distinction was made between their initial education and that of the only son, other than the fact that he was given the opportunity for higher education and professional training at Gray's Inn.

What is even more remarkable, if the usual picture of relationships between parents and children at this period is to be believed, is the obvious freedom and companionship that existed between the girls and their mother. Though their relations with Judge Fell are less well documented there seems to have been mutual affection and respect between them. In the extensive correspondence which exists between Margaret and her daughters there is little of the reserve and distance which might be expected. When she was away from home Margaret constantly asked for, and responded to, domestic and family details.

In spite of these domestic calls on her time Margaret was able to devote a great deal of effort to the early organisation of the Society. Perhaps her most important role was as a co-ordinator and collator of information. There is clear evidence that she received a constant flow of letters from individuals and from groups of Friends throughout the length and breadth of Britain, and soon – as the message spread – from Europe, the West Indies, Asia and America. Little of her outward correspondence survives, but what remains shows that she continually sent out reports and news of the work of the Friends. This was an essential and invaluable function in a movement so diverse and which so encouraged individuality and equality. Nothing could have been easier than for schism and fragmentation of the movement to have taken place, but the supervision and intelligence collected and co-ordinated by Margaret at Swarthmoor played an important part in preventing this, as she admonished the unorthodox and checked the fanatic. No better example can be found than the *cause célèbre* of James Naylor.

Naylor – a Yorkshire man and ex-cavalry officer from the New Model Army – was one of Fox's first followers and seems to have been gripped by a religious fervour akin to mania; to such an extent that it might be thought he had come to believe in his own divinity. In 1656, unhinged by his enthusiasm and corrupted from his true Quaker principles by the ideas of the Ranters – who preached unlimited personal freedom – Naylor, accompanied by his three female disciples, entered the City of Bristol in such a way that it was seen as a parody of Christ's entry into Jerusalem. Naylor was subjected to horrific punishments for blasphemy. George Fox and Margaret Fell were distressed at this treatment of a man they regarded as a friend. Worse still, the whole matter had a damaging effect on the way in which the Quakers were perceived by the world. It was largely due to Margaret that the impression of the Society as representing a lunatic fringe was overcome, and it was by her efforts that Naylor himself was brought to acknowledge his errors and to be reconciled to the movement.

Not all the cases dealt with by Margaret were so bizarre, but she was seen by the Society as a whole as the arbitrator and definer of good Quaker practice. For example, it was she who established the procedures and system for weddings within the Society. In this matter she was aided by the fact that during the Commonwealth and Protectorate marriage became a civil ceremony, thus eliminating the doctrinal arguments that would otherwise have arisen. The system she devised and recommended involved the participation of the Meetings to vet and approve the marriage, so that matrimony was seen as a grave and serious matter and one in which Quaker principles had a important part to play. The Society was strengthened by the insistence that only marriage between members was possible, whilst anyone marrying outside the Society was cast off. Harsh though this penalty might appear, and restrictive and paternalistic as the interference of the Meeting might be, the seriousness with which marriage was viewed helped to create for the Quakers the image of sobriety and restraint that was to become a valuable asset. It was, for instance, in sharp contrast to the teachings of free love and communal relationships advocated by the Ranters and some other extreme sects.

Another function of Margaret Fell during her Swarthmoor years was to co-ordinate and to some extent control the missionary journeys of the Friends. Many of the early Quakers became convinced that God had directed them to become 'Proclaimers of the Word' in the world and, filled with zeal, they became fearless and intrepid missionaries. Fox, who shared this desire and who himself spent the greater part of his life – when he was at liberty – on preaching journeys could only commend their efforts. The cooler and more mentally-disciplined Margaret could see the importance of ensuring that the fervour was directed to give maximum effect, and of covering the ground as fully as possible by ensuring that the missionaries were not in competition with each other. When it seemed desirable, she would ensure mutual support and companionship by directing additional members to a hard pressed area. The activities undertaken by some of the early proselytizers for the Society of Friends are staggering in their boldness, especially when one remembers that in many cases they came from relatively humble backgrounds and had no previous experience of the world outside their immediate area. Perhaps this is the key to their intrepidity, a mixture of innocence and religious fervour.

Foremost among these proclaimers of the message were the group whose origins were in the household at Swarthmoor. From amongst these earliest converts thirteen undertook missionary work. This figure does not include Margaret Fell and her daughters who subsequently travelled on behalf of the Society. As well as extensive work in all parts of the British Isles, journeys to Holland, Germany, Barbados, New England, Italy and Turkey were undertaken. Perhaps the most adventurous of all these 'Proclaimers' was Henry Fell. He seems not to have been a relative of Thomas Fell, but served in the household as the Judge's clerk. He became 'convinced' in 1655 and began his missionary career with a journey to Barbados. From there he sailed to Boston and made an abortive attempt to plant the seed in New England. On the return voyage to England his ship was captured by Spaniards and taken to Spain. Fell and his comrades escaped, travelled back across France and sailed to King's Lynn in Norfolk and thence to London. After a visit to Swarthmoor he returned to Barbados. Next, he was moved to return to London where he was subjected to a rough handling by the troops of General Monck, who were engaged in the business of restoring Charles II to the throne. For some time he was active in South East England until imprisoned at Thetford in Norfolk on a charge of vagrancy. On his release, he and two colleagues were filled with an even more ambitious plan.

Fox describes the expedition in his *Journal*: 'John Stubbs and Richard Scotsthorp and Henry Fell was moved to go towards China and Prester John's country [a fabled Christian kingdom located in Ethiopia]'. In spite of a warrant from the king and the East India Company they could not find a shipmaster willing to carry them. 'And then they went to Holland and would have got passages there: but no passage there they could get; and then they took shipping to go to Alexandria in Egypt: and so by caravan from thence ... but the English Consul banished them from thence'. Despairing of ever reaching the Far East or Prester John the trio returned through Turkey and Germany. Subsequently Fell made yet another visit to the West Indies and it is thought that he died either there, or in America. It is no wonder that one Myles Halhead's wife complained that she had rather her husband was a drunkard than a Quaker because then, at least, she would know that she could find him in the local alehouse! Another remarkable feature of the Quaker missionaries was that women, as well as men, were active in the field. Two of the Swarthmoor travellers were women, Ann Clayton and Alice Curwen. In later years when Margaret Fell was released from her domestic tasks, she became an itinerant proclaimer of the word and was joined in this work by her daughters Margaret, Bridget, Isabel and Sarah. The activity of the female Quakers is a useful reminder of the recognition and equality that the Society gave to its female members, in sharp contrast to the attitudes of their contemporaries of other persuasions.

As well as trying to keep track of the various missionary journeys and circulating news of their progress, Margaret Fell became involved in the business of attempting to meet the practical needs of Friends who were travelling or who were in distress at home as a result of sickness, poverty, age or privations consequent on persecution and imprisonment. In June of 1654 she established a fund, which came to be called the Publick Stock, to which individual Friends and the local meetings were encouraged and exhorted to contribute. This fund was the origin of the Yearly Meeting Fund which became, and remains, the principal financial basis of Quakerism. The early account books show the disbursements made by Thomas Willan and George Taylor the two trustees appointed by Margaret. The entries are many and varied, ranging from subsidies towards the cost of passage for Friends wishing to travel abroad, to bills for shoe repairs for the itinerants, the cost of clothes – shoes and breeches for Thomas Holme at 10s. 6d. or a hat for Elizabeth Fletcher at 2s. 4d. – the cost of postage (this was a major item in view of the remote location of Swarthmoor) and grants to the impoverished families left behind. In later years much of this 'social' work became the responsibility of the 'Women's Meetings'.

With regard to women, and their place in the Society of Friends, the Quakers found themselves in an ambivalent position. The idea of equality of women in the Church had been adopted by several of the more extreme Puritan sects during the period of the Commonwealth and in those liberal times this did not prove too great an obstacle. However, the Restoration brought not only the return of the king but the re-establishment of the Anglican church and its powers of control over the marriage ceremony. Once again the Quakers showed their ability to adapt to circumstances, and both George Fox and John Banks of Kendal wrote powerfully in favour of equality for women within the Society. In this they were both influenced by the active and vigorous part that female members had taken in the missionary activity and their willingness to share in the hardships of Quaker membership. A specially contentious issue in Restoration England, and for many years afterwards, was the payment of tithes by various non-conformist denominations. The Quakers, who vigorously condemned 'hireling priests', were adamant in their refusal to pay – a gesture which often resulted in imprisonment. At least one Lancashire woman, Elizabeth Wyldman of Tatham Fell, died as a result of the privations of her captivity at the behest of Thomas Sharpe, vicar of Tatham. While the theoretical equality of women was recognised, the Quaker men were of their age, and could not entirely shake off the spirit of their times. Though there was some variation in attitude throughout the movement, in general women were seen as having specific roles; as in other Puritan groups the responsibility of a mother as the essential teacher of godliness to her children was emphasised. The suitability of women to undertake social and charitable work was stressed. Banks reflected the widespread view of women as functioning best as the assistants of men and, in general, being subject to the instruction of men. Banks did realise that the apparent incompetence of women might not result from basic intellectual inferiority, as was usually assumed. He saw it as the effect of a society which expected women to 'put the service of things from themselves, although at time and time something have been required of them; and so have quenched the notion of the good in themselves by looking out at the men, and in so doing nothing, have not been the meet helps unto men as they ought to have been and as it was in the beginning'. It can be seen that his intellectual superiority was not displayed in his prose style.

In 1667 George Fox, whose view of the competence and ability of women must have been strongly influenced by his intimate contact with Margaret Fell, ordered the setting up of Women's Monthly Meetings throughout the country. An early Friend, William Couch, describes one of these first Women's Meetings in such a way that shows the main thrust of the work they undertook: 'And now some ancient women Friends did meet together, to consider of what appertained to them, as their most immediate care and concern, to inspect the circumstances & conditions of such who were imprisoned on Truth's account & to provide things needful to supply their wants'. The first Swarthmoor Women's Meeting was held in October 1671, when the only business transacted was the distribution of money to poor Friends. Subsequently in some cases the donations were made in cash but in others the gift was in kind and might range from the loan of a cooking pot to a cow. Clothing was also given and there is an edifying account of their attempts to recover a petticoat given to an old woman who died shortly after receiving it.

It must be stressed that though the business of women's meetings was limited, and that in their definition of female participation in the affairs of the Society, the Quakers displayed some of the mental conditioning of the age in which they lived, their perception of the role of women was far more progressive and liberal than any other group in England. This very advanced outlook must owe a great deal to the lady of Swarthmoor Hall, who has some claim to be included in feminist as well as Quaker hagiography.

During the years when she was confined to Swarthmoor Margaret's efforts were not all limited to practicalities. She wrote and had published no fewer than four books intended to bring about the conversion of the Jews. Two factors played a part in arousing her interest in, and sympathy, for this cause. In 1656, for the first time since the reign of Edward I, Jews were allowed to settle in England. This new tolerance reflected both the personally tolerant attitude of Cromwell and also the widely held contemporary belief of a connection between the English race and the Israelites. This conviction that the English were in some way descended from the lost tribes of Israel and hence stood in a particular relationship with God, was a common delusion of the times – encouraged by selective and highly subjective reading of scriptural texts. A second factor in the new attitude towards the Jews was the remarkable personality of Manasseth ben Israel. A scholar and a linguist, he had been driven by persecution to Holland from Portugal where he had been brought up among a group who, though they professed Judaism in private, worshipped as Christians in public. This duality gave him a broad perspective and breadth of vision, unique in seventeenth-century Europe. It was Manasseth who had persuaded Cromwell to re-admit the Jews and the Rabbi showed himself to be tolerantly intrigued by the Quakers. It was to Manasseth that Margaret Fell's first book was dedicated – 'For Manasseth ben Israel, the Call of the Jews out of Babylon, which is good tidings to the meek, liberty to the captives, and of the opening of the prison doors' – (proof that even in the mid-seventeenth century a snappy title was essential to commercial success). This work from her pen was followed by four other tracts on the subject. Though some of the Jews found Margaret's writings interesting, the sudden death of Manasseth and his son destroyed one of the most promising contacts. There is a possibility that some of the translation of Margaret's books into Hebrew, carried out in the Netherlands, was done by the philosopher Spinoza, who was a Christianised Jew.

In October 1658 Judge Thomas Fell died. The inheritance of his estates, together with the increasing maturity of her children, gave Margaret the opportunity to enter upon a new phase of her work for the cause of Quakerism. This new freedom coincided with the changed political circumstances of the Restoration. The return to traditional values and organisations that accompanied this reversal of fortunes for the country placed the Quakers in an even more dangerous position than before. All the more extreme sects were objects of suspicion to a government which was continually seeking signs of the revival of rebellion. In the minds of the government the Quakers, with their almost ostentatious parade of their distinctions, were particularly suspect as they were erroneously associated with the Fifth Monarchy Men. The abortive and fatuous attempts of these millenarian fanatics to overthrow the new regime had tended to reinforce the hostile attitude towards religious dissent. Of special importance to the Quakers of the North West was the so-called Kaber Rigg or Farnley Wood Plot of January 1661. This conspiracy by old parliamentarians covered the whole of the north of England: its intention was to force the king to implement his promise in the Declaration of Breda to grant full freedom of worship. The plot, led by a Captain Atkinson, was badly organised and, it is suggested, was from the first penetrated by the government's intelligence agents. As a result it quickly degenerated into farce, but the severity with which those implicated were penalised was far from humourous. Although only one person connected with the Society of Friends was linked with the conspiracy, and despite Fox's pamphlet condemning plots against authority, and Margaret Fell's similar declaration to the Justices at Lancaster, the authorities were convinced of Quaker involvement and a period of particularly severe persecution followed.

The Great Hall of Swarthmoor Hall. Traditionally the location of the first vital meeting between Fox and Judge Fell, the room was much restored in the early twentieth century by Miss Clarke Abraham who was responsible for much of the wood work, including the carved dragons which top the panelling.

During this period, the regard in which Judge Fell had been held in legal circles and the social status of Margaret, were of importance to the movement. Fox and a number of other Friends were arrested soon after the king's return and were accused of plotting against the monarchy. Margaret immediately set out for London and was quickly admitted to an audience with the king, who was accompanied by the Duke of York and Henry, the Duke of Gloucester. While the easy accessibility of King Charles was frequently remarked upon – it was by no means unusual for a subject to approach him as he took exercise in St James' Park – it must be thought that Margaret Fell's position as the widow of a distinguished jurist and as a gentlewoman of considerable estate ensured a more patient hearing. Not only did she harangue Charles on the innocence and loyalty of the Quakers but she also bombarded him with written submissions. Charles II preferred a woman of soft submissiveness, but even he seems to have been impressed and moved by Margaret's passion and fervour. According to an account written to Fox, 'she had full and large time to lay all things before him of the Friend's sufferings. He was very moderate and promised fair things'. Charles II was to become notorious for his fair promises. She also bombarded other members of the royal family with her missives: her targets included the Queen of Bohemia, the king's aunt: his sister the Princess of Orange; and, even less likely to be favourable to her cause, the Dowager Queen Henrietta Maria. However, at last her barrage achieved results, and probably to bring an end to a tiresome nuisance, the king and the

Council gave an order by which four thousand Quakers were released.

At the time of the Kaber Rigg plot Margaret was unable to leave Swarthmoor as two of her daughters, Margaret and Bridget, were to be married in 1662. However, in May, two months after Bridget's wedding, the mistress of Swarthmoor set out on her second journey to Court on behalf of the Society of Friends. She writes in her *Brief Relation*, 'I was ... then moved by the Lord to go to London again, not knowing what might be the matter or business I should go for ... I met with an Act of Parliament, made against the Quakers for refusing Oaths. And when I came to London I heard that the King was gone to meet the Queen and to be married to her at Hampton Court.' (The queen was Catherine of Braganza, the Portuguese princess. The marriage took place on 21 May 1662.) She also found that in London the Quaker meetings were being violently dispersed by armed soldiers and two Friends had died as a result of the injuries they

had received. Undeterred by the impending marriage Margaret 'went to the King and the Duke of York [the future James II] at Hampton Court and I wrote several letters to them and therein gave them to understand what desperate and dangerous work there was in London'. At last the king succumbed once more, and gave orders that the prisoners should be released and that the interruption of the meetings was to cease.

There is one last area of Quakerism to which it seems likely that Margaret made a substantial, if usually unacknowledged, contribution. The intense pressure brought to bear on the Society during the 1660s made some form of organisation and control essential if the movement was to survive. A structure was needed that would bring together not only Friends in one district at their usual Meeting for Worship but would also bring them into contact on a regular basis at a regional, national and even international level. There already existed in the North a Meeting for Discipline, which had oversight of the members, and supervised the relief of sufferers and the regulation of marriage. In the period 1666–7 Fox initiated a system of weekly, monthly, quarterly and yearly meetings at which representatives could come together to supervise and direct the work of the Society. The Weekly Meeting for Worship was the equivalent of the parochial structure; the Monthly Meeting, attended by representative members of each Weekly Meeting within a local area, might be seen as the equivalent of a deanery. The Quarterly Meeting was made up of members from a larger region and is roughly paralleled by the diocesan structure of the established church. At the Yearly Meeting held in London Quakers from every Quarterly Meeting throughout the world would come as delegates, and so it might be seen as equivalent to Convocation or a General Synod. The great danger that threatened the Quakers was that the Society would be rent by

Miniature of Charles II as a young man. The original portrait on which this is based was painted by Des Granges about 1651 and shows the King, aged 21, at the time of the ill-fated Worcester campaign. This painting was copied and given as distinguished rewards to faithful supporters of the exiled King. Later portraits show how the hardships of the years of the Interregnum and the bitter experiences of duplicity and failure, together with a debauched lifestyle gave him a more cynical look – the look it would have borne during his interviews with Margaret Fell.
NATIONAL PORTRAIT GALLERY, LONDON

George Fox. This nineteenth-century engraving from an earlier portrait probably provides a rather romanticised picture of Fox. It emphasises the simplicity of his dress: a plain coat in a drab colour and a simple band. Especially distinctive is the low crowned hat, which he insisted on wearing at even the most inopportune times, a serious breach of the etiquette of the period.

internal divisions: this was especially likely in a denomination which stressed individuality and divine guidance and rejected most forms of control or supervision. We have already seen the part played in the early years of the Society by Margaret Fell acting as a central co-ordinating influence. As the Society grew in numbers, and developed from a group confined to a relatively compact area in the North West, some more structured organisation was essential. George Fox is very reticent about his thinking in the period prior to the establishment of the Meeting system. It followed almost immediately on his release from imprisonment at Scarborough. In his *Journal* he writes 'And the Lord opened to me and let me see what I must do, and how to order and establish the Men's and Women's Monthly and Quarterly Meetings in all the nation and write to other nations, where I came not to do the same'. Fox was a man of outstanding physical and moral force, and a charismatic leader, but not one who was concerned with administration and organisation. Though the inspiration to set up the meetings might be divine, this does not preclude the possibility that some human agent acted as intermediary. We know that

Margaret Fell was a woman who had gained a great deal of experience in the administration of her estates and had proved a skillful manager. In addition she had wide experience, gleaned from her correspondence, of the potential problems that could beset the Society.

Consequently, it would seem highly likely that the plan for the establishment of the administrative meetings was suggested by her to Fox. Though this must remain speculation, we know that an even closer relationship was developing between them at this time: their marriage took place in 1668 the year after the establishment of the Meetings.

It could be suggested that Margaret Fell had another vital role in the early development of Quakerism, a role that was psychological rather than practical. Many religions have had to wrestle with the problem of trying to accommodate the place of the male and female elements in their structure. In many of the ancient religions the pre-eminent position was given to the female as the source of fertility. In others the problem was resolved by polytheism giving a pantheon of both gods and goddesses for worship. However, in the great monotheist religions of Judaism, Christianity and Islam, the theology is based on a male, authoritarian God. As a result, in Christianity there had been, at various times, attempts to provide a feminine figure of adoration to represent the essential duality of human society and to allow some recognition of the female contribution of caring, nurture and maternal sympathy. In the Catholic Church of the Middle Ages the immense popularity of the Virgin and of the female saints had proved the depth of this need. The Reformation had seen a return to the stern, masculine Jehovah of the Old Testament in the theology of the established churches, though it may be that at a popular level reverence for the Virgin and the old saints persisted. It could possibly be that one of the reasons for the failure of the other Puritan sects of the mid-seventeenth century to grip the hearts and minds of the general populace was this failure to provide a focus for the female characteristics.

There can be no doubt that for many of the Friends Margaret Fell assumed a firm hold on their affections and gave to the movement the warmth of the feminine role model. The letters she received are full of lavish comments on her beauty and her significance to the writer. Indeed, if read out of context they often assume the character of love letters: Henry Fell writes from London in 1660 'Dear Hearts, truely my love flows forth unto you, and I should be glad to see you (if the Lord so order it) that I might have more time with you than I had last', while John Rous wrote from Barbados, three years earlier, 'often in the night do I behold thee and am refreshed upon every remembrance of thee. Thou art dear to me as my own life. I would greatly desire to see your face in the flesh but I see no way as yet'. Seventeenth-century literary style allowed for a much freer expression of feelings and sentiments than would be usual today and there can be no suggestion that there was any impropriety in Margaret's relationships with these impressionable and emotional young men or that they were aware of the implications that might be perceived in such effusions. Perhaps a truer appreciation of their feeling towards the constant companion and wife of their leader is given by the frequent references to her as 'Dear Mother', or the soubriquet of 'Nursing Mother' that was so often applied to Margaret.

The Religious Society of Friends has proved one of the most enduring legacies of the period of transformation that occurred in the middle decades of the seventeenth century. Its place of origin was in a Lancashire house, and its early roots among the people of Furness and Cartmel. Without Swarthmoor Hall and the patronage of the Fell family none of its subsequent development might have taken place. Pre-eminent was the contribution of a remarkable woman whose faith, constant religious conviction, steadfast loyalty and unshakeable adherence to the cause could withstand persecution and ridicule, condemnation and contempt, imprisonment and mockery. Truly, Margaret Fell deserves to be remembered as an outstanding character in the pageant of Lancashire personalities.

CHAPTER 8

Speke Hall and the Rise of Liverpool

F EW NATIONAL TRUST PROPERTIES are in a situation as immediately
unpromising as Speke Hall, yet concealed amidst housing estates,
industrial premises and re-developed airport buildings is one of the best
examples of Lancashire's vernacular architecture. In the house the North-
Western tradition of florid, highly decorated timberwork reaches its peak. Once
the visitor is through the gates today's world recedes into the distance, the
airport runway is hidden by trees, and within its now dry moat the house stands
like a jewel set on the green velvet of its lawns and framed by flowering shrubs.
It is a very remarkable transformation. Yet it is perhaps appropriate that
the house should be surrounded by the sprawl of the great city in the development of which its original owners and builders played a prominent part at a
crucial time.

The Norris family had held lands in Lancashire ever since the Norman
Conquest or perhaps even earlier – a suggested derivation for their name is
'Norseman' or 'Norman' – but until 1272 their main properties were located at
Blackrod near Bolton, and at Formby some fifteen miles northward of Speke.
About that time, two brothers of the family married the two daughters of the
Lord of the Manor of Speke and each received half that estate as the dowry of
their brides. In the next generation Patrick, the only son of the elder brother,
died without heirs and his moiety of the manor was passed to the younger of
the two brothers, his uncle John de Norris, from whom the family descended
until its extinction in the eighteenth century.

Little is known about the early generations of the family at Speke and they
are unimportant for our purposes, though it was at this time that the military
tradition of the family was established. Of the house in which they lived only
the faintest traces remain. In the present kitchen is a stone-mullioned window
of a design which is not found elsewhere in the house and which predates the
walls that surround it. It is possible that this window is a survival from
the previous house. There is a suggestion that some of the material used in the
stone plinth of the present house was quarried from an earlier building. It has
also been postulated that the now dry moat which surrounds the hall was a
defensive feature of the earlier house, and that the original building might have
been a pele tower.

The approach to Speke Hall over the moat is dramatic. The bridge was part of the development of the Hall carried out by Edward Norris in 1598 to give access to the new wing he had added to transform the house to a quadrangular plan.

PHOTOGRAPH COPYRIGHT WOODMANSTERNE

A section of John Speed's map of Lancashire, showing the county at the beginning of the seventeenth century. Speke lies just to the south of Toxteth Park.

During this early period (and up to the early sixteenth century), although their name appears in the municipal records, the Norris family seems to have taken little interest in the new town of Liverpool which was growing on the banks of the Mersey some seven miles from their house. Founded by King John in 1207 as a base for military operations in Ireland, the new borough made slow but steady progress during the Middle Ages. Its harbour was guarded by a small castle built on a rocky promontory between the Mersey and the Pool, the shallow muddy estuary of a small stream. Along the three simple streets, forming an H shaped plan, which comprised the town were the burgage plots: long narrow rectangles of land, the ownership of which conveyed civil and political rights. The town's economy was based – as it would be for centuries – on port activity, with ships trading along the west coast of Wales and to southern Scotland as well as to the Isle of Man and, most importantly, to Ireland. Within the town though, there was a wide range of crafts and trades of which the most significant seems to have been leather working. In addition, Liverpool was a local market centre, important for the sale of agricultural produce, much of which came from its own town fields. The burgesses had rights to grow crops and to pasture animals on these long rectangles lying north of the town towards the Kirkdale boundary. The

founding of new towns was a frequent early medieval activity, but they met with varying fortunes. Some flourished and became major centres: for example Wyke, renamed Kingston upon Hull by Edward I, became a major trading and commercial port. Others were less successful. Some, such as New Winchelsea, succumbed to the forces of nature; some, such as Newton le Willows, never became anything more than villages or hamlets; and some did none of these things but survived and grew slowly. Liverpool fell into this last group.

It might seem surprising that the Norris family, important landowners only seven miles from the town, showed so little interest in Liverpool. Perhaps they were far enough away in their rural fastness for it to seem of little more than passing concern to them. Their interests were primarily agricultural and urban affairs would seem irrelevant. They may well have considered the much more important and well established town of Warrington to be their local market centre. We will never know, but the family was not significant in Liverpool affairs for four centuries after the town was founded. Instead, they devoted their efforts to improving the estates.

In about 1490 Sir William Norris decided to rebuild the family home. He had chosen the right side – or at least the winning side – in the Wars of the Roses, no doubt under the influence of Thomas Stanley, first Earl of Derby, who was stepfather to King Henry VII. Stanley was the man whose intervention at Bosworth had ensured the triumph of the Tudors, even though his activities and loyalties before this moment were ambiguous. Two years after Bosworth William Norris was knighted for his part in the Battle of Stoke, which brought to an end the challenge for the throne by Lambert Simnel. Perhaps on his return home the new knight foresaw that more peaceful times lay ahead and that the cramped fortifications of Speke would be needed no more. Perhaps he felt that his new dignity of knighthood needed to be sustained by a more luxurious house. Whatever the reason, he decided to build in the latest style, and in a style that would reflect the new age. However, even if the style of the house was modern, its design was firmly rooted in the past.

It was to be a dwelling centred around the great hall. This was to serve as a communal dining and living room for the whole household. It was entered at its lower end through two opposed doors, which were separated from the body of the hall by wooden screens. At the upper end of the hall, standing on a raised dais, which was probably enhanced by a canopy, was the high table at which the Norris family would eat with their guests. It is likely that, on either side of the high table, doors led to a wing reserved for the family. On the ground floor was a parlour and on the upper floor one, or possibly more, bed chambers. In the roof-space garrets children and servants would sleep. It was common, by this time, for these adjuncts to the hall to be set at right angles to the main axis of the house.

At the other end of the hall, either in another similar wing or in a separate building to reduce the fire risk – always great in a timber framed building – would be the kitchen with its ancillary rooms, the pantry for dry goods, the buttery in which wine and ale was stored, and a scullery. In this wing, or in other nearby buildings there would be the dairy (or deyhouse as it was often called) where the household supplies of butter and cheese were made, and the brew house with its elaborate equipment for the preparation of the large amount of ale and beer consumed by the household, for whom it was the everyday drink. Though parts of the great hall survive at Speke the house is so altered and changed by later building work that a description of the original dwelling can only be speculative.

This house sufficed for Sir William and his son and heir, Henry. Henry Norris had fought at the Battle of Flodden, among the troops commanded by Sir William Mollineux of Sefton. Henry was married to Clemence Harrington and a memorial brass to the couple survives in the parish church at Childwall. Their family was small and the house built by his father provided adequate accommodation for them. Henry died in 1524 and for the next forty-four years the house was in the occupation of his son, the second William Norris. William II was an indefatigable builder who was constantly adding to and modifying the house. One of his incentives to expand its size was the fact that

The Great Wainscot, Speke Hall. This striking piece of wood carving, intended to give consequence to the table used by the owner of the house, his family and his guests, when dining in the hall, appears to be of Flemish origin. The decoration is interesting in that it shows the reproduction of Corinthian columns and busts in the classical mode, an early example of the growing dominance of Renaissance motifs.

PHOTOGRAPH COURTESY OF WOODMANSTERNE

he had married twice and had nineteen living children. In 1557 he was declared too infirm for military service.

The first part of his plan was to render the great hall more comfortable. It is uncertain how it had been heated prior to this time. In earlier days it had been usual to warm these medieval halls by an open fire that burned on a hearth in the middle of the room, under a louvred lantern through which the smoke eventually drifted. By the time the first Sir William built the initial stage of the great hall the innovation of a chimney and a side-wall hearth had been introduced in many houses. It is unclear if this was the case at Speke but it seems unlikely, to judge from the plan carried out by the second Sir William. He enclosed the screens passage with permanent walls, rather than wooden screens, and against one of these walls built the huge fireplace with its enormous and lavishly carved bressumer (the beam spanning the fire-place arch), above the fire is a bizarre decoration of crenellations, and what are said to be portrait heads of the family. The position and organisation of this fireplace would suggest that it had no predecessor and that it was intended to replace an open hearth. The construction of this central chimney stack formed a room within a room in the warm and relatively private space around the fire.

It is possible, too, that at this time the great wainscot was installed behind the high table. Tradition has it that this lavish panelling, carved with portrait busts and heads, was brought home by Sir William after his service at the Battle of Pinkie (1547) in which he distinguished himself by the capture of a Scottish standard and in which his eldest son was slain. After the battle Sir William took part in the sack of Holyrood House and the city of Edinburgh. Certainly

Genealogical overmantel, Speke Hall. One of the outstanding characteristics of the Tudor gentry was overweaning pride in their family and lineage. Sometimes this was expressed in a wealth of heraldic decoration in their houses and rooms or, in this case, in a depiction of three generations of the family. Sir William Norris is shown with his two wives and his 19 children on the central panel. On the left are carved his father and mother, Henry and Clemence. On the right-hand panel is Sir William's son, Edward, who became the heir after his elder brother was killed at Pinkie. The dead man is shown at the base of the overmantel, stripped and lying on the battlefield.

the wainscot is of Flemish design and manufacture and bears a close resemblance to work in Holyrood. That he took part in the pillage of Edinburgh is proved by his own hand. He records in his papers the 'Fourteen folio volumes taken when Edenbrow was won, gotten and brought away by me William Norris of Speke K[night] the eleventh day of May aforesaid'. However he makes no mention of the Wainscot, which could hardly have been overlooked, so some doubts about its provenance and acquisition must remain.

Having improved the comfort of the great hall the next stage of the building project was to provide more luxurious family accommodation by demolishing the old parlour wing and building anew. The result is the sumptuous great parlour, a room that still impresses in spite of the loss of both the original wall panelling and the oak inlaid floor. It impresses by size and by the flood of light which comes through the large and numerous windows and glistens on the replacement panelling of the walls, and on the largely Victorian furniture with which it is now fitted. Above all, the eye is caught by the plastered ceiling with its panels laden with swirling foliage, bunches of grapes, pomegranates and birds. This ceiling was probably added by Sir William's grandson in the early years of the seventeenth century and is of English workmanship, though inspired by Italian patterns. The other feature of the room which it is impossible to overlook is the huge, carved genealogical overmantel. In three oak panels this tells the story of the three generations of the Norris family from Henry Norris to Sir William and his numerous children. The death of his son in battle is indicated by a recumbent figure at the base of one of the columns, and the story concludes with the portrayal of his son and heir Edward, with Edward's wife and the two of his eventual nine children who had been born at the time of the installation of the chimneypiece.

Having completed work on the parlour Sir William returned to the great hall and added the two oriel windows, which with their displays of carving and coloured glass not only provided two pleasant nooks but also gave the opportunity to display armorial bearings that would impress the onlooker with the family's ancient lineage. However, this was a minor work in comparison with the next stage of Sir William's plan, which was to extend the two wings at either end of the hall so that the house would occupy three sides of a quadrangle. His motives for this development were probably a combination of the need to increase the accommodation available for his large family and a response to the increasing demand for comfort and privacy in domestic design. The series of interconnecting rooms on two floors allowed both these functions to be fulfilled. Somewhat to the detriment of the ideal of privacy, no corridors were provided and access to the rooms was by a series of connecting doors. It was part of the contribution of Edward Norris, in the next generation, to add the corridors that now run on the inner side of these blocks, next to the courtyard. When he had completed the construction of these new wings to the house, Sir William's final scheme was to turn the old service area of the hall into further family rooms and an additional parlour, now known as the Blue Drawing Room. It is not clear whether all this work was completed by the time of Sir William's death in 1568, but it mattered little as his heir, Edward, was as interested in building and adding to the house as his father. We have already mentioned his addition of the corridors, but far more significant was his scheme to complete the possible development of the house by enclosing the courtyard with another wing across its north side. This is the façade which one sees today when approaching the house: the bridge across the moat, added by Edward, leads one to the entrance gate over which is proudly inscribed 'This worke 25 yards long was wholly built by Edward N. Esq 1598'.

It is not known what prompted Edward Norris to build this new wing, but there are two possible reasons. First, it would create a more impressive seat for the Norris family if the house was in the form of a quadrangle. This was a rather old-fashioned view which harked back to the Middle Ages, a period that was architecturally obsessed with quadrangular buildings – castles, colleges, houses and monasteries all used the enclosed quadrilateral as their basic plan. One might suggest that this tendency reflects the introspective attitudes which prevailed in the medieval period, and that the tendency for buildings after the Renaissance to be outward-looking is a reflection of the more extrovert nature

SPEKE HOUSE, near LIVERPOOL.

Speke Hall from the south west, lithograph by James. This early nineteenth-century view shows the house as it was when occupied by the Watt family and makes an interesting comparison with the same aspect of the house today. The gabled wing nearest the observer is the Great Parlour and the western wing can be seen projecting to the left beyond it. The two gables adjacent to each other are the former service rooms, later converted to use as an additional parlour. The Great Hall is concealed, though its tall chimney can be seen in the centre of the picture.

PHOTOGRAPH COURTESY OF CHETHAM'S LIBRARY

of the European mentality in the later period. On the other hand – on a less metaphysical plane – the quadrangle had the advantage of being easily defensible, and as this necessity dwindled in importance the plan lost popularity. The other factor in Edward Norris's decision may have been the changing religious climate of the period. The increased severity of the penal laws against recusants made it essential that Catholic households which, like the Norrises, were determined to adhere to the old faith had to take more elaborate precautions. There had probably been a chapel in the house for many years: the stone bowl now in the courtyard is thought to have been its piscina. But now a more secluded location was needed, and the new wing provided the opportunity to build anew. It was probably also at this time that the hiding places, secret escape routes, and spy-holes of the house were built, those of Speke being genuine examples, unlike many which are displayed in other places.

In 1605, 'Being himself aged and sickly and his children many in number', Edward Norris released his land to his son – yet another Sir William – who had received his knighthood two years earlier at the Coronation of King James I. This Sir William made only minor additions to the house, including a door from the great parlour and the gateway from the screens passage to the garden. It was also during his time at Speke that the plaster ceiling was added to the great parlour. Although a recusant and thus in theory excluded from the Court, Sir William seems to have maintained links with London and it was he who, in 1617, took John Middleton, the 'Childe of Hale', to court. Once there, the nine foot three inch giant fought the king's wrestler, whose thumb he broke. For this feat King James, with unaccustomed generosity, rewarded him with a gift of £20.

The latter part of Sir William's life was clouded by financial and family difficulties. As we have seen, this was a period when many gentry families found themselves trying to maintain an appropriate standard of living but with an inadequate and declining income. Like many of his contemporaries Sir William tried to rectify the situation by the sale of property. In his case he decided to sell to the Crewe family a house at Blacon near Chester. At the time the house was occupied by his eldest son and heir, William. The younger William had not been informed of the proposed sale and when told of it absolutely refused to vacate the house. After much acrimonious argument the sale was cancelled, the younger William remaining triumphantly at Blacon. Another son, Captain Henry Norris, was serving with the Spanish army in its campaigns in the Low Countries against the Protestant Dutch rebels. It was quite usual for young gentlemen to seek military experience in the service of foreign powers as part of their education. Continental service provided the only opportunity for those who wished to make a military career, there being no English standing army. Service in a Catholic army, fighting against Protestants was seen by most Englishmen as close to treason. Sir William Norris was, perhaps, unfortunate that his financial support for his son was deemed to be a case of sending arms and money to the king's enemies beyond the seas, and to have been punished by a heavy fine.

In 1631 Sir William himself fell foul of the law. The churchwardens of Childwall, the parish which included Speke, called him to account for his non-attendance at church. This was the preliminary step to indictment before the ecclesiastical courts as a recusant. Sir William, a man of irascible disposition, was furious at their presumption and stormed out of the meeting. He apparently felt that the warden's action had been inspired by the enmity of Sir John Moore, the leading Puritan magistrate of Liverpool. Shortly afterwards the two men encountered each other on a Sunday morning in Childwall churchyard. What followed is best told in the words of the Star Chamber records. 'The defendant [Norris] being as it should seem discontented at the Plaintiff [Moore] about the matter of presentment … told the Plaintiff he had been too precise [officious] in examining his, the said Sir William's not coming to church and that it was ungentlemanly dealing'. Moore hotly denied this accusation and 'Said he did therein wrong him. The Defendant, Sir William, gave the Plaintiff the lie and he returning it in his throat, the said defendant drew his sword and struck the Plaintiff twice, he being a Justice of the Peace'. The case ended with Sir William being fined £1000 and £50 costs.

More lay behind this costly quarrel than mere hostility over the particular incident. It is possible to detect economic, social and religious rivalry between the two men. As we have already seen, the Moores and the Norrises were on opposite sides of the great religious divide of the period and each family would have regarded the other as a potential enemy even if there had not been deeper rivalries. The Moore family were deeply rooted in Liverpool, and their rise to fortune had been closely tied to the emergence of the port as a commercial centre. Their houses were at the Old Hall in the town and at Bank Hall in Kirkdale, and it may well be that Norris saw their intrusion into Childwall as an incursion into his territory and an expansion of urban power into a rural setting. It is probably also true that he regarded the Moores as a parvenu family, jumped-up tradesmen and his social inferiors. The rivalry was accentuated by the fact that the Norrises were beginning to take an interest in the affairs of the town and, this had probably aroused the resentment of the Moore family. However, it was not Sir William who had to pay the fine: he had died before the case came to trial, and it was left to his son, the stubborn tenant of Blacon, to meet the debt.

The new William Norris took little part in the Civil War but his son, Edward, served as a royalist colonel. William gave him moral and financial support, and as a result he was fined in 1645 and the estates were plundered of timber for the repair of war damage in Liverpool. In 1651 he faced the sequestration of his properties. These lands were lost until 1662 when, following the Restoration, the 'Manor and Capital Messuage of Speke, with the Demesne thereof, three cottages, two windmills, two watermills and lands to the yearly value of £224 5s. 8d.' were returned to the family.

By this time the owner of the estates was Thomas, the son of William, and he made the vital step of conforming to the Church of England, which allowed the family to take its place in the local and national life from which it had previously been excluded by its Catholicism. The first Thomas Norris does not seem to have seized the opportunities which were offered. However, in 1689, he was elected as one of the two members of parliament for Liverpool as a result of his opposition to the policies of James II. He was High Sheriff of Lancashire in 1696. By this time there had been another election and Sir Thomas had resigned his seat in favour of his brother, William, later Sir William. As members of parliament William and his colleague, Sir Thomas Johnson, played a vital part in the emergence of Liverpool as a great mercantile and commercial centre. Perhaps the most extraordinary aspect of his career was his selection in 1698 as Ambassador to the Court of the Great Mogul of India. The purpose of the mission was to negotiate a trading treaty on behalf of the 'New' East India Company, which had been set up as a Whig rival to the predominantly Tory 'Old' East India Company. The embassy reached Massulipatam on 16 September 1699 and then had a lengthy struggle to overcome the obstacles put in its way, not only by Indian officials, but also by the representatives of the

'Old' Company. Eventually the ambassador and his retinue struggled to Delhi and had a series of unsatisfactory interviews with the Mogul Arunzagreb. By means that are not altogether clear, when he returned to the *China Merchant* for the voyage back to England Norris was able to load 87,000 rupees' worth of his own property and a meagre 60,000 rupees' worth of Company property into the hold. They sailed for home in April 1702, but Norris died at sea, leaving his brother Edward, who was serving as his secretary and physician, to bring back the news and the treasure.

Speke was inherited, after the deaths of Edward and Richard Norris, by their niece, William's daughter Mary. She was married to Lord Sydney Beauclerk, fifth son of the Duke of St Albans, who was in turn the son of Charles II and Nell Gwynn. Beauclerk, known as 'Worthless Sydney', was a rake and a wastrel who destroyed both his own fortune and his wife's. The Beauclerks never lived in the hall after their marriage in 1736 – so much for the ghost story of Speke that tells of Mary's murder of their child and suicide in the Great Hall – and the house was let to tenant farmers. It was neglected and dilapidated until it was bought by Richard Watt in 1797, from the son of Topham Beauclerk, the friend of Dr Johnson. The Watt family did much to restore its former glory, and ultimately it was Miss Adelaide Watt, the last of her family, who bequeathed the house to the National Trust at her death in 1936.

Speke Hall from the south west. This modern view may be compared with the earlier drawing made from nearly the same point (see page 181). Changes in the height of the chimneys are apparent but the main differences, apart from a general tidiness, are in the shape and disposition of windows and the disappearance of the arched windows in the far gables.
PHOTOGRAPH COPYRIGHT
WOODMANSTERNE

Drawing by Bryan Blundell of the ship *Mulberry*. Bryan Blundell was a ship owner, merchant and philanthropist who was central to the establishment of the Blue Coat School in Liverpool. During his days at sea he kept a journal, illustrated with colour washed drawings of his ships. The *Mulberry* shown here was one of his commands, and was the first ship to enter the Dock when it was opened in August 1715. It can be established that she was built for the transport of timber: the square ports in the ship's quarters were for the purpose of loading lengths of timber.

One of the outstanding interests of the later members of the Norris family was their increasing involvement in the affairs of Liverpool. As we have seen, in the Middle Ages they took little or no interest in the town but by the end of the seventeenth century were active in promoting the well-being and advancement of its interests. In part this may reflect their expansion to fill a power vacuum created by the rapid decline in the influence of the Moore family, who sold all their property in Liverpool in the period 1709–12. At the same time, the influence of the two great local aristocratic families, the Earls of Derby and of Sefton, was also in decline for a variety of reasons, so that there were opportunities for the Norris family to establish themselves as a powerful force in a town which was already in a period of rapid expansion.

It may be, too, that the Norrises' new interest in the town reflects the changing attitude and response of the old landowning families to different economic conditions. Income from land, whether derived from farming or from rents, had always been the criterion by which gentle status had been judged. It gave a cachet that could not be matched by money derived from trade or manufacture. Possession of land brought responsibilities and burdens – all

East view of the OLD EXCHANGE built about 1674-taken down in 1748.

direct taxation was based on landed property until the introduction of income tax by the younger Pitt during the Napoleonic Wars. It brought obligations of service in local and national government and it imposed certain duties with regard to the administration of law and social responsibility within the local community. On the other hand, it was the key to entry to the social polity of the country. The right to vote at every level, from elections for the local vestryman to those for parliamentary representatives, depended on the ownership of land. It allowed one to belong to the ruling class, and to enter the fields of administration and the professions which might in themselves provide additional income. This was a time when an official expected a gift before he would carry out the functions of his office.

While one must be careful not to generalise, by the seventeenth century attitudes were changing in the face of increasing economic pressure. We have seen how, in other cases, landowners were looking for ways to supplement their rent rolls. In some instances exploitation of mineral resources, such as coal deposits, provided a valuable new income. Where this was not feasible an alternative was to engage in mercantile or commercial activity. The effectiveness of this route to greater fortune must have been emphasised for contemporaries by the spectacle of rich merchants, such as Humphrey Chetham, buying out the ancient families of the Ratclyffes, the Orrells and the Byrons. It is significant that in their turn the Norris heirs, the Beauclerks, were to sell Speke to the family of a man who was of no birth but who had made a fortune from the Guinea Trade, as the slave trade was euphemistically called. The rise of Richard Watt, from his post as the driver of the town of Liverpool's first

Liverpool town halls, from Lacey's *Stranger in Liverpool*, 1844. The old Exchange building of 1674 replaced an earlier market building, corporation rooms and a mansion house for the mayor. In 1748 this building was demolished and replaced with an elegant classical building designed by John Woods of Bath. Gutted by fire in 1795, James Wyatt was employed to rebuild and refurbish the interior. He also added the dome and terracotta figure of Minerva. The projecting portico was added in 1811.

PHOTOGRAPH, AUTHOR

hackney coach to one whose heir could buy the estates and hall of Speke, is a clear example of the potential wealth that could be derived from commerce, and also of the emergence of a new squirearchy.

In 1686 William Blundell, the squire of Little Crosby, a few miles north of Speke, was asked to supply information about those aspects of Lancashire that were intriguing or remarkable. The details which he gave were to be included in a projected new edition of Camden's *Britannia*. Among his tales of fishes ploughed up on the mosses and of knick knacks made of coal he wrote 'The buildings and people of Liverpool, our next post town, are certainly more than doubly augmented and the customs eight or tenfold increased within the twenty eight years last passed'. In this passage he does not suggest any reasons for the sudden and rapid expansion of what was now a 450-year-old town which, had until this time been a small and undistinguished haven for the coasting trade and for administrative purposes was regarded as mere creek to the port of Chester. However, in his other writings, he inadvertently gives some clues to this sudden development. Some years twenty years earlier he had invested £40 in supplying a portion of the cargo of the ship *Antelope*, one of the first – if not *the* first – Liverpool ship to make the perilous transatlantic voyage to 'the Barbadoes'. He invested his money in a lading of 'Amongst other things ...

TOWN HALL, LIVERPOOL.

3,332 yards of linen cloth, 61 pairs of men's superbest French falls, 2 hundred-weight of candles, 2 barrels of beef, 120 pounds of butter, 20,000 spikes etc etc'. It should be noted that all these items were, or could have been, made in the south west of Lancashire. His investment was amply repaid at 100 per cent and, thus encouraged, such voyages became a regular trade. The ships returned from the West Indies laden with sugar and tobacco. In 1666 Mr Smith, a well-established London sugar baker, had fled from the ravages of the plague and set up Liverpool's first sugar refinery, located in Dale Street. It has been suggested that Smith was not the only refugee to establish himself in the town at this period, bringing new trades and skills.

Liverpool's developing trade with the Americas reflected a national trend. England's overseas trade expanded rapidly, and with government encouragement, English merchants were now regularly trading to Africa, the Middle and Far East, the Levant and the Mediterranean, to Muscovy and the Baltic and to North and South America. In the main these ships were based in London, and in many cases they belonged to the great charter companies such as the East India Company and the Hudson's Bay Company. The second half of the seventeenth century also saw England embark on that prolonged series of wars, first against the Dutch and then later against the French, inspired at least to a degree by commercial rivalry, which was to continue until 1815. In these wars both sides made extensive use of letters of marque, by which privately-owned warships were empowered to attack the commerce of the enemy nations. The

'View of Liverpool in Lancashire' Engraving by Buck from 'The Modern Universal Traveller', 1727. This engraving shows the town of Liverpool at the mid points of its rapid development between 1660 and 1760. In the foreground we see the River Mersey thronged with shipping, both coastal vessels and ocean-going ships. The town is still confined to its original peninsular site with the high ground behind it still very rural. Prominent among the buildings is St Nicholas Church on the extreme left, Liverpool Tower on the waterfront, the Town Hall flying a flag, St George's church (not actually completed until 1734) and the new dock, behind which is the octagonal steeple of St Peter's church.

success of England's continental rivals in this form of warfare made the passage up the English Channel or down the North Sea to reach London very hazardous, and this danger gave a new impetus to the west coast ports. Merchants were quick to perceive that the use of Liverpool or Bristol eliminated the most vulnerable portion of the voyage.

Nor was Liverpool's expanding trade entirely based on distant waters. After the Restoration trade with Ireland increased. Cargoes of linen, flax yarn and wool were imported into England, while coal and manufactured goods were exported. The Isle of Man was another frequent destination for Liverpool ships. Goods could be unloaded in the Island without paying any duty, though this became payable if they were sent on to a mainland port. As a result of this system the sailors of Liverpool developed a flourishing smuggling trade in wines, spirits and tobacco. Nicholas Blundell, the grandson of William, records in his *Great Diurnal* his dealings with the smugglers and the excisemen and the part played by his village priest in concealing the evidence.

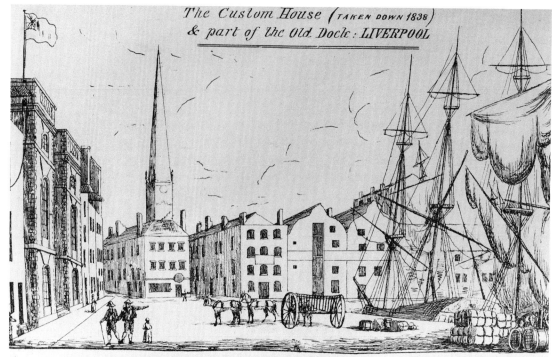

The Custom House (TAKEN DOWN 1838) & part of the Old Dock: LIVERPOOL

St Thomas' Church:

In the 1690s, when Sir William Norris was involved in the affairs of the town, these conditions were bringing Liverpool a new prosperity and encouraging ambition and expansion. Celia Fiennes visited the town in 1696, and wrote; 'It is a very rich trading town, the houses of brick and stone built high and even, that a street right through looks very handsome, the streets are well pitched; there are abundance of persons you see very well dressed and of good fashion, the streets are fair and long, it's London in miniature as much as ever I saw anything'. In this opinion she foreshadowed the view expressed by Defoe, some sixteen years later, that it was 'A large, handsome, well built, increasing and thriving town'. At almost the same time another visitor to the town foresaw a problem which might curtail the apparently rosy future. Greenville Collins in his *Coasting Pilot* (a handbook of information about ports and navigation) wrote 'The ships lie aground before the town of Liverpool; 'tis bad riding afloat before the town by reason of the strong tides that run here; therefore ships that ride afloat, ride up the Slyne where there is less tide'. As trade and the size of ships increased the old methods of cargo-working, by either beaching the ships and unloading directly into carts or the ships lying-off and discharging into lighters, were becoming too slow and too hazardous. Some new provision had to be made.

Had Norris not be sent on his mission to India he would certainly have found himself involved with the scheme to build the first dock. In 1698 a wet dock had been added to the naval yard at Portsmouth, another had been built

Liverpool's first dock, from Lacey's *Stranger in Liverpool*, c.1844. The dock gave more than three acres of safe water which could be entered at most states of the tide. The Custom House, seen on the left, was built at about the same date as the dock and was demolished in 1838. St Thomas' was the fourth church built in the town (1750). Its spire was demolished as unsafe in 1822. The warehouses with dutch gables were built to raise funds for the building of the dock.
PHOTOGRAPH, AUTHOR

St Nicholas' Church from a nineteenth-century engraving. This picture is of the new tower, designed by Thomas Harrison, to replace the steeple which collapsed in 1810. The view emphasises the way in which the church was located on the actual waterfront of the town. The vessel in the foreground is moored in George's Dock, opened in 1767 as Liverpool's third dock. The celebrated trio of waterfront buildings, including the Liver Building, were erected on the site when the dock was filled in in the early twentieth century.

PHOTOGRAPH COURTESY OF BOYDELL GALLERIES, LIVERPOOL

for commercial use at Blackwall on the Thames, while George Sorocold was working on another at Howland in Rotherhithe. A fresh impetus was given to harbour improvements in Liverpool by the great gale of 1703 which had decimated the shipping of the port. As result the Corporation and Sir Thomas Johnson began to develop a dock scheme for Liverpool. Sorocold was invited to the town and prepared an ambitious plan to excavate a basin which would be accessible at most states of the tide. A Bill was presented to parliament but encountered fierce opposition from the unlikely source of the London cheesemongers. They had an arrangement with the port of Chester for the duty-free use of that port, the administrative limits of which included Liverpool. If a dock was built they would be compelled to pay the toll of four pence per ton on their shipping in the Mersey. However, Johnson and his colleague Clayton, who had taken William Norris's place, managed to circumvent the opposition and the Bill was passed. No sooner was this done than Sorocold died and a new engineer had to be found. His replacement was Thomas Steers, who had learned his trade as a military engineer in the army of King William III. His revised and less costly plan, to build the dock in the mouth of the Pool and then fill round it, was carried out and Liverpool's first dock was completed.

Norris was instrumental in two important civic projects during this time. The first was the granting by William III in 1695 of a new charter for the borough. This replaced the more restrictive one granted in 1625, and made the corporation free from the last vestiges of royal and feudal power. It was under the terms of this charter that the town was governed until the Municipal Corporations Act of 1835. Another sign of the growing stature and independence of Liverpool was the Bill of 1699, introduced and piloted through the House by Norris, which conveyed parochial status on the town. Until then, in ecclesiastical terms, Liverpool had been a mere chapelry of the large parish of St Mary, Walton on the Hill. A chapel of Our Lady and St Nicholas had existed since the fourteenth century but it was subordinate to the Rector of Walton.

Now, the town and the chapel were to enjoy full parochial status, and the event was celebrated by the building of a new joint parish church, St Peter's, in 1702.

That a third church was needed by 1715, when St George's was built on the site acquired by the Corporation on which the castle of Liverpool had formerly stood, is a good indication of the rapidly increasing population. It was calculated at the time that in the two decades after 1700 the population of Liverpool had doubled.

In part, this growth was due to the increased trade to the Americas which became possible after the Treaty of Utrecht in 1713. This had gone some way to opening up the South American market to English traders, hitherto excluded by the Spanish authorities. Within the Spanish colonies there was an insatiable demand for slave labour, while at the same time the British colonies in the West Indies and southern North America were experiencing a rapidly increasing demand for their products – sugar, rum, tobacco, rice, indigo and other exotic crops – from a buoyant home market.

The Liverpool merchants were a rough and aggressive group, untramelled by the polite frills and social

right Liverpool, looking north from Toxteth. This view from the vicinity of St James' Church shows the town in the early nineteenth century. Notable is the forest of masts of shipping in the docks. St Nicholas Church, the Town Hall and the steeples of St Peter's and St George's church can be identified.

PHOTOGRAPH, AUTHOR

LIVERPOOL

pretensions of the merchant princes of London and Bristol. As a result they
were able to undercut the shipping rates of the older ports and enhance their
own profits. This is suggested as one of the principal reasons why Liverpool
was to achieve increasing dominance in the slave trade. In 1701 one ship sailed
from Liverpool on a slaving voyage; by 1804 126 ships were engaged in the
trade. Another factor was that the immediate hinterland could supply a wide
variety of acceptable trade goods. The Lancashire textile industry could
produce cheap, light cloths which were more popular in tropical climates than
the heavy West of England woollens offered by the Bristol merchants. The
metal-working districts around Wigan and Ashton-in-Makerfield provided
abundant supplies of nails, spikes, knives, pots and pans all of which were much
in demand on the west coast of Africa.

There was, and still is, much hypocritical condemnation of Liverpool's part
in the slave trade as though the town was isolated and discrete from the rest
of the country's economy. In fact, whoever used sugar, smoked a pipe, wore
clothing made of cotton or drank a glass of punch was benefiting from the
trade. This was also true of the mills and factories and workshops which made
the goods that were exported to be exchanged for slaves, of the shipyards and
the timber merchants who built the ships, of the rope walks and anchor smiths
and a thousand other trades that, directly or indirectly, supplied the 'Guinea
Merchants'. This does not make the trade any more moral, but at least deflects
the obloquy from the town of Liverpool alone. However, the profits of this
evil trade were enormous: it is calculated that in 1730 alone, when fifteen ships
cleared the port for Africa, the profit from the voyages was £214,672 15s. 1d.

The ships used in the African trade were ideally suited to adaptation as privateers or letters of marque, being fast, well armed and able to carry large numbers of men. During the almost continuous French Wars of the eighteenth century this became a popular and profitable trade for the Liverpool seamen. Quick fortunes could be made by lucky owners and captains such as Fortunatus Wright and William Hutchinson. Few were as successful as Captain Dawson of the *Mentor*. In 1778 this ship was considered so unseaworthy that her original owners refused to accept her from the builders. In desperation she was fitted as a privateer and sent on a cruise. On this first voyage Dawson and his crew captured the French Indiaman *Carnatic* and a cargo valued at £135,000. Less fortunate, perhaps, was the *Active* which captured a prize whose cargo included a live zebra.

This new-found wealth was used by the town on a continuous programme of civic improvement. We cannot trace this in detail here but a few highlights will suffice to show the increasing affluence and sophistication of Liverpool. In 1709 some of the mercantile wealth of Brian Blundell was used to found the Blue Coat School, where forty boys and ten girls were to be instructed in reading, writing, and arithmetic, and to learn the craft of spinning cotton. The school buildings of 1716–26 remain as the oldest buildings in the City of Liverpool and have been beautifully restored following severe damage in World War II. In 1745 the first public infirmary was set up and in 1749 a new

The former Blue Coat School, School Lane, Liverpool. Bryan Blundell, a seaman, merchant and philanthropist, used some of the profits of his voyages to found a school for the care and education of orphans of the town in 1716. The building underwent considerable alteration and additions before being heavily damaged by bombing in 1941. Now fully restored, it serves as a gallery and arts centre and is the oldest surviving building in Liverpool.

PHOTOGRAPH, AUTHOR

Early nineteenth-century view of the Mersey, from Lacey's *Stranger in Liverpool*, *c*.1844. This shows the entrance to the George's Dock Basin, constructed in 1767. It conveys some of the bustle of the expanding port and the multitude of ships of all types that could be seen. The two single-masted vessels in mid-stream are 'flats', the sailing barges used to link the town to the Weaver Navigation and the Bridgewater Canal at Runcorn. The steamer is one of the early ferry steamers, which were first used in 1812. The absence of building on the Cheshire side of the river is most noticeable.

PHOTOGRAPH, AUTHOR

Exchange building and Town Hall was erected to the designs of the fashionable John Woods of Bath. In the same year yet another church, St Thomas', was built and in 1762 the cosmopolitan nature of the population was indicated by the building of the first Jewish synagogue and a Catholic chapel. In 1760 the principal streets were paved and all the time the line of docks along the river front was growing. The new areas of the town were lined with fashionable housing, in Clayton and Williamson Squares and along the new streets named Duke, Hanover and Cumberland to emphasise the town's commitment to the House of Hanover. In less than a hundred years the transformation from a third rate market town with a small coasting port to a major city which could claim to be the second city and port of the Empire was completed.

While these changes to the town were in progress, considerable efforts were being made to improve the port's connections with its industrial hinterland. In 1720 an Act was obtained in parliament to make the River Weaver navigable and thus allow the easier movement of Cheshire salt and Staffordshire pottery to the Mersey. At about the same time Thomas Steers, the dock engineer, was planning a similar project to open the River Douglas to navigation and thus make Wigan coal available in the port.

In 1726 the first Lancashire turnpike road was opened between Liverpool and Prescot, primarily to allow the coal from the pits and the mugs from the potteries of that town to reach the docks. In 1738 the new Salthouse Dock was opened, its name an indication of an innovation in the industry of the port. It is calculated that the triangular estuarine trade in coal, salt and manufactured goods contributed as much as the Guinea trade to the wealth of the town. In 1755 Henry Berry, the dock engineer, was employed by the merchants and corporation of the town to construct the Sankey Brook Navigation, which was in effect England's first canal and a few years later the port became the terminus of the Duke of Bridgewater's canal from Manchester. It was a port which by 1760 had a population of 25,787 and was the home of 226 ships with a total tonnage of 23,665 tons. In 1767 a further dock, St George's, was opened and a pilotage service was introduced.

We could go on to trace the growth and development of the town in the latter part of the eighteenth century and during its heyday in the hundred years that followed, but the intention is to show the links between Speke Hall and the Norris family in the first stages of this transformation. The transfer of the

Memorial to Richard Watt in the Church of St Wilfrid, Standish. This elaborate memorial, carved by John Bacon Junior, dates from 1806 and commemorates Richard Watt, who was born in Shevington but made his fortune in the West Indies and Liverpool. The urn incorporates a portrait bust while the two supporting figures lean on a bee-hive representing industry and a compass to illustrate his seafaring activities. On the base is an interesting and detailed view of the Liverpool waterfront. The spire on St Nicholas Church still stands and the domes of the Town Hall and St Paul's Church can be discerned.

PHOTOGRAPH BY LEN FENDER. REPRODUCED BY KIND PERMISSION OF THE RECTOR, CHURCH OF ST WILFRID, STANDISH ownership of Speke from the Beauclerks, heirs of the Norrises, to Richard Watt is in itself indicative of the growing social importance of the wealth and commerce of the town. About 1745 carriages were a rare sight in Liverpool; Mrs Sarah Clayton owned the first one to grace its streets, in about 1730. However, a publican named Dimmocke had a chaise which could be hired out, together with a boy to lead or drive the horse. This boy was Richard Watt and he, like many Liverpool lads, believed that the opportunity to make his fortune was to be found at sea. He shipped out of Liverpool in a Guineaman and for a long time no more was heard of him. Eventually merchants in the town became aware of the rise of a firm of West India merchants, Messrs Watt and Walker. Richard returned to the town, his fortune made after his years in Jamaica, but he did not forget his origins and settled £100 a year for life on the remaining members of the Dimmocke family. Watt continued to trade in the town and it was his nephew, also a Richard Watt, who inherited his fortune and used some of it to buy Speke Hall.

So the threads come together in the house. We can trace the ancient lineage of the Norris family, their interest in the closing years of their fame in the commercial growth of the town, the way in which the new facilities and governmental structures set up by their efforts aided the rapid commercial expansion of Liverpool. In turn these allowed the diligent, the determined and, no doubt, the unscrupulous to make the fortunes which created a new aristocracy.

All this was epitomised in the mission of Sir William Norris to India. He was helping to lay the foundations not only of commercial success, but ultimately of imperial expansion. So it is perhaps appropriate to recollect that at his audience with the Great Mogul he was preceded by a ceremonial sword of state, a symbol of his plenipotentiary powers. When his baggage eventually arrived back in this country the sword was given to the corporation for use on ceremonial civic occasions. It is still kept among the mayoral regalia and bears on its blade the inscription

> This sword of state, carried before his Excellency Sir William Norris of Speke, in his embassy to the Great Mogul, given as a memorial of respect to this Corporation Anno Domini 1702 John Cockshutt Mayor.

This sword, still the symbolic expression of the powers of the lord mayor and corporation of the city, is also an emblem of the part played by the Norris family in creating the town.

CHAPTER 9

Rufford Old Hall and Martin Mere

'BY NOT GOING THROUGH ORMSKIRK I avoided going by the famous mere called Martin Mere, that as the proverb says has parted many a man from his mare. Indeed it being near evening and not getting a guide I was a little frightened to go that way, it being very hazardous for strangers'. The writer of this passage was not some nervous traveller frightened by their own shadow, but the intrepid Celia Fiennes, whose solitary journeys on horseback in the last decades of the seventeenth century took her the length and breadth of the country. It is obvious that the reputation of the trackless mosses and meres of Lancashire was well known even in her native south country, and that the prospect of traversing them daunted even her independent spirit. In fact this passage written in the 1690s is an epitaph for the old mere as it had been over the centuries and coincides with the first efforts to reclaim the wasteland.*[1]

The mere had existed ever since the retreat of the ice at the end of the Pleistocene period (10,000 BC) when the slow dissolving of a huge block of ice created a clay-lined hollow on the Lancashire plain. This filled with meltwater and the rain that ran off its gently sloping sides to become a shallow lake, some three miles by two. At its western end it was separated from the sea by a narrow spit of sand hills and moss land. It was on this slender piece of solid ground that the later villages of Crossens and North Meols were to grow up. It might be expected that the natural drainage of the mere would have been into the sea or the Ribble estuary at this point and some historians postulate such a channel. However, the main point where the water drained out over the lowest point on the rim of the mere was at its eastern extremity and the outlet flowed through a marshy channel into the River Douglas. It was this stream that was crossed by an uneven ford on the road between Ormskirk and Preston.[2] At the ford a settlement grew up which took its name from its position and was known as the Rough Ford or Rufford. In earlier times such settlement as there was around the mere was in scattered hamlets and villages, where the people made a living by a combination of farming the drier land and supplementing the produce of their fields and their cattle by fishing and wildfowling on the mere. Traces of

---

* The notes and references for this chapter may be found on pages 262–3.

Rufford Old Hall from the north. The three major building phases of the house can be seen in this view. On the left is the brick wing added in 1662 to provide new kitchen and service accommodation. The gable end to the right of this wing represents the old service rooms, largely rebuilt about 1725 and refurbished in 1820–23 by John Foster. The Great Hall is now all that remains of the house built *c*.1530 by Sir Robert Hesketh. The former west wing that had contained the private rooms of the family disappeared in the early eighteenth century.

PHOTOGRAPH, AUTHOR

these early days on the mere are confined to a few scattered finds and the remains of the dug-out boats recovered during the operations to bring the former lake bed into agricultural production during the last century. In his History of the Parish of North Meols, Farrer describes such a find on the farm of Robert Ashcroft at Rufford in 1869. When excavated the boat was found to be 13 feet in length, 2 feet 10 inches in beam and drew 20 inches of water. It had four seats hewn in it and a strange row of holes a few inches below the prow, perhaps to allow some sort of screen or shield to be affixed. When discovered the boat was lying on a sloping sandy bed which showed ripple marks, thus indicating that it had been beached and abandoned. Dating these craft is difficult as they were not found in association with other objects and similar types of boat were used over a very long period. They have not been subjected to radio-carbon dating. It used to be assumed that they dated from the Iron Age, but modern investigation ascribes a date in the eleventh century to the example in the Southport Museum.[3]

Life in the district probably changed little between the Dark Ages and the Middle Ages, though the rights to the lake and its resources were transferred from the lords of Lathom to the priors of Burscough when that Augustinian house was founded at the end of the twelfth century by Adam de Lathom. There is a document from the reign of Edward III by which the prior leased, to one Thurstan de Northleigh, fishing rights together with a small plot of land on Blakenase, one of the several small islands in the mere. This plot, some 90 feet by 20 feet was too small to be farmed and was presumably intended as a base for Thurstan's fishing.[4]

The Great Hall, Rufford. In this view the camera is looking from the 'upper end' of the hall towards the 'screens passage'. This entrance corridor, in which the doors which formerly led to the kitchen can be seen, is separated from the hall by the spere trusses extending from each side of the wall and the central movable screen. The columns of the speres are thought to be survivors from the earlier hall. The most notable feature of this hall is the very fine hammer-beam roof with its armorial carving and angelic decoration.

At the Dissolution of the Monasteries, rights on the mere passed into secular hands. The new owners included three of the most important local landed families: first, the Stanleys of Lathom, the Earls of Derby; second, the Scarisbricks of Scarisbrick; and finally, the Heskeths of Rufford. Some other less important families also had shared rights over the mere, and at least one portion of its shore line, at Burscough, was in common ownership. Today, when visiting Rufford Hall it is difficult to imagine it perched on a low eminence on the edge of a large lake but the mere can be shown to have played an important part in the domestic economy of the Heskeths and their household.[5]

The origins of the Hesketh family are obscure, although it seems certain that they originated in the village of that name near Tarleton. The name Hesketh is derived from the Norse word for a 'horse racing course'. It was by marriage into the powerful Fitton family in 1285 that they acquired two of their most important estates – Martholme near Padiham, and Rufford itself.[6] We know nothing of their earliest houses at Rufford. Although the moated site some half

The Drawing Room (*top*) and Dining Room, Rufford Old Hall. These rooms occupy the space devoted to the service rooms in the original house, which became redundant after the building of the 1662 wing. They were rebuilt for their present purpose by Thomas Hesketh, *c.* 1725. The roof trusses visible in the drawing room are of sixteenth-century date, but are not part of the original con-struction. Much of the decoration of these rooms dates from Foster's work in the early 1820s.

a mile north of the Old Hall has been suggested as the possible location of their original home, it seems rather too small to have contained any - considerable house.[7]

The first house of which any trace remains is that built by Robert Hesketh (1429–91). In the Great Hall of the present house are the two great spere trusses, which can be dated to this period by their style. These are massive oak columns, each hewn from a single tree trunk. Their purpose is to support the two short wooden-panelled walls which separate the entrance passageway from the hall. The carved decoration upon them is of a quite different style to that found in the rest of the house. However, this decoration bears a close resemblance to that on similar spere trusses at Adlington Hall, Cheshire, which was the home of Robert's sister-in-law. Perhaps the same carpenter was responsible for both works. This house was demolished by Robert's great grandson, another Robert, who built the present hall during the 1530s.[8]

The intervening generations of Heskeths had grown in wealth and prestige, largely due to their close association with the Stanley family. The Stanleys had played a prominent part in the enthronement of the Tudors and had been rewarded with the earldom of Derby. Thomas Hesketh, the son of Robert, held the post of Receiver in the household of Lord Derby. This position gave him charge of the supply side of the vast Derby fortune, and he also seems to have been the *de facto* accountant of the household. In his will he describes himself as 'Acomptante' to both the first and second earls. Such a post, in the loose moral climate of the day, gave considerable scope for self enrichment. During Thomas' lifetime estates at Croston, Tarleton, Bretherton, Ulnes Walton, Howick, Wrightington and Shevington were acquired. At his death, among considerable endowments to charities, he left no less than 1,400 pounds weight of gold and silver plate in the safekeeping of the monks of Whalley, until it could be claimed by his heir.[9]

The transfer of Thomas Hesketh's estate was complicated by his rather chequered matrimonial career. He had been married twice, first to Elizabeth Fleming of Croston, a marriage that ended in divorce after sixteen years, on the grounds of her adultery with Thurstan Hall by whom she had a child. In 1492 Thomas remarried. The bride was Grace Towneley of Towneley, by whom he had one son, William, who died young. In addition to his two marriages Thomas Hesketh had had a long standing relationship with Alice Hayward, by whom he had three children. The eldest of these, Robert, was named as his heir. This will was hotly contested after Thomas' death in 1523 by his three sisters, Margery, Dowsabel and Maud, all of whom were married into powerful families. Eventually, in about 1528, Robert's succession was established. It is thought that to mark the event, and to proclaim his undoubted Hesketh descent, he demolished the existing house and built himself a new home which would be a statement of his new-found glory. His ancient descent was proclaimed in a wealth of armorial carving in the timbers of his new great hall and in the coloured glass of its windows. It is likely that the shields carried by the angels in the hammer beam roof were also heraldically painted. The walls were decorated with other associated coats of arms. By these means Robert Hesketh made any challenge to his right to the Lordship of Rufford seem absurd. Building is often much more than the simple provision of shelter but can be a means of expressing status and aspirations.[10]

The new house, on which work must have begun in about 1530, was built on very traditional lines and with the traditional local building materials. It comprised a communal great hall with two wings disposed at right angles at either end. These wings have now disappeared: the west, or family, wing was demolished at an unknown date in the early eighteenth century, while the east, or service, wing was subjected to two rebuildings and alterations which have left only traces of its original form. Today, one can see in the screens passage, at the lower end of the hall, the doors which originally led to the kitchen, buttery and pantry, but these doors became redundant when the former service wing was rebuilt by Thomas Hesketh in about 1725. At this time the service rooms were converted into a dining room and drawing room using material from the decayed Holmeswood Hall, which stands on the edge of the mere some two miles west of Rufford. These rooms were refurbished a hundred years later when the house was brought back in to family use by Sir Thomas Dalrymple Hesketh.

Of the original structure only the Great Hall retains something of its initial appearance. Particularly striking is the so called moveable screen, a rare feature which has been retained in few other houses of the period. This, together with

the spere trusses, separated the living areas of the hall from the entrance or 'screens passage', which had an external door at either end. That at the southern end was blocked and converted into a window, probably during the nineteenth-century refurbishment when among other works the floor was flagged. It seems that the hall was always heated by a fire on the south wall and never had a central open hearth, the present lantern and apparent smoke hole being installed to light the billiard table in Sir Thomas Dalrymple Hesketh's time. The other striking feature of the great hall is the splendid hammer beam roof, the only one in Lancashire to have angelic decoration. This ecclesiastical touch perhaps hints that the roof might have been acquired from Burscough Priory at the Dissolution.[11]

The next phase of building work at Rufford occurred in 1662 when the estates were in the hands of John Mollineux of Teversal, Nottinghamshire. In 1653 the Hesketh properties had been inherited by Thomas Hesketh, whose father had died when Thomas was an infant. His mother, Lucy, had remarried John Mollineux who was appointed as one of the child's guardians. Mollineux proved a faithful and diligent stepfather who did much to restore and revive the estates after the ravages of the Civil War. He rebuilt the manor house on the lands at Becconsall, and at Rufford he ordered the building of the new brick service wing. It must be assumed that the old kitchen block was very dilapi-

The kitchen of 1662, Rufford. The primary purpose of the wing added to the hall by John Mollineux, on behalf of his step-son Thomas Hesketh, was to provide a new kitchen and service wing. This intention is somewhat obscured by the fact that the modern entrance to the property is through the former kitchen. The vast open fireplace under its stone arch has been greatly reduced by the installation of a nineteenth-century grate.

PHOTOGRAPH, AUTHOR

dated and was perhaps no longer suitable for the needs of the day. The new block, built of brick in a style which shows the influence of Renaissance ideas, contained a kitchen and its attendant store rooms on the ground floor, while the floors above were used for additional family bed chambers and for servants' accommodation. This is clearly discernible in the inventories of the house made in 1685 and in 1696/97. These documents also show that the old service wing was still in use for storage and work rooms.[12]

At this time the west wing, whose presence is now indicated by the doors at either side of the high table in the hall, and possibly by a shallow depression which is visible in the ground at the west end of the hall, was still in existence. It may subsequently have been destroyed in a fire, as local tales relate, or it may have been demolished. Whatever the reason for its loss, it is not shown on the sketch of the hall included in a plan of the area made in 1736 though the 1696/7 inventory proves that it existed at that date. Its disappearance therefore can be dated between 1697 and 1736.[13]

In the eighteenth century the Heskeths were spending less and less time at Rufford, which was small and unfashionable. For a period they used Ribbleton Hall at Preston which they had purchased, and the Old Hall was let to tenants. In 1723 the surrounding grounds had been let to Thomas Sharrock and the house itself to a gentleman named George Wharton, a fact which can be discovered from a lease by which the property was let by Elizabeth Bellingham of Preston, formerly the wife of Robert Hesketh, to her son Thomas. By this lease Thomas was to have the use of material from the derelict Holmeswood Hall to restore Rufford. Wharton, already the tenant, was to continue living in the house 'Until a convenient dwelling be found for them'. He was also to continue to 'Enjoy the little garden leading to the Necessary House [privy] and convenient Out Housing for his Cattel and forage' during his stay there. It is not clear whether after the rebuilding of the east wing which followed this agreement Thomas Hesketh actually returned to dwell at Rufford. It seems more likely that he remained at Ribbleton. His son, also Thomas (created the 1st Baronet Hesketh in 1760), felt that the old house was not consonant with his new dignity, and it was again let to tenants. He built a neo-classical house on a site some half a mile from what then became known as the Old Hall. It was an unassuming building with an Ionic colonnade on its façade but no evidence as to the identity of its architect or records of its building survive. We know that in 1779 the Old Hall was leased to a gardener, Thomas Low, at an annual rent of £22 16s. 0d.[14]

The 3rd baronet was Sir Thomas Dalrymple Hesketh (1777–1842) who succeeded his grandfather to the estate in 1798. He felt the New Hall was inadequate and employed the Liverpool architect, John Foster senior, to build a huge extension wing. The baronet was an enthusiastic builder and in 1815 he ordered the refurbishment of the Great Hall in the Old Hall for use as a village schoolroom at a cost of £300.[15] In the summer of 1820, the school having been removed to a new building in the village, a long programme of refurbishment of the Old Hall began, using John Foster junior, the son of the architect of the

New Hall, to direct the work. The impetus for this work was provided by the impending marriage between Sir Thomas' only son, Thomas Henry, and Annette Bomford from County Meath. Though the bridegroom died in 1843, his widow continued to live at Rufford until her death in 1879. By this time the Hesketh family fortunes had been revolutionised by the marriage of Lady Annette's son, Thomas George, into the Fermor family. Eventually his wife, Lady Arabella, inherited the huge estate of her brother, the 5th Earl of Pomfret. The inheritance included the Hawksmoor designed mansion at Easton Neston near Towcester, and this became became the principal home of the Heskeths. Rufford went into a period of decline, as the family began the process of selling off its Lancashire estates.[16]

During the renovation of the Old Hall by Foster little change was made to its exterior, except for an attempt to give a 'Tudor' appearance to the east wing (which had been rebuilt in 1725) by affixing sham timbers to the walls and adding elaborate barge boards. At the same time the 1662 wing was extended eastward, with a whole new block of rooms and staircase turret being added. In this new building Foster took care to harmonise both the material and the style to the existing 1662 wing.[17]

The major building works undertaken by the Hesketh family at various times, but especially in the early nineteenth century, reflect the measure of prosperity that accrued to them from their various estates. The account books preserved among the Hesketh family papers show that the greater portion of their wealth was derived from agriculture and rents. However, as early as 1620 the coal mining which was carried out on their lands at Shevington and Wrightington was highly valued.[18] Martin Mere was a minor factor in their income in the earlier years: in 1744 it contributed £29 4s. 5d. in rents, boons, chief rents and demesne to the annual revenue of £1,722 3s. 1¼d. received by the estate. It became increasingly important in the later period, the turning point being the decision in 1694 by Thomas Fleetwood of Bank Hall at Bretherton to attempt the drainage of the mere.[19]

Until this time the main value of the mere to its proprietors had been as a source of fish and they had also harvested the abundance of birds to be found on the mere. Writing at the end of the seventeenth century in his *Natural History of Lancashire and Cheshire* Dr Charles Leigh, a friend of the Heskeths says, 'In it were found great Quantities of fish such as Roach, Eels, Pikes, Perch and Bream ... and vast quantities of Fowls, as Curlews, Curleyhilps, Wild Ducks, Wild Geese and Swans, which are sometimes there in great numbers'. Evidence for the importance of fishing on the mere is borne out by the few references to the area from the Middle Ages. We have already mentioned the use of the mere for fishing by the Priory of Burscough and it is significant that the modern road from the mere to the village of Burscough is known as Fish Lane. This would have been the route used by the fishermen to take their catch either to the priory or to market at Ormskirk. In 1354 two men, one from Rufford and one from Holmeswood, were accused of taking bream to the value of £1 from the waters assigned to Richard de Aughton in North Meols.[20]

Rufford Old Hall from the gardens. This southern aspect of the Great Hall shows the massive chimney of the fireplace. There is no evidence that Rufford ever had a central open hearth and the lantern on the roof is not a Victorian replacement for a louvre but was added to provide light for the billiard table. The large window next to the gable was added either during the conversion of the hall for use as a school in 1815 or when it was restored to family use in the 1820s. It marks the former main door of the house, and is matched by a door on the north side.

PHOTOGRAPH, AUTHOR

In October 1557 Sir Thomas Hesketh was sued in the duchy court by Henry Banastre of Bank Hall and one of his serving men, John Hunter. According to the, no doubt, partisan accounts given, the previous March some men from Bank Hall were fishing in what they claimed to believe were the waters assigned to their master. A party of Hesketh's servants attacked them and caused them to flee, leaving their nets behind. In the afternoon Hunter and William Dobson went back, peaceably as they claimed, with no other weapon than a staff 'such as they usually walked with' to recover their equipment. They were accosted by Hesketh's men and, despite their pleas that they had no intention of fishing, were attacked and beaten up. Further witnesses were called on both sides and gave interesting testimony on the distribution of fishing rights on the mere.[21] Cases like this prove the importance of the mere as a source of fresh fish, which would have been doubly welcome in the winter when fresh meat was in short supply: one can imagine that Martin Mere was used as a huge stew pond by the Heskeths.[22] The proprietors of the mere seem to have allowed the local people the opportunity for unrestricted angling from the bank, but more commercial fishing on the mere itself was strictly controlled and rented. For this privilege a cash payment was made and also payment in kind in the form of a specified number of live pike.

There is some documentary evidence in the Hesketh and the Scarisbrick papers for the fishing techniques used on the mere. The inventory of Holmeswood Hall attached to the will of Robert Hesketh 1620 includes a boat and six 'owers for a boat'. These were valued at one shilling and the boat at ten shillings.[23] It has been suggested that the tower at Holmeswood, now the only remaining part of the hall, was intended as a lighthouse to guide benighted fishermen on the mere. A similar tower at Martin Hall, Burscough, was used in this way. The inventory of Edward Scarisbrick of Scarisbrick includes details of fourteen bow nets, which were nets fixed to a wooden hoop rather like a large shrimping net, and in addition he had a number of pike nets.[24] It is also known that pytchs or wicker fish traps were used. These cones of basketwork were set in blocks across channels used so that once fish had entered the pytch they were unable to escape. Long lining was also used, in which lines carrying numerous baited hooks were fastened to posts set below the water level.

Those proprietors whose portion of the mere, like that of the Scarisbricks, lay to the south, enjoyed a considerable advantage in fishing. As a counsel's opinion puts it, 'That part of the Mere lying in Rufford and Holmeswood was a shallow and having no cover for fish was of little value'.[25] The reason was that in this part the bottom of the mere was sandy and sterile, while further south a muddy bottom encouraged the growth of weeds and provided a more congenial habitat for the fish. Rivalry over control of the best fishing areas gave rise to many disputes between the proprietors. As early as the fourteenth century the families of Hesketh and Scarisbrick were in conflict over fishing rights on the mere.[26] Fish were marketed widely, and we know that the Shuttleworth family of Smithills Hall near Bolton bought 'fish from Martin Mere' in the 1580s.

It was in the eighteenth century, after the draining of the mere, that the fiercest dispute between the two families took place. There are extensive documents concerning this action preserved in both the Scarisbrick and the Hesketh archives, but curiously none of them is dated. They appear to date from about 1725 and are mainly concerned with the boundaries between the lands available to the various proprietors. It seems that although each family knew the extent of its fishing rights while the mere was flooded, after it had been drained new boundaries (or meres, as they were confusingly called in the Lancashire dialect) had to be defined. These papers provide valuable insights into the way the mere had been used before its reclamation. We have already emphasised the importance of fishing, but they also contain references to wildfowling. These can be found in a deposition made in a document in this series. The witness deposes that 'The ... owners and proprietors ... of the said Mere & their ancestors & tenants had & have likewise sole rights of catching or killing of all swans & other wildfowl that were or bred or made their nests in & upon any parts of the Mere ... Also to take the eggs of Swans & other wildfowl breeding there'.[27] The birds not only provided fresh food in the winter, but the feathers and down from the nests were a valuable commodity. The inventory of 1620 shows that all but a few of the beds at Rufford Hall (and there were more than fifty) were of feather, as were the bolsters and pillows. Robert Hesketh and his son enjoyed the delights of down mattresses, but even the servants, except the lowliest, had feather beds. The depositions referred to above also give some clues about other uses made of the mere. 'They ... received the yearly proffits arising therefrom by getting and cutting reeds or grass growing thereon or by digging mosswood or stocks

[the semi-fossilised remains of tree trunks or roots dug from the peat] or by grazing or de pasturing the same with horses or cattle'. The turf cuttings could be used for fuel or even as a building material and thatch was the indigenous roofing method of the area. As late as the mid-eighteenth century the outhousing and farm buildings at Rufford Hall were thatched; the roof of the coach house was renewed in 1744 at a cost of £1 5s. 5d.[28] It is apparent that the reference to pasturing cattle refers to the practice of 'scoring' cattle on the islands within the mere. As the water was shallow they could easily be reached by wading or swimming the animals across to the island grazing grounds.

While we have considered the economic potential of Martin Mere it must not be forgotten that although it was the largest of the Lancashire freshwater meres it was by no means unique. South of Martin Mere in the districts east of Ainsdale and Birkdale were at least three other similar if smaller lakes – the Black and the White Otter Pools and Gattern Mere. These were surrounded by mossland which, though perhaps slightly drier in summer, must have been covered with flood water for much of the winter. East of Rufford, between the village and its parish church at Croston, lay the Fenny Pool, which seems to have been a semi-permanent feature of the landscape, though at its greatest extent in winter. The authors of the Commonwealth Church Survey of 1651 wrote of Rufford 'The waters lying between the saide towne and the Parish [church] of Croston are for the most part not passable'.[29] To the north of the Ribble similar conditions prevailed in the Fylde: Marton Mere, to the east of modern Blackpool, was little smaller than its southern namesake, though the different spelling has been retained by historians to distinguish the two. It can therefore be assumed that a similar economic use was made of the very extensive meres and mosslands. In his *A Description of the Country for Thirty or Forty Miles Around Manchester* Aikin makes an estimate of the extent of the mosslands of Lancashire at that time (1793) as 26,500 acres and to this he adds 482,000 acres of moors, marsh and commons. These figures were calculated when a good deal of the land which had been waste had been reclaimed, and it would not be unreasonable to suggest that in the early seventeenth century a total approaching double Aikin's figures would be closer to the truth. The draining of Martin Mere, however, was the first major effort made within the county to reclaim by draining the meres and wet moss lands.

In the earlier part of the seventeenth century Dutch engineers had begun the drainage of the fens of East Anglia. The schemes had, in general, been successful, although they had provoked considerable hostility from the local people who saw their way of life disappearing. However, in Lancashire nobody had attempted any considerable reclamation plans and the landowners had contented themselves with small, piecemeal, schemes.

The instigator of the Martin Mere drainage, Thomas Fleetwood, had his roots in Staffordshire. He had acquired his interests in Bank Hall and the surrounding area through his marriage to Anne Banastre, the heiress to that family's estates. Perhaps the fact that he was a stranger to the area caused him to look with new eyes at the problem and decide to attempt the drainage of the mere. One can imagine the incredulity and perhaps alarm with which Fleetwood's proposal to reverse the flow of Martin Mere by cutting a new drainage channel was received. The inscription on his monument in St Cuthbert's Church, North Meols describes it as 'A Deed which older generations dared not attempt and the future will scarce believe'.

No contemporary papers relevant to the drainage of Martin Mere exist to give any insight into either how the work was carried out or by whom it was supervised or to indicate local reaction to the works. It is sometimes suggested that Dutch engineers and workers were brought in, possibly men with experience in East Anglia, but this can be no more than supposition. Only two sources give any significant detail of the work.[30]

The first is a copy of the original agreement between Fleetwood and the other proprietors of the mere, which survives in the Scarisbrick family archives. The parties concerned are Lord Derby, Robert Hesketh of Rufford, Richard Bold, William Dicconson, Robert Scarisbrick, Barnaby Hesketh of Meols, Peter Ashton and Roger Hesketh of Aughton. These eight landowners agreed to lease their land and rights on the mere for the lives of Thomas Fleetwood, his daughter Henrietta Maria, and a period of thirty-one years after the decease of the survivor of the two. The agreement also gave Fleetwood the right to make drains and sluices and it was agreed that any legal charges which might ensue would be met by Fleetwood. In return Fleetwood undertook to compensate the proprietors for the value of the fishing or other profits from the mere. This passage confirms the impression already gained, that fishing was the most important contribution of the mere to the economy of the area. Fleetwood undertook to return the lands to their original owners at the end of the term, together with any improvements that he had made. The lands would be returned in proportion to the original holdings on the mere. In the meantime the owners were to have the right to 'fish and foul' in 'such channels as shall be left in and upon the said Meare and New Intended Improvements for their owne pleasure and recreations only BUT not otherwise'. This is yet another - indication of the importance attached to fishing on the mere both for food and recreation.

Nearly a hundred years after Fleetwood's scheme had been put into execution an account of it was written by Thomas Eccleston who had inherited the Scarisbrick estates and put into operation a more elaborate plan to recover the lands of the mere. The success of this scheme led to Eccleston being invited to write an account of his activities, and for this he was awarded a gold medal by the Royal Society of Arts. This is the second source of information about the drainage of the mere. Eccleston writes

> About the year 1692 Mr Fleetwood of Bank Hall, proposed to the several other proprietors to drain Martin Meer on condition that a lease of the whole of three lives and 31 years should be granted him; which they agreed to; and Mr Fleetwood obtained an Act of Parliament the same year to empower him to effect it. The following year he began the work; his plan being to discharge the waters immediately into the sea at the mouth of the river Ribble, which had before forced themselves a passage into the river Douglas when the Meer [sic] waters raised above their usual height by the land floods, as is noted by Camden in his Britannia. The intervening ground between Martin Meer and the Douglas, lying considerably higher than the Meer, occasioned the stagnation, and kept it full. Mr Fleetwood began the undertaking by making a canal or sluice, twenty four feet wide, of a depth sufficiently lower than the Meer, which he cut from the Ribble Mouth, through an embanked salt marsh, and then through a moss or bog in North Meols about a mile and half in length; he continued it through the lowest parts of the Meer. To prevent the sea from rushing up the canal and overflowing the Meer, which lies ten feet lower than the sea high water mark at spring tides, he erected in his canal near the sea, a pair of flood gates, which shut when the sea water rose higher than those in the canal, and opened again by the sluice stream when the sea retired.

He goes on to expound the problems of silting and erosion which bedevilled this system. The long outfall across the sands at Crossens allowed silt to be deposited in the lock and thus prevented the gates closing properly, and the sea swirling around the lock at high tide washed the banks from round the masonry. Subsequently, Eccleston tells us that to try to rectify these faults Fleetwood's executors extended the outfall channel. Fleetwood died in 1717 and his daughter in 1719. Consequently the lease on the mere lapsed in 1750, a great deal earlier than had been anticipated. Eccleston goes on to state that some efforts were made to keep the works in operation but partly due to neglect and the result of damage suffered in a severe storm in 1755 the mere reverted to its natural state: 'The lands upon the Meer became again of little value, being covered with water all winter and liable to be flooded by very trivial summer rains'.[31]

In general Eccleston's account of the state of affairs on Martin Mere prior to the commencement of the new work in 1782 has been accepted by historians as an accurate account. As a result the tendency has been to dismiss the work of Fleetwood as a brave try, but one that achieved little success. This traditional view must be critically examined. In the first place, it can be shown that the account by Eccleston contains errors of fact. For example, the agreement between Fleetwood and the proprietors was drawn up in 1694 and not 1692 as he states. There is also a misunderstanding of the agreement in his statement that it was for three lives, when, in fact, it was for two plus thirty-one years.

While in themselves these errors are not especially significant, they must make us view other statements with some caution. Had he wished to, Eccleston could have checked the agreement from his own muniments; that he did not do so indicates no firm desire to give an accurate account of Fleetwood's actions. It might be supposed that Eccleston was anxious to minimise the achievements of his predecessors in order to enhance his own results. Evidence will be adduced to show that the description of his work is designed to exaggerate the degree of success that it achieved.

While we may regard the statement on the Fleetwood memorial that he 'Had converted the Great Martensian Mere into firm dry ground' as an over-statement, his work seems to have been more successful than is generally thought. It created enough dry ground for Fleetwood to be able to sell or to let three farms to intrepid settlers on the mere. These three hardy souls were John Berry, whose name is perpetuated in Berry House at Tarlscough, Henry Low and William Wiggins, remembered in the lane and bridge called after him. In the words of the lawyer who drew up a document, 'The said tenants or farmers have built and erected upon their said farms or tenements dwelling houses & out houses for the better occupying, improving and cultivating of the said farms'.[32]

Further evidence of the financial rewards of a holding on Martin Mere, in the years between the drainage works of Fleetwood and Eccleston, comes from the Rufford stewards' accounts. That for 1744, drawn up by Alexander Radcliffe of Ormskirk (a most conscientious and meticulous steward) shows that the annual return from Martin Mere was £29 4s. 5d.[33] It is to be presumed that this includes the annual compensatory payment by Fleetwood's executors for the loss of the fishery. To put this figure in perspective, it should be noted that revenues from nineteen different estates are listed and Martin Mere is ninth in order of magnitude. While it is tiny compared to the £660 from Rufford or £225 from Croston it is considerably greater than the £1 10s. 3d. from Hutton or the miserable 4s. 2d. from Newton in the Fylde, while even Wrightington with its coal mines was worth only £25 4s. 6d. It must be remembered that this amount in the accounts records only revenue from land and it is known that in 1723, a Mr Halywell paid £17 4s. 0d. rent for the coal mines at Wrightington.[34]

These figures prove that Martin Mere was a far from negligible part of the Hesketh estates. It seems that the Martin Mere lands had the additional advantage that they were comparatively free from a burden of either local or national taxation. It is possible that they were assessed at a lower rate than the better drained agricultural lands that surrounded them. Perhaps the amount of the assessment had been fixed prior to their improvement and had not been amended. In the year covered by the account the charge for land tax was 2s. 2d. The customary rate of assessment for this tax was four shillings in the pound. If the Martin Mere lands were charged on this basis it would indicate that the Hesketh property on the mere was deemed to be worth only ten shillings a year. In addition to this moderate charge, local taxes had to be paid.

The total of these, made up of the constable's levy, poor rate and church tax, was a further 4s. 1d. The income derived by the Heskeths from their lands on the mere would seem to contradict the assertions made by Eccleston about the low value of land on the mere, and his claim that he could only let land at 4s. per acre. It must be admitted that he is speaking of a period some forty years later when there had been a collapse of the earlier drainage works.

It is now time to examine the nature of Eccleston's activities in draining the mere. Having secured the permission of the other proprietors on the mere in 1782, he consulted John Gilbert who, as steward and land agent to the Duke of Bridgewater, had played a major part in the construction of the canals envisioned by his employer. Gilbert had considerable expertise in hydraulic engineering and it has been suggested that he, rather than James Brindley, was the engineering genius of the early canals. He advised the construction of a new set of triple lock gates at Crossens, and a lowering of the threshold of the lock to stimulate the flushing action of the stream. While construction work at Crossens continued, further gangs of men were employed on deepening and increasing the gradient on the main drainage channel on the mere, the Great Sluice. The year 1783 saw the mere more than usually flooded but after the completion of the work on the sluice dry ground had appeared. The next stage was to complete the enlargement and extension of the sluice and to dig an extensive pattern of feeder ditches totalling over 100 miles in length. The new technology of agriculture, in part made possible by the Industrial Revolution, came to Eccleston's assistance in this major project. He wrote

> I procured a draining or guttering plough, on Mr Cuthbert Clark's construction, which was drawn by eight, sometimes ten able horses, and which I can certainly recommend as a most useful implement in all fenny countries. I am most greatly indebted to the inventor, for with this, in one day, I cut drains eight miles in length, thirteen inches in depth, twenty inches wide at the top, and five at the bottom ... which would have cost, if done by hand, seven pounds, five shillings and ten pence.

It is a matter of regret that he does not give the actual cost of the work using the plough.[35]

All this work occupied the year 1783 and by the end of that year some land was drained. In the following year several acres were dry enough to be ploughed and were used to produce a crop of spring wheat. The other dry land was either used as pasture or for the growing of a crop of hay, which Eccleston describes as very inferior in quality. In 1785 he was able to plough some '200 large acres' on which crops of barley and oats were grown with considerable success. He recounts that he had been able to sell the barley for £11 17s. 6d. per large acre, 'the produce of land which before let at no more than four shillings the acre'. (By the term 'large acre' Eccleston is referring to the 'customary acre' or 'Cheshire acre', which was widely used in Lancashire and was of something more than twice the size of the statute acre.) Other parts of the newly-drained lands were used for pasture and for meadow. Scotch cattle and horses did well on the new pasture lands and the meadows, after the first years, produced fine quality hay. We know from other sources that Eccleston specialised in the breeding of coach horses, and cattle of the Suffolk Poll breed. The latter were widely bought by local landowners including the Heskeths.[36]

What is noticeable in this account by Eccleston is that nowhere does he specify the actual amount of newly drained land that resulted from his scheme. The impression gained is that the whole of Martin Mere was rendered fit for cultivation by his efforts. Further study shows that this was very far from the case. While one must exempt the flooding of the mere in 1789 which he reported in a subsequent letter to the Royal Society, since it was caused by both the River Douglas and the Rufford Branch of the Leeds and Liverpool Canal breaking their banks after excessive rains, much of the mere must have remained waterlogged. It was probably these marshy areas that provided grazing for the large flocks of geese that are mention in Holt's *General View of the Agriculture of the County of Lancaster*, written in 1795, as being fattened for the winter market.

In 1785 William Yates published his map of Lancashire, the first accurate, measured survey of the county. Yates was keen to indicate evidence of industrial and economic developments – for example wind and water mills are shown and differentiated, the new cotton factories are marked and the canals are delineated. However, on Martin Mere no indication is given of the work in progress when the survey was carried out and it bears the rather depressing legend 'Dry in the summer season'. While it may be true that Eccleston's success postdates the survey work for the map, one might have expected that Yates, who must have have been aware of the drainage work, would have included some reference at the time of publication.

It is true that portions of Yates' map, especially in the most rural areas, are less carefully surveyed and drawn, but the recovery of Martin Mere from the waters could hardly be overlooked. More concrete evidence that much remained to be done comes from the Hesketh papers. On Friday 21 November 1823 William Shakeshaft, steward to Sir Thomas Dalrymple Hesketh, attended a meeting at the Ram's Head in Tarleton called by the principal landowners on the mere. Its purpose was to discuss the feasibility of making a new sluice from the Great Sluice at a point known as Crostone's to Hundred End. Shakeshaft and Robert Holmes were appointed by the meeting to investigate and report back on Monday 1 December. What they proposed was a ditch some 2 miles in length, which would be 18 feet wide at ground level and 12 feet wide at the water. The average depth of the cutting would be 8 feet 8 inches. They calculated that the whole work would occupy seven large acres of land (15.2 statute acres, 6.02 hectares) and would cost £5,000.

The report goes on to say that 'Two thirds of the length of the sluice runs through peat bog which is now very wet, consequently it is the opinion of Robert Holmes and William Shakeshaft that the new sluice will be of great service to that land' and estimated that approximately 1833 Cheshire acres would be recovered. This description, written some fifty years after Eccleston's report suggests that his picture of Martin Mere as a drained, fertile area of rich farmland and pasture can – may one say it – hardly hold water![37]

The existence of ill-drained land remaining on the mere is confirmed by the fact that when, in 1849, steam pumping was introduced another 800 acres were brought into use. The instigator of this development was William Boosie, the steward of the Rufford estates. Even so, quite extensive areas of marsh were still shown in the area, subsequently to be developed as the wildfowl reserve, on the Seventh Series Ordnance Survey map of 1954. It was probably the improved drainage created by pumping that allowed for the improvement of communications on the mere. Eccleston had built many miles of road on a foundation of faggots covered with a thick layer of sand; roads which are now causing severe problems because of the weight of modern traffic.[38] In the period between 1850 and 1855 the Southport and Manchester Railway, later absorbed into the Lancashire and Yorkshire Railway Company, built its line across the mere between Burscough and Blowick. This development was timely, in that it enabled the mere farmers to shift the emphasis of their cultivation away from the cereals, especially barley, which had been grown in large quantities on the magnificently fertile soil. The huge barns attached to the older farms – for example at Berry House – show the size of the yields in these early days. By the 1860s and 70s English grain producers were suffering from competition with the cheap imports from the new prairie farms of Canada and the United States. In many areas this inflicted serious damage on farming, but on Martin Mere the farmers were able to adapt to grow vegetables and potatoes for the mass market of the nearby industrial towns. The rail link allowed the rapid transport of fresh produce to markets in Manchester, Liverpool and the towns of east Lancashire. The cultivation of vegetables was not entirely new; in his reply to the questions sent to him by John Holt, who was compiling the first survey of Lancashire agriculture in about 1795, Thomas Eccleston describes the cultivation of carrots as an important local activity.[39]

The draining of Martin Mere was of crucial importance, not just to the immediate area of South West Lancashire, but to the county as a whole. The economic development of the shire had been seriously handicapped by the great extent of non-productive land. Not only had this rendered farming difficult and of low profitability but it, together with other natural obstacles, had seriously obstructed communications within Lancashire. In consequence the county had remained backward and fragmented, socially, economically and intellectually. Various small-scale attempts had been made to reclaim limited areas of land – we find these recorded in manorial records and *post mortem* inquisitions of the seventeenth century – but the wholesale recovery of a large area of ground from beneath the waters of a lake had never even been contemplated. At this distance in time it is impossible to draw any firm conclusions about the success of Fleetwood's plan. There seems little doubt that it did convert a sizeable area of the former mere into land of agricultural value, and transformed the rest from a lake into an area of ill drained moss. The maps of the period following his work and the attached descriptions give no indication that there was any body of standing water remaining throughout the year. Constant vigilance and thorough maintenance were needed to keep the land dry, as indeed they still are, and it may very well be true that by the 1780s, especially after the damage to the sea gates incurred in the great gale of 1755, the mere was in poor condition. However, it may perhaps be considered that Fleetwood's achievements have been underestimated by historians too influenced by Eccleston's account. Other evidence suggests that there still remained much work to be done on the mere even after Eccleston had completed his plans.

Whoever is to have the credit for the drainage of Martin Mere, both principal protagonists were driven by the same motives. Though many of the landed families of Lancashire supplemented their income by the exploitation of mineral reserves on their lands – a method used not only by the Heskeths but also by the Bradshaighs and the Gerards among others – or by commercial or mercantile activity, like the Blundells and the Norrises, the main source of income, and the one which was considered to be the most important, was the revenue derived from land. This was made up of two components. The first was the profit from the demesne lands, which were farmed by the lord directly and provided both for his immediate needs and a surplus for sale. The second component, the bulk of the income, was derived from boon rents and rents on leasehold and copyhold land. This income could be increased either by raising rents and fines at the change of occupancy or by having more land available for rent. The first method had the inherent defect that excessively high rents discouraged the tenants and created resentment and discontent. Though rents did increase during the seventeenth and eighteenth centuries, the augmentation in Lancashire was moderate. It was generally recognised that increased rents could only be demanded if the profitability of the farm was increased by some means. This might depend on the fluctuation of prices of the commodities produced, or on improved methods of cultivation leading to higher yields.

The second method of increasing revenue, by the letting of more land and thereby having an increased rent roll, could only be achieved if hitherto unused and waste land was brought into cultivation. This was the incentive that drove both Fleetwood and Eccleston, and made the other proprietors of the mere so willing to give their concurrence and co-operation to the schemes.

In the case of Eccleston and Sir Thomas Dalrymple Hesketh, 'the improvers', they were also encouraged by the changed economic climate in England, which by the latter years of the eighteenth century was becoming an increasingly urban society. This was especially true in the North West, as the Industrial Revolution seized Lancashire in its grip. The many workers in factories, mines and mills were drawn from a class of rural workers who had previously grown much of their own food. Their new lives made this impossible. As a result the farmers found themselves faced with a double challenge. They had to feed a greatly increased overall population – it is considered that the population of Britain doubled between 1700 and 1800, and then doubled again every fifty years until the beginning of the twentieth century. In addition, the percentage of the population who could be expected to produce any contribution to their own diet declined sharply. By 1851 the majority of English people lived in towns.

These conditions obviously placed the farmer in a position of potentially making great profits, especially as there was little or no food available for import and the protective tariffs of the Corn Laws reduced foreign competition. Though the increased yield could be matched by rises in rents payable to the landowning families, agriculture and land ownership remained a lucrative activity. It was in these conditions that Thomas Eccleston and Sir Thomas Dalrymple Hesketh saw the benefits of investment in the expenses of drainage on Martin Mere.

Rufford Hall has many attractions to offer the visitor but there is little to remind one of the days when it stood on the brink of an inland sea; a sea which provided food and sport and fuel to its inhabitants. Building material in the form of reeds for thatch and wattles for wall panels came from the fringes of the mere, cattle grazed the damp pastures beside the lake and on its islands, and wildfowl were harvested from the water's edge. When the time was ripe the Hesketh family were fully prepared to support the visionaries who believed that it could be drained. The house is a reminder of the beginnings of a most important advance for Lancashire. The success achieved on the mere encouraged similar ventures on other sites and the nineteenth century saw most of the mosslands subjected to a drainage scheme of some sort. The reclaimed land was then brought into highly profitable cultivation. As a result the mysterious wildernesses of the county largely disappeared and the face of Lancashire took on a new look. Though perhaps less obvious, the process initiated on Martin Mere was as important to the county's economic future as the revolution in textile manufacture that was occurring at the same time and is the subject of the next essay.

CHAPTER 10

Hall i'th'Wood, Samuel Crompton and the Industrial Revolution

T UCKED AWAY ON THE FRINGES of Bolton is a house which, even if it is not so architecturally distinguished as others we have discussed, has a significance in the history not only of Lancashire, but of Britain and the world, which might be expected to make it a place of pilgrimage. However, it remains little known and untroubled by hordes of visitors. Its fame rests on the accident of history that, in the years of its decline and decay, it became the home of an untutored genius who was to revolutionise the world around him. It is in many ways a sad and ironic story of inventive genius and missed opportunities, of trust and deceit, and of a malign fate that dogged the footsteps of the inventor with a dreadful persistence.

Hall i'th'Wood, its rustic name belying its modern surroundings of a major paper mill and a housing estate of the 1960s, dates from the second half of the fifteenth century. It was probably built circa 1480. The original builder was Lawrence Brownlow, a successful clothier. Clothiers, at this time, were the men who bought the cloth made by the independent textile workers, and saw to its transport and sale in the appropriate markets. In the early years of the development of the Lancashire textile trade they were not involved in commissioning work or in the supply of raw materials. Brownlow had been successful in his business and wished to demonstrate that success by building himself a new house. Its design was typical of the middle-ranking houses of the period, with a communal living room or hall. Probably there were wings attached to the main hall, containing the kitchen and service rooms at one end and the family rooms at the other. Traces of the family wing can be seen intermingled with the next, Elizabethan, phase of building.

The prosperity of the Brownlows continued over the next three generations and in 1591 Lawrence's great grandson, also a Lawrence, built the cross-wing at the eastern end of the house and set at right angles to the main axis. This wing contained a withdrawing room or parlour and a bedroom or chamber with a loft above it. The loft was probably used either for storage or as accommodation for children or servants. By this time changes in fashion – or the

Hall i'th'Wood, watercolour by J. Nash. This rather romantic and idealised painting was probably intended to show the house as it might have been at the time the Cromptons rented a tenement there. It shows two of the three major building phases of the house. In the foreground is the timber-framed original Brownlow dwelling, while to the left is the porch and the wing added in the post-Civil War period by Alexander Norris. The rural setting shown in this painting is a strong evocation of the origin of the name of the house.

greater prosperity of the Brownlows – required building in stone. This Elizabethan wing is not easy to see and it is necessary to make one's way round the back of the house to appreciate it. The windows are square headed with a drip mould over them and on the first floor the bed chamber has a eight-light mullioned and transomed window. On the east end of the house a privy is cantilevered out from the chamber wall.

Shortly after building this extension to their house the Brownlow family fell on hard times when, for some unknown reason, their business collapsed. They were forced to put the house on the market, and it was bought by another Bolton clothier, Christopher Norris. He needed to borrow £2,000 from his son Alexander to complete the purchase, and when Christopher died in 1639 Hall i'th'Wood became the property of Alexander Norris. At the time the Bolton area was one of the strongholds of Puritanism in the North West and was known as the 'Geneva of the North'. The town gave unconditional support to the parliamentary cause in the county. It successfully resisted royalist attacks until 1644, when it was stormed by the troops of Prince Rupert with great loss of life and property. Foremost among the Bolton men was Norris, who worked

in the treasury of the county and was responsible for the confiscation and sale of royalist estates. By some strange chance while, or shortly after, he had carried out these responsibilities Norris was able to build a whole new wing on to Hall i'th'Wood. Constructed in stone, it comprised an imposing two storey entrance porch, a parlour on the first floor and a large dining room on the ground floor.

The days when a master and his household ate together in the hall were gone, and the hall was modified to become a kitchen and servants' dining room. Access to the new wing involved the construction of an elaborately carved staircase with the balusters and newels turned in decorative patterns. Nothing was spared in the building of this new extension to the house, as Norris asserted his increased social status. The exterior of this wing is well endowed with those curious pyramids, obelisks and spheres of stone which were used in the first half of the seventeenth century as the outward and obvious signs of a gentry house.

The rooms as we see them today are the result of the extensive restoration of the house by Lord Leverhulme in the early part of the twentieth century. The house, long in the hands of tenants, during the nineteenth century had fallen into dereliction and decay. In 1899 Viscount Leverhulme, the Bolton born, millionaire manufacturer of Sunlight Soap, bought the remains of the house and in 1900 gave it to Bolton Corporation together with a - considerable sum of money for its restoration. During the repairs that were carried out the rooms were restored to something resembling their original appearance.

Hall i'th'Wood.
This early nineteenth-century depiction of the house emphasises the elaborate timberwork of the original Brownlow house and gives a less romanticised view of the house than that shown by Nash. It bears a close resemblance to the picture by Selim Rothwell in its realistic treatment of the environs of the house.
PHOTOGRAPH, AUTHOR

Lord Leverhulme continued to buy furniture for the hall until his death in 1925 and much of the fine furniture and furnishings in the house are the product of his generosity. However, more far-reaching work was needed as floors, ceilings and wall panelling had been destroyed. To rectify this damage suitable examples were sought around the country and either purchased or replicas made. Therefore, today, the panelling is correct in period but not of local manufacture: that in the withdrawing room is from Ashford in Kent, and in the dining room from a house at Buntingford in Hertfordshire. The plaster ceilings, too, are copies of mid-seventeenth-century examples. One is a reproduction of a ceiling at Chastleton manor in Oxfordshire and the other is based on a ceiling in the Old Woolpack Inn in Bolton.

The place of the Norris family in Lancashire society was firmly established in 1654 when Alexander's daughter married John Starkie of Huntroyd. The Starkies, too, had been in the forefront of parliamentary activity in the county and this was probably a political as much as a romantic marriage. It certainly proved deeply unhappy. As part of her marriage settlement she was given the reversion of Hall i'th'Wood, and for a time it was part of the Starkie estates. The house was used by her son periodically but by the early eighteenth century was considered old fashioned and uncomfortable and was let out in tenements: the gentry no longer wished to live there.

The Norris Dining Room Hall i'th'Wood. This room on the first floor of the stone block is one of those restored and refurbished by Viscount Leverhulme. Though not all the material is original the effect is a realistic recreation of a room of the mid-seventeenth century.

Less than a mile from Hall i'th'Wood is a remarkable survival, Firwood Fold, which is now preserved as a conservation area. It is a rare and almost untouched example of the type of hamlet in which many Lancashire people lived in the seventeenth and eighteenth centuries. A dozen or so houses – part farm, part workshop – are built round a central paved or cobbled area. In the eighteenth century it housed a community which tilled the surrounding lands but was also heavily involved in the spinning and weaving of cloth. It is difficult to know which of these was the primary employment and it probably differed from family to family and from year to year. The oldest of the cottages, stone built, thatched and of mid-seventeenth-century date, was the home in 1753 of the Crompton family.

They had come down in the world. Their ancestors owned the original Firwood Farm, but that had been lost in the previous generation and now they merely farmed some of the land as tenants. It was in the cottage that Samuel, the only boy among their three children, was born in December 1753. When he was five the family moved to occupy one of the tenements at Hall i'th'Wood.

However, their new home brought misfortune. Shortly afterwards the father died, leaving the mother to bring up the children. Times were hard but Mrs Crompton made every effort to earn an adequate income. She continued farming the patch of land they retained, she was famous for the quality of the butter she made, and at Hall i'th'Wood she had hives of bees in the garden and sold honey. But the main source of income was the cloth that she and an elderly crippled uncle, Alexander, made. Mrs Crompton was held in high regard by her neighbours and was appointed as overseer of the poor. This post made her the executive for the poor law administration of the township, responsible for the collection of the poor rate and the disbursement of payments to the

South front, Hall i'th'Wood. Two of the most important stages in the building of Hall i'th'Wood can be seen here. The right-hand gable marks the Great Hall of the house built by Lawrence Brownlow in about 1480. The elaborate and highly decorative timber-framing is typical of the district and the period. The complete change in style that took place between the building of the original house and its enlargement by Alexander Norris is clearly exemplified by the porch and family rooms added by him immediately after the Civil War.

PHOTOGRAPH, AUTHOR

Elizabethan wing and the Norris additions. The sharp contrast in styles between the Elizabethan wing on the left and the Norris additions to the house is apparent. However, Norris, building in the Restoration period, was apparently a man of conservastive tastes. His porch and wing are of a design that might have been used 50 years earlier. The new ideas beginning to permeate taste can be seen exemplified in buildings such as the 1662 wing at Rufford (see page 199) or even more remarkably at Astley Hall near Chorley refurbished in or about 1653 (see page 244).

PHOTOGRAPH, AUTHOR

poor and needy. It carried a small salary and perhaps partly as a result of this she was able to keep Samuel at school until the unusually late age of sixteen. However, much of his time out of school was spent helping her spin cotton yarn on a sixteen spindle jenny.

The jenny, a crude hand-operated machine, was the first of the great eighteenth-century spinning inventions which were to revolutionise textile production. It had been devised between 1764 and 1768 by James Hargreaves, a weaver of Stanhill near Blackburn, but was not patented until 1770. It was based on the cottage spinning-wheel previously in use but was able to spin a number of threads because the yarns, instead of being pulled out by the spinner's fingers, were held in a moving carriage that slid along rails. At the same time, the spindles on the machine were turned through ninety degrees and were vertical, rather than horizontal as they were on the spinning wheel. Incidentally the name, around which several legends have arisen was derived from 'ginny', which was in turn a contraction of the word 'engine'. Though the jenny could produce a useful yarn, it was a yarn of coarse quality and not particularly strong.

The impetus for the improvement of spinning machines had come from a development in weaving which had taken place some thirty years before. John Kay was the son of a yeoman farmer of Walmersley near Bury. He was trained as a reed maker; that is, one who made the brass-wired combs which were used on looms to press together the fibres as a piece of cloth was woven. At this time (*circa* 1730) two factors were combining to put pressure on the textile industry to increase production. The first was the increase in exports to all parts of the world as the British commercial empire expanded. The second was the rising demand at home resulting from the increase in population and the greater prosperity of the people, who demanded more and different types of cloth.

The manufacture of cloth is divided into three major activities. The first of these is the preparation of yarn. This involves the process of carding – combing the fibres to remove dirt, knots and tangles. At the same time the wool, cotton or flax filaments are made to lie parallel with each other. This is a necessary preliminary to spinning, in which the separate fibres are made into a continuous thread. In spinning it is essential that two forces are simultaneously applied to the yarn. It must be twisted so that the separate components interlock. The tighter the twist, the stronger the yarn is. At the same time, it must be pulled out to the requisite length and fineness, this operation is known as 'drawing'. In all forms of spinning these are the basic requirements and the various machines, however simple or sophisticated, are designed to give these two motions.

The second stage is the conversion of the yarn into cloth either by weaving or knitting. Knitting was the first mechanised textile-manufacturing process, the knitting frame being designed and manufactured as early as 1589 by the Reverend William Lee. It was used mainly in the stocking industry of the East Midlands, and despite the introduction of the knitting frame in that district, hand-knitting remained an important trade in other parts of the country, especially in Yorkshire and Cumbria. Weaving, in which two sets of threads running at right angles to each other were interlaced, was carried out on a wooden frame, known as a loom. The fixed set of threads, the 'warp', was

The Great Hall, Hall i'th'Wood. Originally the main communal living and eating room of the Brownlow household, by the mid-seventeenth century this fine room had been reduced to the status of a servants' hall. Its present appearance reminds us of the sparse furnishings and absence of comfort in early Stuart houses. In those times chairs were a rarity and reserved for the most important members of the family, while others sat on stools or benches.

stretched across the frame vertically. The weaver (or as they were frequently called using an older term, webster) passed the movable or 'weft' threads alternately over and under the warp, using a large wooden needle or shuttle. By the eighteenth century hand-looms were considerably more elaborate than this description implies, but the basic principles were unaltered.

The final stage of cloth manufacture was appropriately known as 'finishing' and gave the requisite colour and texture to the cloth. Though the details varied according to the effect required, finishing involved such processes as bleaching, dyeing, fulling and raising the cloth – that is, creating a nap on the fabric. Whereas spinning and weaving were mainly domestic occupations, of necessity the finishing was usually carried out in small workshops.

In the early eighteenth century spinning, carding, and weaving depended on hand tools, including the simple spinning wheel and the handloom. It required the output of three spinners to maintain the productive capacity of one weaver working on a handloom. Often cloth was made by family groups, with the women and children carrying out the preparation and making of the yarn, (hence the derivation of the word 'spinster') while a male member of the household did the weaving. Over the years a balance between the number of spinners and weavers had been achieved, so that yarn and cloth production matched each other in a mutually sustaining relationship.

This equilibrium was destroyed in 1733, when John Kay devised his flying or wheeled shuttle. This incorporated two developments. First, instead of the

shuttle being slid across the taut warp threads, from hand to hand by the weaver, the Kay shuttle was driven from side to side of the loom by spring-loaded hammers. The second improvement was that the shuttle was fitted with wheels and ran in a trough or runway across the loom. This was especially important, as previously a single weaver could only make a piece of cloth as wide as the span of his arms – about 27 inches being usual. For greater widths two weavers had to be employed, passing the shuttle from one to another. Now, by using a flying shuttle 'broadcloth' could be produced at half the labour

John Kay, inventor of the flying shuttle. Born in 1704 at the Park, Walmersley, near Bury, Kay belonged to a prosperous yeoman family. By 1730 he was in business as a reed-maker in Bury and made significant improvements to that process. This was followed by the invention of the flying shuttle in 1733. In 1745 he perfected a mechanical small-wares loom. However, in 1753 his house was attacked by a mob and his property and machines destroyed. In disgust Kay emigrated to France, where there was considerable interest in new textile machinery, but he died there in obscurity.

PHOTOGRAPH COURTESY OF CHETHAM'S LIBRARY

charges. The flying shuttle increased the weaver's capacity both by the superior speed at which he could work and by the greatly increased width of cloth.

As the flying shuttle gradually came into general use the balance between spinning and weaving was destroyed. A fly-shuttle weaver could utilise the production of six or more spinners. For a time the spinners responded by increasing their workforce, but eventually the only way to meet demand was to find some means by which an individual spinner could produce more than one yarn at a time.

Various attempts were made to devise improved spinning machines, of which Hargreaves' jenny was one of the more successful. Most of these attempted improvements, like the jenny, tried to adapt the technology of the spinning wheel, which had limited potential. In the Midlands an entirely new principle of spinning was devised by Lewis Paul and John Wyatt. On their machine the essential stretching of the yarn or 'draught' was provided by passing the thread through a series of rollers turning at different speeds. The machines were relatively successful, but this did not prevent their factory becoming bankrupt about 1753. Some of their machines were then sold to a Lancashire spinner and set up at Brock Mill near Wigan, which can claim to be the first spinning-mill to operate in the county.

There is no proof, but it is likely that these machines had been seen by, and inspired, the man who was to be responsible for the next step forward. Richard Arkwright was born in Preston in 1732, one of a large and impoverished family of thirteen children. He became a barber and wig maker and after his marriage to a daughter of Robert Holt of Bolton removed to that town. How and why he became involved in attempts to develop a new spinning engine, and the sources of his inspiration, are obscure and a subject of controversy. In 1769 Arkwright patented a new machine called the 'water frame' which, like the spinning engine of Wyatt and Paul used the roller principle. It may be that in his travels to purchase hair and to attend on clients Arkwright had visited Brock Mill, and seen the newly installed machines. Subsequently there were furious arguments and law suits about the origin of Arkwright's invention, but what is important is not its technical detail but the way in which it was to revolutionise textile production.

Since the time of the Brownlow family the role of the clothier had changed. Cloth was still made on the domestic system by operatives who worked in their homes but the type of fabric made was commissioned by a clothier. He also controlled the supply of raw materials, transport and the marketing of the finished product. The machines used were small, and easily made by the local carpenter and blacksmith, and the power was provided by the operative's muscles. The water frame was a large machine and required an external source of power.

At first Arkwright used a donkey walking a circular track, but soon substituted a water wheel – later steam power was utilised. The size and expense of the machine, and the necessity for a source of power, ensured that the water frame could not be used in the domestic system but required special buildings and, therefore, a work force brought in from outside. The textile mill had been born. Arkwright may not have been a particularly original engineer and inventor, but he was a shrewd businessman who saw the potential of the machine and realised the changes in the

Samuel Crompton. This portrait in oils is by Charles Allingham, about whom little is known other than he was a peripatetic portrait painter working between 1802 and 1812. At this time Crompton's prospects seemed brightest with the imminent prospect of the government's reward. Even at a period of hope the painting emphasises Crompton's sensitive, withdrawn and introspective character – even in a picture he avoids direct contact with the observer.

structure of the industry which it would bring about. To obtain the necessary capital to exploit his machine he went into partnership with a wealthy Derbyshire clothier, Jedediah Strutt. In 1776 the partnership built its first mill, situated at Cromford near Derby. The success of this project led to the building of several other mills in Staffordshire and Derbyshire. In 1777 Arkwright returned to Lancashire, and built a mill at Birkacre, near Chorley, which was powered by the waters of the river Yarrow. A few years later his company constructed a large mill in Miller's Lane, Manchester. Most of these early mills were still situated in rural locations. They were often built in valleys on the moorland edge, where cheap land and abundant water power were available, and so were often in quite remote areas. This made it difficult to find an adequate supply of labour, and soon villages began to grow at the mill gates. Arkwright was one of the first mill owners to provide accommodation for his workers.

The demands of fashion, and the greater availability of cheap cotton brought from India and the West Indies, placed the emphasis of much of this new production on cotton cloth rather than wool or linen. Cotton spinning had initially proved difficult, but gradually the techniques had been evolved. Although at first the cloths of Lancashire were mixtures of cotton and linen or cotton and wool, by the early decades of the eighteenth century pure cotton calicoes were being made. In 1721 this trade had been given protection from the import of Indian calicoes, but it had proved impossible to spin yarn fine enough to reproduce the delicate muslins, which were still imported, and sold at very high prices. It was apparent that anyone who could perfect a way of spinning a very fine cotton yarn would have a fortune within his grasp.

At this point (*circa* 1777) we can return to Samuel Crompton, who was now working full-time in the family's cloth-making enterprise. He was constantly hindered in his work by the inefficiency of the jenny on which he was trying to spin yarn, and this annoyed him greatly. As a relatively small and hand-powered machine, the jenny enjoyed great favour among the Lancashire spinners, who could make use of it in their homes – in contrast to the massive Arkwright frames. However, jenny yarn was coarse and soft and subject to frequent breakage when it was spun. To reduce these irritations Crompton began to contemplate making modifications to the jenny. He seems to have begun work when he was about twenty-two, in 1775, and for four or five years to have tried various experiments. He had no training as a craftsman, though obviously he had an aptitude for this type of work. He lacked tools as well as training, and according to accounts of his life took a job as a violinist in the Bolton theatre orchestra, having first made his own fiddle and taught himself to play it. The 1s. 6d. a night earned in the pit was spent on buying equipment and materials for use on his experimental machines. Crompton himself described this period of experiment 'as a continual endeavour to realise a more perfect principle of spinning. Though often baffled I as often renewed the attempt, and at last succeeded to my utmost desire, at the expense of every shilling I had in the world'.

Success came in 1779. He had decided to combine the two methods of drawing the yarn then in use – the moving carriage of the jenny and the rollers of the water frame. On Crompton's new machine, after passing through rollers, the thread was further drawn out by a moving bar to which it was clamped. It was this use of a hybrid design which gave it the name 'mule' (which eventually became the recognised designation of the machine): it was a cross-breed between the two previous machines. It was also known in its early period as the 'muslin wheel' or the 'Hall i'th'Wood wheel'.

Crompton worked on his machine in secret and often at night. The strange noises and shaded lights had given rise to stories of hauntings in the old house but probably many of his neighbours knew that Crompton, a secretive and reserved man, was working on some new device. However, there was amazement and consternation when he offered the first products of his new machine for sale. Yarn of such fineness and strength had not been seen before, and it could command a very high price. Later, Crompton wrote of how he obtained 14s. a pound for the spinning and preparation of No 40s but after a short time he got 25s. a pound for the spinning and preparation of 60s. He then spun a small quantity of No 80, to show that it was not impossible to spin yarn of that fineness 'with the greatest ease'. For the spinning and preparation of this he got 42s. a pound. These numbers (40, 60, 80 etc.) refer to the 'count', the fineness of the yarn. It was determined by the number of 'hanks' of yarn of 840 yards length that can be obtained from a pound of raw material. Now that he could produce such high counts fame and fortune seemed just around the corner, as it was these very fine threads which were needed to produce the gauzy cloths that were in such demand. With his expectations of prosperity raised Samuel ventured to marry a Miss Mary Pimlott, the daughter of an impoverished West India merchant and described as 'A handsome, dark haired

Contrasting timber work at Hall i'th'Wood. Both these photographs are of the framing of the west front. The plain herring bones are located above the ground-floor windows, while the barbed timbers are from the upper stages of the gable where they are more visible to passers-by. The infill was often white or colour-washed to protect the vulnerable daub from rain and the depredations of animals. Timber was not usually treated and was left to weather.

PHOTOGRAPHS COURTESY OF BOLTON MUSEUM AND ART GALLERY

woman of middle size and erect carriage'. She had been forced to earn her livelihood as a spinner at Turton because of her father's circumstances.

No sooner was the prototype of the 'mule' complete than it faced destruction. In 1779 a series of machine-breaking riots took place in Lancashire as the hand operatives became afraid that the new spinning machines would deprive them of their livelihood. The attentions of the rioters were not only directed at the water frames, which they saw as the chief danger, but also at those using other machines in the preparation of yarn. These innovations were seen as detrimental to the domestic trade at a time of recession. The rioting was widespread and damage was done to machines throughout the county. Serious incidents occurred at Aspul, Birkacre (where Arkwright's mill was destroyed), Westleigh, Worsley, Golborne, Little Bolton, Pemberton, Wensleyfold, Blackburn and Balderstone. A contemporary account says

> In the course of a few days they pulled down and broke in pieces several hundred of the Carding, Doubling, and Twisting engines and large Jennies; and being irritated by the assistants of the owners of the Patent Machines shooting one [of the rioters] and wounding many of their fellow sufferers both men and women, they unhappily set fire to and burned down one of the large patent machines [Birkacre]. Among the other places attacked were premises at Preston, Altham and Folds near Bolton.

Folds is very near Hall i'th'Wood, and no doubt Samuel was well aware of what was going on. Conscious that it was known that he had a mysterious spinning machine, he feared a visit from the jubilant rioters. The mule was dismantled and parts hidden in the garrets of the house. A trap door in what is known today as Crompton's Room is thought to be the entrance to the place of concealment. In the nineteenth century a Mr Bromeley recorded how he was shown the trap and told the story by Crompton himself. After the trouble had died down the machine was reassembled, and production resumed.

Crompton was a mechanical and inventive genius but he seems to have been totally unworldly and devoid of any business sense. He also lacked the vital factor of good fortune and was continually dogged, throughout his life by mischances. For example, there is a story that about this time Arkwright, intrigued by the stories of Crompton's fine thread, visited him. The two men had a distant relationship, Samuel's wife being a remote cousin of Arkwright's first wife.

The wealthy manufacturer used this relationship as a pretext for the visit, but almost certainly he wanted to investigate the machine. It is also suggested that he had it in mind to offer Crompton a partnership should the machine live up to the current reports. They did not meet, as Crompton was out collecting the poor rate on his mother's behalf. If they had done so it might have resulted in an operation in which Crompton's technical skills would have been combined with Arkwright's business acumen. This would have provided a considerably better future for the Cromptons.

Instead of founding a successful business Samuel found himself bombarded with enquiries and offers and spies, one of whom is reputed to have hidden in the attic for three days watching the Cromptons at work through a hole he had bored with a gimlet. Others brought ladders and tried to see through the windows so that Crompton had to erect a screen to conceal the machine. In spite of all this activity and interest he seems to have had no grasp of the potential value of his invention, or of the urgent need to protect it by patent.

The constant badgering had serious effects on Samuel, a shy and retiring man who found contact with strangers taxing and difficult. As he wrote in a later letter to a friend 'I found to my sorrow I was not calculated to contend with men of the world; neither did I know there was such a thing as protection for me on earth. I found I was as unfit for the task that was before me as a child of two years to contend with a disciplined army'. The family moved away from Hall i'th'Wood to another farm, Oldhams, a few miles away. Of this period Crompton subsequently wrote,

> During this time I married and commenced spinner [sic] altogether. But a few months reduced me to the cruel necessity either of destroying my machine altogether or giving it up to the public. To destroy it I could not think of; to give up that for which I had laboured so long was cruel. I had no patent nor the means of purchasing one. In preference to destroying it I gave it to the public.

His claim to be unable to afford a patent is possibly only part of the story. Probably the truth is that he was unaware of the procedure and lacked the confidence to enquire.

Views of Hall i'th'Wood. Both of these pictures show different aspects of the west front of the house. Most marked is the difference between the extravagant timber framing of the hall wing and the much more restrained masonry of the Norris wing, though the influence of the Gothic style can still be seen. The way in which the stonework of the Norris porch has been integrated into the timber framing of the original house is clear in this picture. The presence of the trees and flower beds does much to soften the severity of the lines.

In this account Crompton does not tell of how he consulted a Mr Pilkington, a cotton manufacturer of some importance and standing in Bolton, who offered him the 'completely disinterested' advice that he should make his invention public. In return Pilkington undertook to raise a subscription among the main manufacturers and eighty of them agreed to pay a total of £66 6s. 6d. On the strength of this verbal promise alone, Crompton not only explained the principle but actually handed over the prototype. His naiveté was such that he did this before he had received the money. It took him many years to extract what he was owed from the subscription, and he only ever realised about £60 of it.

He used the money to build a new and slightly enlarged machine with fifty-two rather than forty-eight spindles. Among the manufacturers who did pay, and who tried to befriend Crompton, was Sir Robert Peel, the father of the future prime minister. Crompton took offence at what he saw as Peel's patronage and became very touchy and reluctant to be involved.

In 1812 Peel raised the issue of Crompton in parliament pointing out that although by his invention a whole new industry and considerable wealth had been created, Crompton himself was living in virtual poverty. Peel was supported in his efforts by Mr Blackburne, one of the other Lancashire MPs, and they had some success: the government was persuaded to make an ex gratia payment. It would have been difficult for them to ignore the figures presented on Crompton's behalf: that there were 4.2 million mule spindles in use, compared with 310,516 water frame and 155,880 jenny spindles. It must be admitted that these figures, gathered on Crompton's behalf probably underestimate the numbers of alternative machines that were operating. Crompton himself was called to London to meet the two MPs and discuss the amount of the award. As they were talking in the lobby the Prime Minister, Spencer Perceval, approached and, not recognising Crompton, said 'How much are we going to pay Crompton?', and suggested the sum of £20,000. Deferentially Crompton moved away while the discussion took place, but he had gone no distance when a shot rang out and, pushing through the turmoil, he discovered that Perceval had been shot dead by William Bellingham, a failed Liverpool merchant trading with Russia who blamed government policy for his bankruptcy. When parliament returned to the matter a month later, the sum of only £5,000 was awarded. Even then Crompton's ill fortune was not ended: most of this money was invested in a bleach works but due to his lack of business sense this too failed.

In the later years of his life he was reduced to such poverty that the consciences of the mill owners using the mule were touched. A subscription was raised to buy an annuity of £63. On this modest amount, and with what he could raise by doing various other odd jobs, Crompton lived until 1827. Some years later, in a final irony, the Bolton mill owners who had exploited him shamelessly in life raised a subscription of £2,000 to erect a statue to him in the town.

In the form in which he invented it the mule was still a small, hand-operated machine, though very soon the larger manufacturers were using massive hand-operated machines with as many as three hundred spindles. Many

Handloom weaver's cottage, Diggle. The rapid growth of demand for cloth, following the improvements of spinning machinery, required that houses should be designed to accommodate a loom shop for hand weaving. The weaver required good daylight so the maximum area of windows were provided. As the residents of the house might not be the weavers, a separate entrance was furnished by outside steps and there might also be a room devoted to storage of raw materials and finished goods.

PHOTOGRAPH, AUTHOR

improvements and additions had to be made to the basic design until it came to dominate the spinning industry. Three of the first improvers to work on the mule were Henry Stones of Horwich, Baker of Bury, and Hargreaves of Toddington. In 1790, at New Lanark Mills in Scotland, William Kelly adapted the machine to water power and at about the same time Wright in Manchester devised the double mule, which became the backbone of the Lancashire spinning industry. In 1825 Richard Roberts of the Manchester engineers Sharp Roberts and Co. perfected the self-acting mule and 520 of these, carrying 200,000 spindles, were in use in the county by 1834.

The impetus to the improvement and devising of spinning machines had been the need to satisfy the greatly increased capacity of the weavers who used the flying shuttle. With the rapid expansion of spinning capacity following the invention of the machines a new imbalance was created. The capacity of the spinners outstripped the ability of the weavers to turn yarn into cloth. The clamour now was for weaving to be accelerated in order to use this surplus output. It was deemed impossible for weaving to be mechanised, and so frantic efforts were made to find new handloom weavers. For a time these efforts were successful, and the handloom weavers, whose skills were at a premium, were able to demand increased payment for their work. For a brief period the handloom weavers found themselves the aristocrats of the textile trade. One, writing in later life of this time, said 'With old loom-shops insufficient, every lumbern room [sic] even old barns, carthouses, and outbuildings of any description were repaired, windows broke through blank walls and all were fitted up for loom-shops. This source of making room being at last exhausted, new weavers cottages with loom-shops rose in every direction'. A startling example of this phase of activity was encountered at Shaw Lee, Diggle, a hand-loom weaving community, where, during this period one dwelling was described as having been converted from a 'Necessary House', or privy. Radcliffe, the source quoted above, continues to describe the prosperity of the weavers.

> In these years [1788–1800] the operative weavers on machine yarns, both as cottagers and small farmers, even with three or four times their former rents … might be truely said to be placed in a higher state of wealth, peace and godliness by the great demand for, and the high price of their labour than they had ever before experienced. Their dwellings and small gardens, clean and neat – all the family well clad – the men with a watch in their pocket and the women dressed to their own fancy.

Doubtless there is a element of nostalgia in this account, but its general accuracy is attested by the comfortable stone-built weavers' cottages that crowd many Pennine villages.

However, nemesis was on hand in the unlikely presence of Edmund Cartwright, a clergyman who lived in Kent but had Lancashire origins. He tells the story of how he stopped at an inn in Macclesfield when returning to his parish, and fell into conversation with some Manchester merchants who were bemoaning the absence of improvement in weaving. He raised the suggestion that weaving, too, could be mechanised.

> The Manchester gentlemen unanimously agreed that the thing was imprac-tical, and in defence of their opinion they adduced arguments which I was certainly incompetent to answer, or even comprehend, being totally igno-rant of the subject, having never, at that time, seen a person weave.

His interest in the subject aroused, Cartwright returned to his vicarage and gave the matter some thought.

> In plain weaving … there could only be three movements, which were to follow each other in succession, there would be little difficulty in producing and repeating them. Full of ideas, I immediately employed a carpenter and

Crompton Cottage, Firwood Fold, the birthplace of Samuel Crompton. Many of the earliest concentrations of textile manufacture were centred in the 'yard' or 'fold' surrounding a farm. The occupants of the farm arranged the conversion of existing buildings or the building of new accommodation for their workers. At one time the Cromptons had worked Firwood Farm and this was their home where Samuel was born on 3 December 1753. Firwood Fold is now a conservation area in which this sixteenth-century stone built farmhouse is surrounded by a square of later textile workers' cottages, the whole giving an impression of life in the eighteenth century.

PHOTOGRAPH COURTESY OF LEN FENDER

a smith to carry them into effect. As soon as the machine was finished I got a weaver to put in the warp ... to my delight a piece of cloth, such as it was, was produced.

So in 1785 the automatic or power loom was invented. It was far from being the answer to the problem, as Cartwright was the first to admit, and it was only after a further two years of development work that he took out his patent and submitted his work to the arbitrament of commerce by opening a weaving mill at Doncaster, a venture that proved disastrous.

The power loom eventually came to Lancashire in 1790 when Grimshaws of Gorton built a weaving mill at Knott Mill, Manchester, under licence from Cartwright. They tried to improve the machine but without much success. Over the next twenty years many eminent engineers made contributions to the development of the power loom and gradually it became more satisfactory. By 1813, 2,400 were in use nationally and they were the main target of the Luddite riots of 1812–14. Although mechanised looms were smashed at Westhoughton,

Middleton and other places, the new looms soon replaced handloom weaving in Lancashire for all except specialist fabrics. Handloom weaving of these persisted until the First World War in some parts of the county.

To trace the evolution of the factory system, and the creation of the great mill towns of Lancashire during the reign of King Cotton, might take us too far from our starting place at Hall i'th'Wood. So let us return to the house and to Crompton. Two men, Arkwright and Crompton, both associated with the Bolton area, did more than any others to create the new industrial society which emerged in the early nineteenth century. Arkwright's invention, the water frame, was of only temporary importance in itself but the imperatives that it set created the need to bring production out of the houses of the operatives and centre it in specialised buildings. Though at first these were in remote areas which provided good sites for water power, the transition to the use of steam engines made it important for the costs of fuel transport to be reduced. The newer mills were therefore built in areas nearer the coalfields.

The geography of Lancashire meant that they were situated on the plain, and nearer to the coast and the port of Liverpool which was the main source of their supplies of raw cotton. The flat plains of south-west Lancashire were ideal country for the development of improved transport links, and it is no accident that it was in these areas that the earliest developments of canal and rail transport took place. In these new locations textile production became an urban, rather than a rural, occupation. Arkwright foresaw the development of this pattern and, with his business sense, was able to exploit the new system. He died, rich, respected and titled, a tribute not so much to his engineering skills as to his commercial ability. Samuel Crompton was an inventor of genius and a talented technician but was totally lacking in the ability to develop and exploit his genius, he died, poor, neglected and ignored by those who benefitted from his invention.

Hall i'th'Wood can be seen as a link between the Lancashire of the Middle Ages, when the county was remote, underdeveloped, impoverished and neglected and the changes that were to metamorphose the region into the workshop of the world. Here, it can be claimed, the world's first industrial society had its origins. The impetus for this development came, at least partly, from the growth of a textile industry that came to dominate the economy of the county and of the nation. In the house at Hall i'th'Wood all theses changes are exemplified. The name suggests the medieval landscape, little modified by the hand of man; the house was built by a family engaged in the early textile trade; and in its period of decline as a house it was the home of the man who transformed his world. Traditionally it is artists who starve in a garret, and not the inventors of machines which created a world centre of industry and formed the nucleus of an industrial nation's economy. In the 1850s and 1860s half of England's exports were textiles and most of these were made in Lancashire on the machines that Crompton devised, but he, the inventor, had died, if not in a garret, certainly in depths of poverty and obscurity. It is a sad and poignant story.

CHAPTER 11

Other Interesting Houses in Lancashire

I F YOU HAVE FOUND visiting or reading about these houses interesting, you might also like to explore the history and the architecture of some others located in the historic county of Lancashire. All the houses listed here are open to the public at some time during the year. The present visiting arrangements may be subject to change and a preliminary telephone call should always be made. Although every care has been taken in preparing this gazetteer, neither the author nor the publisher can be responsible for any errors or omissions.

Note: All the properties have adequate car parking facilities.
Admission charges. The amount of these is indicated by the £ sign which represents the full adult charge. Concessions and party rates may be available.

> £:   Under £5
> ££:   £5–10
> £££:   £10–15

In the directions to each house a four-figure grid reference is given.

Name of house: *Gawthorpe Hall*
Address: Padiham, Lancashire BB12 8UA.
Owners: National Trust, operated by Lancashire County Council.
Locations and directions: Located 1 mile east of the centre of Padiham. The entrance is on A671 east of the town. GR SD 8034
Admission charges: Yes £ (National Trust members free)
Opening hours: Hall open 1 April–31 October, not open Monday or Friday (except Good Friday and Bank Holiday Mondays). Open 13.00–17.00. Gardens daily 10.00–18.00
Disabled access: Grounds only
Restaurant/tea room: Yes
Telephone number: 01282 771004
Email: rpmgaw@smtp.nttrust.org.uk

The Shuttleworth family built this spectacular house between 1600 and 1605 to indicate their increased wealth and status, arising from a successful involvement

Gawthorpe Hall. Though the basic shape and plan of the house derives from the original design of *c*. 1600, with a central core surrounded by symmetrical wings, a great deal of detail dates from the restoration by Sir Charles Barry, 1849–51. This architect was anxious to emphasise those things which he felt gave an air of antiquity. The entrance porch was remodelled, the pierced parapet with its bogus motto added, and the central tower with the disguised chimney stacks was raised in height.

in the law and the church. The originator of the plan was the Rev. Lawrence Shuttleworth. The family at that time were largely based at Smithills Hall but owned an earlier and almost derelict tower house at Gawthorpe. It is thought that the architect employed by the family may have been Robert Smythson, the architect of Hardwick Hall and one of a family of masons and designers who were bringing in many new ideas of domestic design. Gawthorpe's plan of a central doorway, flanked by two equal piles of rooms all built around a central staircase tower reflects the latest design trends of the period and must have amazed local contemporaries. The building of Gawthorpe is especially interesting as a very complete set of accounts survive. These are published by the Chetham Society (Old Series vol. 35 (1856), vol. 41 (1856) and vol. 3 (1857)). These accounts which cover the period from 1582 until 1621 are unusually full and include not only details of the building of Gawthorpe, but domestic and estate expenses for Gawthorpe, Smithills and the Shuttleworth's rented house in London. Taken together the accounts give a vivid picture of life in a Lancashire country house in the early modern period.

From these records it can be seen that in the early Jacobean period Gawthorpe was a centre for the theatre in Lancashire and it was on numerous occasions visited by some of the top London companies of players while they were making their winter tours. It is suggested that the Great Hall of the house was designed to provide accommodation and staging for these events and that Shakespeare might have played here.

The Shuttleworths were heavily involved in the Civil War when Colonel Richard Shuttleworth was one of the most prominent parliamentarian soldiers and administrators during the period of the Commonwealth.

By the mid-nineteenth century the house was in a state of disrepair when it became the home of Sir Richard Kay-Shuttleworth, the educational pioneer. He called in Sir Charles Barry, the designer of the Palace of Westminster and one of the most celebrated of the Victorian 'Gothic' architects to undertake a reconstruction and refurbishment of the house between 1849 and 1851. This gave the house its present appearance in which elements of the romantic are emphasised, such as the bogus 'medieval' motto inscribed on the tower, and in a number of other places. The last of the family to live in the house, Rachel Kay-Shuttleworth, was an enthusiastic collector of needlework and her collection is now displayed in a number of rooms.

Though much altered in the Barry restoration, the house still includes three spectacular rooms from the earlier period: the Great Hall with its screens, gallery and dais; the Parlour with spectacular and lavish plasterwork frieze and ceiling; and, on the first floor, the Long Gallery, again with highly decorated plaster. This room is also used to house a collection of seventeenth-century portraits on loan from the National Portrait Gallery.

Name of house: *Hoghton Tower*
Address: Hoghton, Preston PR5 OSH
Owners: Sir Bernard Hoghton
Location and directions: Located on A675 6 miles south of Preston or via
   M65 junction 3. GR SD 6226
Admission charges: Yes £
Opening hours: Contact house
Disabled access: Very limited in the house, grounds available
Restaurant/tea room: Yes
Telephone number: 01254 852 986
Email: mail@hoghtontower.co.uk

Situated on a steep crag overlooking much of the south-west Lancashire plain Hoghton Tower has one of the most imposing appearances of any house in Lancashire. The site attracted an early fortified house which was one of the homes of the Hoghton family. However, during the Elizabethan period and possibly earlier they preferred their house at Lea near Kirkham. The family at this time were among the most prominent of the recusant squires of the county.

In 1565 Sir Thomas Hoghton decided to re-build the old house on its crag. The new house which emerged was distributed around two courtyards, of which the upper contained a strong tower, which was destroyed, probably by an accidental explosion, when the house was captured by the parliamentarians in 1643.

In 1617 the house was the scene of a famous royal visit when King James I

Hoghton Tower. In this picture we see the sham military might of the entrance front to the lower courtyard of the Tower, which exploits the dramatic opportunities of its site on the crag. The apparently imposing battlements and walls are mainly decorative and the original fortifications stood within the upper courtyard prior to their destruction in the Civil war. Much of what is visible here is the result of the vigorous restoration programme of the nineteenth and early twentieth centuries.

PHOTOGRAPH COURTESY OF B. & N. DIXON

stayed there on his way south from Scotland. The occasion was marked by the most sumptuous feasting and revelry. According to legend it was on this occasion that the King knighted the loin of beef, thus creating 'Sirloin'. The Hoghtons had hoped to recoup some of the expense by selling the King a reputed alum mine at the foot of the crag, but he was uninterested and it was years before the family were free of debt. A detailed account of this visit when the drive was covered with scarlet velvet, can be read in the *Diary of Nicholas Assheton* (Chetham Society, old series, vol. 14 (1848)), in which the feasts and the hangovers that followed them are graphically described.

The owner of the house during the Civil War was Sir Gilbert de Hoghton, a Catholic and staunch supporter of the King, but his successor abandoned the family's traditional religious allegiance and the de Hoghtons became leaders of the Lancashire Nonconformists. In both 1715 and 1745 Sir Henry Hoghton was a leader of the government forces resisting the Jacobite incursions. The house was so much damaged in the Civil War that it was little used, and the family were based at Ribbleton Hall near Preston while the old house fell into disrepair until in the nineteenth and twentieth centuries strenuous efforts were made by the antiquarian Sir Henry de Hoghton to reclaim it and large sums of money were spent in gradually reconstructing much of the ruined parts, notably the lower courtyard, though the original tower, destroyed in the explosion was never replaced.

Visitors today can see the original Great Hall located in the upper court and according with the medieval design of a courtyard house. Various other rooms, most of which show evidence of the reconstruction of the house can be seen. These include the rooms occupied by King James and his favourite, George Villiers, the Duke of Buckingham. The cellars, which contain a deep well, can also be visited.

> Name of house: *Scarisbrick Hall*
> Address: Kingswood College, Scarisbrick near Ormskirk
> Owners: Kingswood College
> Location and directions: Located on the north side of the A570 half way
>   between Southport and Ormskirk. GR SD 3912
> Admission charges: Yes £
> Opening hours: It is open occasionally for visits. For details of visits
>   contact the Domestic Bursar
> Disabled access: Ground floor only
> Restaurant/tea room: No
> Telephone number: 01704 880200
> Email: kingswood@indschool.org

The family of Scarisbrick had lived on the same site for several centuries before the present house was built. They had always been an influential family in the south-west Lancashire region and had been involved in many ways in the running of the county. They were among the proprietors who supported the

attempt by Thomas Fleetwood in 1694 to drain the large post-glacial lake, Martin Mere, which filled much of the land between Ormskirk and the present site of Southport (see Rufford Old Hall, chapter 9). The limited success of this scheme inspired Thomas Eccleston, who though a Scarisbrick by birth, had adopted the Eccleston name in order to inherit their estates, to carry out more extensive drainage works which resulted in some of the area of the Mere becoming valuable agricultural land. This and other successful investments created a vast fortune for his successor, Charles, who was reputed to be the richest commoner in the country, a fact which perhaps explains his often very eccentric behaviour.

Our knowledge of the old hall is limited to one sketch made in the early nineteenth century which shows a sprawling house, presumably built around a courtyard, with a great hall, numerous mullioned windows and what appear to be extensions built in the seventeenth century. The picture gives little information about the materials used to build this house which appears to be covered in a rendering. It is likely that the house was of timber-frame construction and some evidence of this has been uncovered.

Flushed with his new fortune, Thomas Scarisbrick employed Humphrey Repton to landscape the park in 1803 and in 1815 decided to modernise the house. The architect was either Thomas Rickman or John Foster the younger of Liverpool. Some of their work can still be seen in a new west wing, but the major project was encasing other parts of the house within a stone carapace. On the death of Thomas he was succeeded by his brother Charles whose fortune was augmented by money derived from the development of the new resort of Southport. Charles was obsessed with the new romantic attachment to the Middle Ages and in 1836 employed a largely unknown young architect, Augustus Welby Pugin, to design a house which would hark back to the medieval splendours of the Scarisbrick family, provide a fitting setting for Charles' collection of English and European medieval wood carving, and represent the strong devotion of the family to the Roman Catholic church. It was on his design for Scarisbrick that Pugin's rise as one of the great Victorian architects was founded.

The result is a dazzling house which displays the skill and originality of its architect who was then only in his mid-twenties but to the modern taste seems almost psychotic in its bewildering complexity. At every opportunity the heritage of the family is driven home by the innumerable heraldic symbols and monograms. Nevertheless the opulence and craftsmanship in the Pugin rooms is breathtaking. Highlights of a visit are the Great Hall, the King's Room and the Red Drawing Room where the contrast between the full-blooded style of Pugin with the rather anaemic efforts of the architects of the earlier alterations in the former library is striking.

Charles Scarisbrick spent his last years in total seclusion, not even speaking to his steward, and died in 1860, leaving the house unfinished. During his last years he had tried to prevent the estates passing to his sister, Anne Lady Hunloke, but without success. Lady Anne seems to have been as obsessive as her brother and began building work again. By this time A.W. Pugin was dead and her choice as his successor was his son, Edward Welby Pugin. Between them they produced a plan for the east wing even more extravagant than the previous work. Their close co-operation is commemorated in a stained-glass window on the staircase in the wing. The main feature was a tower which surpassed the modest effort of his father – which has been seen as a prototype for the Clock Tower at Westminster. While the first Pugin was a keen student of the archaeological Gothic, the son was freer in his treatment and more inclined towards the Hammer Horror school. The east wing is dominated by flying, predatory birds which perch on every conceivable pinnacle, presumably a reference to the falcon of the Scarisbrick arms.

After her death, Lady Anne's property passed to her daughter, who had married a French-Spanish aristocrat, the Marquis de Castlela. Their adopted son was killed in the First World War, and on the death of the Marquesa much of the property was sold off. The Hall became a part of the Church of England Teacher Training College, St Katherine's, evacuated from Liverpool during the Second World War. On the return of the College to Liverpool the property was bought by the Oxley family who turned it into a boys' boarding school. In turn the school was amalgamated with a Southport school to form the present Kingswood College.

On the sale of the Hall following the departure of St Katherine's College some portions of the furnishings and rooms were bought by Lancashire County Council, although they remained in the house. Consequently, as the house contains publicly owned works, the house is required to open its doors to the public on occasions.

Name of house: *Astley Hall*

Address: Astley Park and Museum, Chorley, PR7 1NP

Owners: Chorley Borough Council

Location and directions: The park is located off the
  A5106 near the centre of Chorley or can be
  accessed from the A581 GR SD 5718

Admission charge: Yes £

Opening hours: April–October, Tuesday to Sunday
  12.00–17.00. Also open Bank Holiday Mondays

Disabled access: Very limited on ground floor only

Restaurant/tea room: No

Telephone number: 01257 515 555

Email address: www.astleyhall.co.uk

Overworked as the phrase 'hidden gem' may be, it can be appropriately applied to this house, owned by Chorley Council and tucked away in the middle of an extensive public park which is flanked by a large modern housing estate. The house was given to the Council by the last of its Tatton owners as a war memorial for the town, a function which it still fulfils, as in the house a room is devoted to the casualties of the First World War. Approaching through the park the visitor is confronted by a most unusual façade. The south front consists of a central doorway flanked by two strange and primitive Ionic columns. The door is set between two five-sided bays, almost totally glazed, which extend through three floors. On the third floor a continuous run of windows makes up one side of the long gallery. Above this is a parapet pierced by blind oval niches and crowned with a balustrade. Today the whole front is covered in a rather sombre cement rendering, although a painting in the house shows that it was originally built of a warm, red brick. The building history of the house is very complicated and does not seem to have ever been totally unravelled.

Broadly speaking, the core of the house was built about 1575 when the Charnock family, who had owned it ever since the fifteenth century, decided to make it their principal home. The first house was a conventional courtyard house built in the Lancashire timber-framed tradition. This courtyard still lies in the centre of the house but found itself overtaken by the startling developments which followed. The Charnocks were a family of moderate influence but like many of the county's gentry families proved stalwart in their adherence to the Roman Catholic faith. Several became priests and one was implicated in the Babbington plot to assassinate Queen Elizabeth I. During the Civil War they supported the king and suffered for his cause. The last of the family, Thomas, died in 1648 leaving the estates to his daughter who married Richard Brooke of the Norton Priory family. It seems that it was at this time that Astley went through its great transformation into a wonderful showpiece. It may be that this was the time when the extraordinary façade of the south wing was created but it was certainly the time when a transformation took place indoors. Nothing about the exterior prepares the visitor for what awaits them. The main

Astley Hall. The remarkable extent of the windows in this façade at Astley is what gives the house an appearance which is unique in Lancashire and unusual anywhere in England. Though a matter of some argument, this façade probably dates from the middle years of the seventeenth century when the remarkable refurbishment of the interior was carried out. The doorway is surrounded by a barbaric attempt to reproduce an Ionic entrance and the bay to the right probably occupies the site of the Great Hall's oriel window. The rendering of the walls is not original and the oldest painting of the Hall shows it to be built with a brick of soft, pinkish colour.

door leads directly into what was the great hall but is now an entrance chamber which extends through two floors. In the left-hand corner a wide, newel staircase with energetically carved balustrading of the 1660s winds upwards. A large fireplace with an exotic riot of pilasters stands opposite the door. But these are almost overlooked as the eye takes in the ceiling. Panelled by large beams it displays swags, fruits, cherubs, lovers' knots, heraldry of the Charnocks and the Brookes and extraordinary mouldings. The whole is in white, although all is not as it seems and not all is plaster; in some parts the putti are of lead and the coiled mouldings of the beams are twisted and painted leather, but nevertheless it is a tour de force.

However, the hall has not yet rendered up all its delights. The walls are panelled and within an arcaded framework are panels depicting a most eclectic collection of portraits of great men. These seems to date from the last years of the Charnock occupation of the Hall. One can discern some pattern in their selection in that several can be paired as adversaries, Tamerlane and Sultan Bajazet, Skanderberg and Mohammed II, Philip II, Queen Elizabeth, Francis Drake and the Earl of Leicester represent the almost contemporary war with Spain, Alexander Farnese and his opponent King Henry IV of France, Spinola and Gabor Belem, opponents in the Thirty Years War. Others are prominent in other fields, Columbus and Magellan represent the navigators, but why is William III there? Surely only as a statement of political adherence after 1685.

Leaving the Great Hall, the visitor wanders into the drawing room. Here in some ways the plaster work, obviously by the same hand, is even more extraordinary and is described by Pevsner as 'barbaric'. The ceiling is much lower, the room is fully furnished and the whole array of a central roundel, more cherubs, scallop shells and palm leaves that look like the rib cage of vast sea monsters close in to dominate and overwhelm. Continuing down the east wing are the library and drawing room. These were rebuilt in 1825 but are furnished with their original geometrically inlaid panelling.

There are some other interesting rooms on the ground floor and on the upper storeys but the other jewel at Astley is the Long Gallery. These adjuncts to houses were fashionable in the late sixteenth and early seventeenth centuries. They served variously as places for games, rooms in which a promenade could be taken in inclement weather and as picture galleries and also – if evidence of probate inventories is to be relied upon – as a domestic dumping ground. The Gallery at Astley was uncertainly inserted across the original gables of the front and seems to hang insecurely balanced on them. Its floor waves and dips like a ship at sea, and it contains one huge piece of furniture which must have had the gallery built around it. This is the shuffleboard table, over twenty feet long and supported on ten pairs of legs. The outer wall of the gallery consists almost entirely of glass and looks surprisingly modern in its concept.

In the opening paragraph Astley was described as a gem. It is more than that; it is a treasure that should be visited by anyone who enjoys old houses or who is interested in the history of Lancashire.

Name of house: *Leighton Hall*

Address: Carnforth, Lancashire LA5 9ST

Owners: Mr and Mrs R. Gillow-Reynolds

Location and directions: Near the village of Yealand Conyers. M6 Junction 35, follow A6 Kendal or, alternatively, use A6 from Lancaster or Kendal. The house is signed from main road. GR SD 4974

Admission charge: Yes £ Adults £5 Children £3.50 Senior citizens £4.50

Opening hours: 1 May–30 September, Tuesday–Friday & Sunday 14.00–17.00. Also Bank Holiday Mondays. During August 12.30–17.00.

Disabled access: To grounds only

Restaurant/tea room: Yes

Telephone number 01524 734474

Email address: info@leightonhall.co.uk

Leighton Hall. The way in which its setting enhances the architecture and appearance of Leighton Hall is evident in this picture. The central block is the original house, though enlivened by its 'Gothick' façade of about 1810. To the left is the wing added in 1870 by Paley & Austin. The right-hand pavilion and orangery add to the asymmetrical charm of the house, which contributes to the illusion of a fairytale castle in an entrancing landscape.

The quiet peninsula which extends to Silverdale and the estuary of the River Kent has something of the air of a land which time forgot. Isolated from the main routes, it is served by a network of lanes which wind through woodland and pasture. It almost seems appropriate that this delightful wilderness area should contain a fairytale castle. The white stone of Leighton gleams against the emerald of its half-saucer of surrounding, lime-fed lawns and trees. Its tower and battlements seen from a distance, must be the home of Rapunzel. In the best tradition of fairy stories much of this is an illusion. Closer inspection shows that the frontage of the house, with its balanced centre section and two wings is a product of the Georgian fascination with the 'Gothick' and conceals a much more standard Georgian rear elevation of about 1760. Even this is to some extent a deception as there are three strange buttresses and concealed within the masonry are some recently discovered gothic arches. There is a record of a fortified house being established here in 1246 but these must date from the late fifteenth century when the house was the home of the Middleton family. On either side of the central block are two pavilions, one contemporary with the main house. The left-hand pavilion is of a later date and is the work of the Lancaster based firm of architects, Paley & Austin. Built in 1870 it has something of a lighter feel. The ground floor contains a splendid music room in which recitals and concerts are still held.

The Middletons were notorious in the mid-seventeenth century as staunch recusants, who had a resident priest, and as pinch-penny landlords – their tenants repaid them in the Civil War by supporting the cause of Parliament *en masse*. The family paid for their loyalty to the royalist cause with a fine of £2,646 imposed by the new Commonwealth government. In the early eighteenth century the house passed to a grandson whose son-in-law and heir, Albert Hodgson, was captured at the battle of Preston in 1715, when Leighton was sacked and burned by government troops. His right to the property was cancelled by the government and for the first and only time the house came on the market. It was bought back for Hodgson by a friend, but Hodgson, when eventually released from gaol, was ruined in health and wealth. His daughter had married George Towneley of the Towneley Hall family. A portrait of George is among the six 'lost' paintings recently recovered at Towneley, where it can now be seen. About 1790 the house passed to the Lancaster banking family of Worswick. Alexander Worswick was married to Alice Gillow. After the bankruptcy of Thomas Worswick the house was eventually sold to Richard Gillow who began the transformation of the house by his 'Gothick' additions. The architect responsible is unknown, though some involvement by Thomas Harrison of Lancaster or Richard Gillow himself have both been suggested. Harrison worked extensively in the town of Lancaster and on some country houses in the surrounding district. Though Richard Gillow is best known as a cabinet-maker and furniture designer, there was a wealth of architectural expertise in the family. His father, also Richard, was the architect of the Custom House on St George's Quay in Lancaster (now the Maritime Museum) while his brother Robert designed the house of Clifton Hill at Garstang. Whoever was responsible, they were prepared to make use of the new building technology which had become available and they fitted cast-iron tracery and mullions in the windows and used iron structurally in the house.

The interior of the house is especially notable for the remarkable collection of Gillow furniture which it contains, some pieces of which are unique. The development of Gillow's furnishings in Lancaster is one of the great Lancashire success stories of the eighteenth and nineteenth centuries. The cabinet-making trade was started by Richard's grandfather, Robert. He is recorded in the records of Lancaster as 'a joyner' specialising in coffins, mangles and pig troughs. About 1740, when Lancaster was making remarkable progress as a port trading with the West Indies, he started to buy the mahogany and other tropical hardwoods which were being brought into the town, often as 'dunnage' or packing of the more valuable cargoes. He found a ready market for furniture among the planters of the Sugar Islands who found these hardwoods were more resistant to rot and the boring beetles of the tropics than European timbers. By the 1770s he and his son Richard were working as architects and building contractors in Lancaster. By the early years of the next century Richard had joined the Lancashire gentry. It is suggested that the subsequent fame of Gillow rested on their meeting a market for men of similar origins, not quite top drawer, but socially ambitious, who appreciated craftsmanship and value for money and who sought to make an impression of gentility. One of their special-ities was the making of billiard tables, and the dining room at Leighton was designed to hold one of these so it has lighting from an overhead skylight as well as windows in the gothic manner.

The room which lingers in the memory after a visit to Leighton is the light, spacious and elegant hall. On entering, one is confronted by a screen composed of three lofty four-centred-arches supported by cast-iron clustered columns. Through the screen can be seen the main staircase, curving gently to the right. The steps are cantilevered from the wall and unsupported while the balusters are miniature copies of the main columns. All are painted in light tones and illuminated by a long window on the turn of the stairs.

Today Leighton is also famous for its collection of birds of prey and these are frequently shown in free-flying displays. The house and the beautifully landscaped and maintained grounds ensure that, though one has to seek it out, Leighton Hall provides a memorable visit.

Name of house: *Ordsall Hall*
Address: Ordsall Lane, Salford M5 3AN
Owners: Salford City Council
Location and directions: In Ordsall district, near Salford Quays. The
    house, less than a mile from the end of the M602 motorway, is signed
    from most major road junctions. Accessible by public transport buses
    71, 73, 84, 92 GR SJ 8196
Admission charges: None
Opening hours: Monday–Friday, 10.00–16.00.
Disabled access: Ground floor only
Restaurant/tea room: None
Telephone number: 0161 872 0251
Email address: www.ordsallhall.org

One of the most distinctive forms of house in Lancashire is the timber-framed, black and white manor house. A good number of these have survived, although many more have been lost in the last hundred years. Timber framing was a standard method of building throughout those parts of the country where good building stone was in short supply, but where large timbers could be easily and cheaply found. The timber frames could be shaped and jointed on the ground, carried to the site and re-erected using marks to ensure that the correct joints were assembled. Fixing was done with wooden pegs, known as trenails and the oak timbers gradually hardened and became more durable with age. The spaces between the frames could be filled with a variety of materials; sometimes brick was used, but much more common was the use of daub. This mixture of clay, water, straw and cow manure, was smeared over a light framework of wattles or slightly larger timbers known locally as clam staves. While daub might deteriorate with age, it was easily and cheaply replaced and could be remarkably durable provided it could be protected from the damp.

To ensure rigidity of the framing, cross braces were fitted in the corners of each frame and these braces could be cut to ornamental shapes. In Lancashire the elaboration of the cross braces was carried to excessive lengths and in some cases they were so large and elaborate that the in-filling was reduced to a minimum and the walls are almost entirely composed of timber. At the same time, when the opportunity presented itself, carpenters would indulge a taste for carving grotesques on any available surface. Ordsall Hall is a good illustration of the Lancashire timbered style.

The earliest record of the hall is in 1251 when it was owned by the Hulton family, who transferred it to the Radcliffes in *c*. 1330. They were a family who, in the sixteenth century, acquired a great reputation for their military prowess. Sir William Radcliffe was knighted in 1544 as a reward for his service in the Scottish wars, especially for his part in the so-called 'Rough Wooing' when the army of the Earl of Hertford captured and sacked Edinburgh in an attempt to force the marriage between the infant Queen Mary and young prince Edward (later Edward VI). At the same time, another member of the Radcliffe family, Sir Christopher, was commanding the gunners of Berwick on Tweed.

In 1596 Sir William's grandson, Sir Alexander, was serving in the expedition dispatched to Cadiz in an unsuccessful attempt to emulate Sir Francis Drake's singeing of the King of Spain's beard. Alexander was succeeded by his brother, John, who was prominent in the Irish Wars of Elizabeth, under the command of the Earl of Essex. He then followed a political career, sitting as one of the MPs for the county in the first three parliaments of Charles I. He returned to the battlefield, joining the Duke of Buckingham in seizing the Ile de Ré to support the French Huguenots who were under siege in La Rochelle. In the confused fighting which followed Radcliffe was killed.

His son and heir, Sir John, was a most prominent royalist leader in Civil War in Lancashire and after his capture in 1644 was imprisoned in the Tower of London. It was in this period of distress that Humphrey Chetham was able to acquire parts of the Ordsall estate (see chapter 5). In 1662 after the return of the King, the Radcliffes decided to sell the property in Ordsall and it was bought by John Birch of Ardwick who had been a leading parliamentarian. Eventually the property passed to the Earl Egerton of Tatton, in whose hands it remained until the encroaching urban sprawl of Salford led them to dispose of it and the Hall went through a period of chequered use until eventually it was acquired by Salford Council and opened to the public.

The house only survives in part. It originally comprised a quadrangle, but two sides, the north and the eastern ranges, have disappeared. However, the two surviving wings provide an interesting illustration of the changes in domestic architecture in the early seventeenth century. The south range is probably the original hall and still contains the Great Hall, the vast, three-bay, communal room in which originally, the household ate – the head of the family dining in state at the raised table on a dais – with the other members ranged at long tables on either side of the central hearth. At the lower end, opposite the high table and separated by screens, lay the service rooms, the kitchen, buttery and pantry. Behind the High Table was the parlour and chambers where the family lived and slept. At Ordsall the hall has not survived unscathed and the present south wall is a Victorian replacement, but the interior gives one a good impression of how one of these houses would have looked in its heyday.

The south range shows how the fifteenth-century hall was still acceptable with some modification, decoration and elaboration in the days of Elizabeth. In the next phase of building in 1639 a very different expectation was held. Bricks, then a newly introduced and prestigious material in Lancashire, were used for the new western extension. Internally, more smaller rooms giving privacy and luxury were needed and provided for.

It is the quaint charm of Ordsall and its incongruity of position which makes it an interesting visit, especially as the associated family's careers touch the wider picture of English history at so many points. As a reminder of this it is worth remembering that the 'Bonnie Earl of Derwentwater' whose quixotic loyalty to the Jacobite cause led him to join the '15 and who perished on the scaffold at the Tower for his efforts, was a member of a different branch of the Radcliffe family.

Name of house: *Smithills Hall*
Address: Smithills Dean Road, Bolton, Lancs.
Owners: Smithills Park Trust
Location and directions: Located on north side of Bolton. The house can best be reached from the A58 Bolton ring road, GR SJ 7011
Admission charges: Yes £. Guided tours available
Opening hours: Winter: Tuesday only 1300–1700. Saturday 1300–1500. Sunday 14.00–17.00. Summer: Tuesday–Saturday 11.00–17.00. Sunday 14.00–17.00
Disabled access: To all ground-floor rooms.
Restaurant/tea room: Machine only (restaurant nearby in coach house)
Telephone number: 01204 332 377
Email address: office@smithills.org

It is a long way from the suburbs of Bolton to the ancient Hospital of St John of Jerusalem, but at Smithills one makes this transition. The house site was

Smithills Hall. This picture illustrates the most important building phases of the house. The stone gable on the extreme left is the Great Hall, while the simple timber-framed gable facing the camera is the later family solar wing of the house. The long timbered façade with the oriel window shows the Great Parlour added by the Barton family c.1530 and the later family wing in the typical elaborate Lancashire style. The stone gable is that of the chapel, restored and rebuilt in the 1840s when large additions were made to the house.

originally owned by the Order of the Knights Hospitaller, set up in the eleventh century to provide escorts and hospital care for pilgrims making the perilous journey to Jerusalem. In England the Order had its headquarters at Clerkenwell and also owned extensive property and smaller houses throughout the country. The lands at Halliwell were one of these estates, and was the site for a house, which according to legend, had been founded in AD 680. This was tenanted by the Hulton family, who were replaced by the Radcliffes in 1335. For some years it was their chief residence before it passed by marriage to John Barton of Newark in Nottinghamshire. The Barton family made it their main home and then as it became unfashionable they rented it out to various other families, including for a time the Shuttleworths of Gawthorpe. It was Robert Barton who was the Justice to whom George Marsh, the Protestant martyr, was first brought, and left his indelible footstep (see Chapter 3). It was this Robert who in 1535 added the spectacular parlour with its extravagant linenfold panelling, liberally interspersed with carved portrait medallions and heraldic symbols, some of which rely on the rebus of a diagonal bar across a tun or barrel — hence bar tun.

It is on the step between this room and the great hall that the martyr's footstep appears. The great hall's earliest parts date from the early fifteenth century. In the hall the spere trusses — the short walls which helped to reduce the area spanned by the screen — still survive as do the doors to the service wing.

Beyond the upper end of the hall, a two-storey wing contains the original parlour on the ground floor and a chamber or bower on the first floor though these have been refurbished extensively in the recent past. The parlour has the convenience of a large stone fireplace built into one wall, an indication of the high luxury of these rooms when they were built and before they were replaced by the great parlour of 1535.

In the mid years of the seventeenth century the estate at Smithills passed into the hands of George Belasyse, Viscount Fauconburg of Newbrugh Abbey in Yorkshire. Fauconburg was an anomaly in the period, in that he showed neither religious or political prejudices: although many of his relatives were Roman Catholic he was a moderate Anglican and though his cousin Sir John was one of the most vehement Cavaliers, Fauconburg was uncommitted. As a man of studied moderation he was selected by Oliver Cromwell as a match for his daughter Mary. The couple were married in Whitehall in 1657, in a union which it was hoped would prove an exemplar of spanning the great divide and prove the moderation of the Lord Protector. It is fair to record that it proved a happy match.

The Fauconburgs retained an interest in the Smithills estates but never lived at the Hall. In 1772 they sold the property to the Byrom family of Manchester. The Byroms remained at the house until about 1822 when it was sold to a local bleachworks owner by the name of Ainsworth. The Ainsworths probably enjoyed the antiquity which gave spurious antiquity to the family but they also wished to live in the most luxurious of modern conditions. This conflict of interest resulted in the construction of a huge new wing to the west of the old courtyard. In keeping with their aspirations this was given an antique appearance. This wing of the house was in use for many years as an old people's home and has lately been refurbished and re-furnished by Bolton Council. It is once more open to the public to provide an interesting contrast of styles and furnishings.

Name of house: *Croxteth Hall*
Address: Croxteth Lane, Liverpool L12 OHB
Owners: Liverpool City Council
Location and directions: East side of Liverpool ring road, Queen's Drive, between A580 and A57. Follow signs to Croxteth Country Park, GR SJ 4093
Admission charges: Yes £
Opening hours: Every day, 10.30–17.00.
Disabled access: Full to grounds and farm and ground floor only of Hall
Restaurant/tea room: Yes
Telephone number: 0151 228 5311
Email address: croxtethcountrypark@liverpool.gov.uk

Croxteth Hall was the principal house of the Mollineux family from the early years of the eighteenth century. They had been important in south-west Lancashire for many centuries before this when they had lived mainly at Sefton. The family originated from the ranks of the followers of William the Conqueror, when William de Molines joined the retinue of Roger of Montgomery and their name, which signifies 'of the mill' is obviously of Norman origin. We know that their family were brought to the area of Lancashire by Roger of Poitou who was given the lands 'between Ribble and Mersey' by the new king. As his reward William de Molines was given, among other estates, the manor of Sefton. His grandson, Richard of Sefton, sided with John, Count of Mortain, later King John, against Richard I and was fined 100

Croxteth Hall. This western wing of the house was added in 1702 by the second Viscount Sefton. The sash window was a novelty in Lancashire and this structure with its eleven bays makes full use of the style. The design is not one for the architectural purist, the pair of windows at either end of the front have been squeezed in and the entrance portal is rather too large. However, the impression made by the raised block on its terrace, pierced with circular bull's eye windows, and the sweep of the double staircase leading to the entrance is impressive.

shillings after the rising was suppressed on the king's return from imprisonment in Germany. In 1260 we find the family being raised to knighthood for the first time. Sir William Mollineux was created a knight banneret – a promotion in the field – as a reward for bravery in the wars in Gascony. It is thought that his effigy survives on a tomb in the parish church of Sefton. His grandson, Sir William, attained the same honour at the Battle of Navarette in 1367 under the command of the Black Prince. Another Sir Richard fought at Agincourt in 1415 and as a reward for his services was made Chief Forester of the Royal lands in West Derby Hundred, Constable of Liverpool Castle, and was granted a park or hunting enclosure at Croxteth. His son was killed at the Battle of Blore Heath in 1459, at the very beginning of the Wars of the Roses, when he was engaged on the Lancastrian side. The family continued displaying military talent. Sir William Mollineux, like many Lancashire men, was at Flodden Field in 1513 and distinguished himself by capturing two Scottish standards. Further members of the family earned distinction and lands in Ireland during the wars of Elizabeth. The family were rewarded with an Irish peerage, as Viscount Maryborough. The second Viscount Richard and his brother and successor, Caryl, played an essential part in the operations of the royalist army and it was the latter who led the storming party which recaptured Liverpool for Charles I in 1644. Caryl was a loyal supporter of the Stuarts after the Restoration and he was one of the few men in England who made any serious attempt to save the cause of James II, when he seized Chester and held it briefly on the king's behalf.

Throughout these years the family's principal house was at Sefton. This has now almost entirely vanished but in the fields opposite the church and now bisected by a new road, the remains of the moat, fish ponds and various irregularities of level mark the site of the house. At Croxteth they had a smaller hunting lodge, which had been built c. 1575 by Sir Richard Mollineux on a site formerly known as Barret's Hall. Some of this original house still survives but it is difficult to see from the outside, having been almost buried in later building and the interior of the house has been so much altered that it is concealed in the service areas. However, a couple of mullioned windows and a studded door are relics of this original house.

It was Richard, the second Viscount Sefton as they had now become, who seems to have made the decision to move the family seat from Sefton to Croxteth. In order to provide a house sufficiently worthy of his dignity he ordered the building of a large new south wing between 1702 and 1714. This is an elegant and typical piece of 'Queen Anne' design. The material is a soft-coloured red brick with white quoins and stone pedimented surrounds to the windows. Its appearance is regular and symmetrical. As was typical of the period, the roof is concealed behind a brick parapet, ornamented with urns. There is a central door surmounted by a trophy of arms, and the whole is very typical of the age of Wren. A peculiarity is the way in which the architect has raised the whole wing on a terrace pierced by oval windows. It may be that he had in mind the design of Italian houses in which the principal rooms were located on the first floor, a style exemplified at Lytham Hall.

The Mollineux family seem to have abandoned both their military and their political interests in this period and devoted themselves to extending their local estates and influence, as well as pursuing field sports. They were especially interested in horse racing. The Earls organised race meetings at Crosby, and then later Maghull and Aintree, one of which evolved into the world-famous Grand National in 1836. These less controversial activities led them to being raised in the peerage as the Earls of Sefton in 1711. The house was enlarged in 1874 by the fourth earl, who extended the east and south ranges and added some of the associated farm buildings and stables. In the early twentieth century the house was greatly extended and re-modelled by McVicar Anderson.

The Mollineux family became extinct with the death of the Earl in 1972 and a few years later the house and grounds passed into the hands of Liverpool Corporation who operate it as a country park and educational resource. It can now be visited, but the displays largely concentrate on recreating the upstairs and downstairs life of the period before the First World War. There is little emphasis on either the story of the Mollineux family or their place in the history of Lancashire.

Name of house: *Lytham Hall*
Address: Ballam Road, Lytham
Owners: Lytham Town Trust & Heritage Trust for the North West
Location and direction: The hall is situated very near to the centre of
    Lytham, near the station. Road access via A584 either from direction of
    Preston and Kirkham or from end of M55 then A5073. GR SD 3527
Admission charges: under review at the time of writing
Opening hours: Pre-booked parties only
Disabled access: Ground floor only
Restaurant/tea room: Yes
Telephone number: 01253 736 652
Email address; Lytham.hall@htmw.co.uk

It was Benedictine monks from the priory of Durham who were the first known inhabitants of the site of the hall. Land in the area had been bequeathed to them and they established a cell with a few monks to manage their lands on the Fylde coast in 1190. The cell had grown sufficiently to achieve a degree of independence as a Priory by 1443. The Priory of Lytham was among the first wave of lesser monasteries closed by Henry VIII in 1536. As usual, the estates were eagerly bought by various speculators and it was in 1606 that it came into the hands of Sir Cuthbert Clifton, whose house lay at the nearby village.

Lytham Hall. Designed by John Carr in 1757–64 for Sir Cuthbert Clifton this house replaced an early seventeenth century house which was, in turn, built on the site of the former Priory. The sophisticated design of the house allowed Carr to create the exterior impression of an Italian palazzo but to make the internal arrangements conform to English requirements. The Clifton family were largely responsible for the creation of Lytham as a resort and sea-bathing place at the end of the eighteenth century.
PHOTOGRAPH COURTESY OF B. & N. DIXON

The Cliftons were a wealthy family who, like many of their neighbours, were active recusant Roman Catholics. Though a drawing of the old house survives, there are now no significant remains. It vanished in 1757 when Thomas Clifton decided to equip the family with a house in the latest taste. In the midst of its extensive wooded park the old house was demolished and the York architect John Carr was brought in to provide a house which is the first large classic Georgian house in Lancashire. The house stands four-square and is built in brick, with painted stone mouldings and architraves. Like Croxteth, the corners of the building are adorned with stone quoins and the whole sits on a plinth of stone. In the centre of the main façade is an Ionic pediment with four pilasters extending from the first floor to cornice level. On the ground floor a central doorway provides the main entrance. This, too, has a pedimented door case, in which Doric columns emphasise strength and stability, and is approached up three steps. On the ground floor the door is flanked by eight rectangular sash windows, each of which has a rusticated 'Gibbs' surround. On the first floor, above a string course, are nine plainer windows, the extra window being over the door, while on the second floor are a similar number of windows, smaller and square, with an even more severe frame to them. The mansard roof of slate is supported on a dentiled parapet.

The impression created is of the classic Italian styled villa on which these houses were modelled. In these the ground floor or *piano rustico* contained servants' rooms and those used by the family for everyday life. On the first floor, *piano nobile*, were the state rooms and those used by the family for ceremonial occasions and for entertaining. Often to emphasise this distinction between the every day and bucolic, and the educated and genteel the ground floor would be built using stone, often rusticated. Here at Lytham this was not done but the windows help to strengthen the impression of solidity and stability. This theme is extended by the simple Doric columns in the door case, while in contrast the upper floors have a much lighter feel to them.

In fact, though the impression is created, the facts are quite different, and the main rooms of Lytham are located on the ground floor and include some in which the changing taste of the 1760s is shown. This new style was due to the influence of the John and Robert Adam brothers. Carr had acted as clerk of works at Harewood House and absorbed the teachings of the new style. This was based on the greater knowledge of the art of ancient Rome which the infant science of archaeology was making known. The difference of approach is made clear at Lytham in the contrast between the plasterwork of the entrance hall and the décor of the dining room. In the hall the remarkable plasterwork ceiling in which Jupiter with his thunderbolts stands in a roundel of scrolls and mouldings, dominates and overpowers. The dining room displays a lighter touch in contrast to the opulence of the hall. Here an oval of fluted moulded plaster fills the centre of the ceiling while the walls are divided into panels by delicate pilasters in a vaguely Corinthian style, the whole has a lightness and airiness which is not evident in the entrance hall, a feeling which is emphasised by the arched niche which contains a mahogany buffet designed for the position. The house has a number of other elegant and pleasing rooms which can be visited, and a feature to look out for is the fine quality of the chimney pieces throughout the house.

Name of house: *Borwick Hall*

Address: Borwick Hall, Borwick, Carnforth LA6 1JU

Owners: Lancashire County Council

Location and directions: Located 3 miles north-east of Carnforth. Access from M6 Junc. 35 & 35A; follow A6 north towards Kendal. After 1 mile turn right on unclassified road to Borwick. GR SD 5273

Admission charges: Yes £

Opening hours: Not regularly open; special appointments and arrangements must be made (usually school holidays are the best time).

Disabled access: Difficult, but some availability on ground floor.

Restaurant/tea room: No

Telephone number: 01524 732508

e-mail address: kathbatly@ed.lancscc.gov.uk

Just as, today, on any motorway journey one can expect to see the smart and well-kept green lorries of Eddie Stobart, the Cumbrian haulage millionaire, so some four hundred years ago a traveller in the North West was very likely to encounter a train of pack horses, the property of the Bindloss family. If the horses were travelling south, the panniers slung over the horses' backs would almost certainly be filled with newly woven woollen cloth, much of which would have originated around the family's Kendal base. The heavy Kendal cloth found a ready market in northern Europe and along the Atlantic coast of France and Spain. Much was exported via east-coast ports such as Hull and King's Lynn, as well as from the Channel ports, of which the most important was Southampton. The route from Kendal to the ports of southern England brought Bindloss ponies through Lancashire, where similar cloth was made and

where the clothiers of Manchester, having bought the cloth from the domestic craftsmen, were eager to use this conduit to the markets. Consequently the Kendal pack trains regularly passed through Lancashire, collecting the kerseys and friezes made in the Pennine areas. On their return trip they brought better quality wools from the Cotswolds and Midlands, which were mixed with local fleeces to improve the standard of the local cloth, together with luxury items and other imports from the Continent.

So successful were the earlier generations of the family that by the last decade of the sixteenth century Robert Bindloss was able to contemplate joining the ranks of the landed gentry through the purchase of Borwick Tower. There is supposed to have been a a fortified house on the site which had passed through a number of hands before Robert decided on his bold purchase.

A pele tower was a stone built, defensible, tower house in which the ground floor served as a cattle pen while the family could take refuge in the upper floors in time of danger. The design had developed along the violent border zone, not only as a protection against marauding Scots, but as a protection from feuding neighbours. Lancashire was frequently subjected to Scots raids, of which the most serious occurred in the reign of Edward II in the early fourteenth century. The oldest parts of Borwick Tower date partly from the fourteenth century, although the interior has been stripped out and rebuilt, probably by Robert Bindloss. Attached to the tower is his new house; the symmetry of whose façade, with gables at either end and a central entrance porch, is broken only by the presence of the tower. The house is approached by a gatehouse which was added about 1650 and attached to this is an array of barns of the same date. It is thought that these may have been built as a stable block in which the pack horses were kept.

A unique feature of the interior is the stone staircase which ascends through the central core of the house. The medieval spiral, essential for defence, has been abandoned in the piping days of peace in the reign of Elizabeth and instead we have an early stone newel stair which rises in short straight flights around a central core. At the head of the stairs is a balustrade of rather crude copies of classical columns and a slab inscribed, 'ALIXANDER BRINSMEAD MASON 1595', a very rare example where the stonemason – who would probably have acted both as craftsman and as architect – signs his work.

So successful was the Bindloss family business that Robert's son was made high sheriff of Lancashire for the year 1612–13, and was knighted during the famous visit of James I to Hoghton Tower in 1617. He later purchased one of the newly created baronetcies. His grandson and heir, Sir Robert, was the wealthiest member of the Lancashire gentry, with an annual income estimated to be £3,240 in 1643. In spite of his wealth and prestige Bindloss played a canny hand during the Civil War, in which he favoured Parliament, though taking care not to cut all links with the King's party. He lost much of his influence with the parliamentarians after 1649 when he strenuously opposed the execution of Charles I. In later years the family's fortune declined, and Borwick was rented to tenant farmers.

The house is of special interest in the way in which it spans the change between the gothic style and the introduction of new ideas derived from classical models. The former can be seen in its mullioned and transomed windows, mock castellations and angular drip mouldings over the windows, while the plan of the house and the occurrence of motifs of classical style indicate future developments in architecture and design.

The house is now an outdoor pursuits training centre operated by Lancashire County Council.

Notes and Further Reading

Abbreviations

C.S.	Chetham Society
o.s.	Chetham Society, old series
n. s.	Chetham Society, new series
3rd ser.	Chetham Society, third series
Deane	*Rufford Old Hall*, National Trust Guide Book, 1991
Farrer	*History of the Parish of North Meols*
L.C.R.S.	Lancashire and Cheshire Records Society
L.C.A.S.	Lancashire and Cheshire Antiquarian Society
L.R.O.	Lancashire Record Office, Preston
T.H.S.L.C.	Transactions of the Historic Society of Lancashire and Cheshire
V.C.H.	Victoria County History of Lancashire

General background reading

The most recent and up-to-date general history of the social and economic development of Lancashire is *Lancashire, A Social History, 1588–1939*, by John K. Walton (MUP, 1985). For a more general view of the history *An Illustrated History of Lancashire* by J. J. Bagley (Phillimore) is rather dated and compressed in its format; however, it covers the entire history of the county and should not be ignored. More up-to-date is Alan Crosby's *A History of Lancashire* (Phillimore, 1998). A more antiquated view is given in *A History of Lancashire* by H. Fishwick (London, 1894; re-printed 1968). The architectural tradition of Lancashire is treated in a general way in *English Vernacular Houses* by Eric Mercer (HMSO, 1975) and a much more specific view is given in *Rural Houses of the Lancashire Pennines, 1560–1700* by S. Pearson (HMSO, 1985). *Lancashire's Architectural Heritage*, J. Champness (Lancashire County Council, 1988) and *Murray's Architectural Guide to Lancashire*, P. Fleetwood-Hesketh (John Murray, 1955) give an overall view of the buildings of the county and are lavishly illustrated. The two-volumes in Nikolaus Pevsner's *Buildings of England* (Penguin, 1969) series are invaluable. A new series of their books is in preparation. The first volumes have appeared as *Pevsner Architectural Guides* (Yale). A new and comprehensive guide to the larger houses of the county has appeared in J. M. Robinson's *Guide to Country Houses of the North West* (Constable, 1991).

For all topics the Victoria County History volumes, though dated in their concept and outdated in the sources drawn upon, cannot be disregarded. All the houses dealt with in this house have individual guide books or publications of varying quality from the excellent to the banal.

1. Browsholme Hall and the Lancashire Forests

A. Winchester, 'Field Wood and Forest in Medieval Lancashire, in *Lancashire Local Studies: Essays in honour of Diana Winterbotham* (Carnegie, 1993).

T. D. Whittaker, *History of the Parish of Whalley* (London, 1800).

R. Cunliffe-Shaw, *The Royal Forest of Lancaster* (Preston, 1956).

A. Harrison, 'Ancient Forests, Chases and Deer Parks in Lancashire', L.C.A.S. (1901).

G. H. Tupling, *Economic History of Rossendale*. C.S., n.s., xxxvi (1927).

J. Porter, 'Waste Land Reclamation in the Sixteenth and Seventeenth centuries', T.H.S.L.C., cxxvii (1978).

J. Porter, 'A Forest in Transition: Bowland 1500–1650', T.H.S.L.C., cxxv (1975).

M. Brigg, 'The Forest of Pendle in the Seventeenth Century', T. H. S. L. C., cxiii, cxv (1961, 1963).

J. Swain, *Industry Before the Industrial Revolution 1560–1640*, C.S., 3rd ser., xxxii (1986).

C. Ironfield, 'The Parish of Chipping during the Seventeenth Century', T.H.S.L.C., cxxvii (1978).

N. Lowe, *The Lancashire Textile Industry in the Sixteenth Century*, C.S., 3rd ser., xx (1972).

A. Vickery, *The Gentleman's Daughter* (Yale and London, 1998).

2. Whalley Abbey and Monasticism in Lancashire

M. E. C. Walcott, 'Inventory of Whalley Abbey' T.H.S.L.C., n.s., vii (1866).

O. Ashmore, 'Bursar's Accounts of Whalley Abbey, 1520'. T.H.S.L.C., cxiv (1962).

C. Haigh, *The Last Days of the Lancashire Monasteries and the Pilgrimage of Grace* C.S., 3rd ser., xvii (1969).

C. Haigh, *Reformation and Resistance in Tudor Lancashire* (Cambridge, 1975).

D. Knowles, *Religious Orders in England*, vol. III (Cambridge, 1959).

3. Sir Richard Shireburne of Stonyhurst and the Lancashire Recusants

C. Haigh, *Resistance and Reformation in Tudor Lancashire* (Cambridge, 1975).

J. Leatherbarrow, *Lancashire Elizabethan Recusants*, C.S., n.s., cx (1947).

W. Rea, 'The Rental and Accounts of Sir Richard Shireburne', T.H.S.L.C., cx (1958).

E. Duffy, *The Voices of Morebath: Reformation and Rebellion in an English Village* (Yale, 2003).

4. Samlesbury Hall and Witchcraft

G. Harrison, *Trial of the Lancaster Witches* (Muller, London, 1971) (Introduction and facsimile of Potts' 'Wonderfull Discoverie').

E. Peel and P. Southern, *Trials of the Lancashire Witches* (1985).

R. Poole (ed.), *The Lancashire Witches: Histories and Stories* (Manchester, 2002).

K. Eyre, *Witchcraft in Lancashire* (Dalesman, 1974).

K. Thomas, *Religion and the Decline of Magic* (Weidenfeld & Nicholson, 1971).

A. Macfarlane, *Witchcraft in Tudor and Stuart England* (Routledge & Kegan Paul, 1970).

A. Kars and E. Peters, *Witchcraft in Europe, 1100–1700* (Dent, 1973).

H. Trevor-Roper, 'The European Witch Craze in the 16th and 17th Centuries', (*Religion, Reformation and Social Change Essays*, 1967).

A. Hodge, *Samlesbury: A Short History* (Carnegie, 1985).

R. Eaton, *A History of Samlesbury in the Hundred of Blackburn* (Blackburn, 1936).

G. Tupling, *South Lancashire in the Reign of Edward II*, C.S., 3rd ser., i (1949).

5. Turton Tower and Humphrey Chetham

F. Raines and C. Sutton, *Life of Humphrey Chetham*. C.S., n.s., vols il and l (1903).

G. J. French, *Bibliographic Notes on Church Libraries of Humphrey Chetham*, C.S., o.s., xxxviii (1885).

N. Lowe, *The Lancashire Textile Industry in the Sixteenth Century*, C.S., 3rd ser., xx (1972).

A. Wadsworth and J. de L. Mann, *The Cotton Trade and Industrial Lancashire 1600–1780* (Manchester, 1931).

S. J. Guscott, *Humphrey Chetham 1580–1653*, C.S, 3rd ser., 45 (2003).

Roberts E. (ed.), *A History of Linen in the North West* (Centre for North-West Regional Studies, 1998).

6. Towneley Hall and the Scientific Revolution

C. Webster, 'Richard Towneley and the Towneley Group', T.H.S.L.C., cxvii (1966).

J. Aubrey (ed.), 'O. Dick', *Brief Lives* (Penguin, 1982).

L. Shepherd (ed.), *Dictionary of National Biography* (London, 1886).

S. Bourne, *An Introduction to the Architecture of Towneley Hall* (Burnley, 1977).

S. Pearson, *Rural Houses of the Lancashire Pennines 1560–1760* (H.M.S.O., 1985).

L. Jardine, *Ingenious Pursuits* (London, 2000)

L. Jardine, *On a Grander Scale* (London, 2002)

P. H. W. Booth, 'From Medieval Park to Puritan Republic', *Lancashire Local Studies: Essays in Honour of Diana Winterbotham* (Carnegie, 1993).

7. Swarthmoor Hall and the Quakers

G. Fox (ed.), J. Nickalls, *Journal of G. Fox* (Society of Friends, 1975).

M. Fell, *A Brief Relation of Margaret Fell* (1710).

I. Ross, *Margaret Fell, Mother of Quakerism* (York, 1984).

M. Webb, *The Fells of Swarthmoor Hall* (London, 1865).

M. Mullet (ed.), *Early Lancaster Friends* (Centre for North-West Regional Studies, 1978).

R. Muschamp, 'The Society of Friends in Lancaster District in the Seventeenth Century', T.H.C.A.S,. xliii (1926).

W. Braithwaite, *The Beginnings of Quakerism* (Cambridge, 1955).

B. Reay, *Quakers and the English Revolution* (Temple-Smith, 1985).

O. Greenwood, *Quaker Tapestry* (1990).

A. Nightingale, *Early Stages of the Quaker Movement in Lancashire.* (1921).

N. Penny (ed.), *The Household Account Book of Sarah Fell* (Cambridge, 1920).

N. Morgan, *Lancashire Quakers and the Establishment 1660–1730* (Halifax, 1993).

8. Speke Hall and the Rise of Liverpool

J. A. Picton, *Memorials of Liverpool* (Liverpool, London, 1873).

G. Northcote-Parkinson, *The Rise of the Port of Liverpool* (Liverpool U.P., 1962).

N. R. Nooks, *Liverpool's Historic Waterfront* (H.M.S.O., 1984).

Anon., *History of Liverpool from Ancient Times* (Liverpool, 1810).

H. Smith, *Liverpool, Its Commerce, Statistics and Institutions* (Liverpool, 1825).

J. Twemlow (ed.), *Liverpool Town Books* (Liverpool, 1918).

G. Chandler, *Liverpool* (Batsford, 1957).

G. Chandler and M. Saxton, *Liverpool in the Reign of James I* (Liverpool, 1960).

G. Chandler and E. Wilson, *Liverpool in the Reign of Charles I* (Liverpool, 1965).

J. Touzeau, *Rise and Progress of Liverpool* (Liverpool, 1910).

R. Muir, *Bygone Liverpool* (Liverpool, 1913).

R. Muir, *History of Liverpool* (Liverpool, 1907).

J. Brownbill (ed.), *The Moore Manuscripts*, L.C.R.S., lxviii (1913).

J. Peet, 'Liverpool in the Reign of Queen Anne', T.H.S.L.C., lix (1907).

W. Irvine (ed.), *Liverpool in the Reign of Charles II* (Liverpool, 1899).

9. Rufford Hall and the Draining of Martin Mere

W. Farrer, *History of the Parish of North Meols* (Liverpool, 1903).

A. Crosby, 'Fowl Play', in *Lancashire Local Studies: Essays in honour of Diana Winterbotham* (Carnegie, 1993).

Thomas Fleetwood and the Draining of Martin Mere, T.H.S.L.C., 152 (2003).

W. Proctor, 'Manor of Rufford and Ancient family of Rufford', T.H.S.L.C., lix (1907).

In view of the paucity of published material on Rufford detailed references have been provided:

1. C. Fiennes, *The Illustrated Journeys of Celia Fiennes* (Macdonald, Webb & Bower, 1982) p. 161.

2. W. Hale, *Martin Mere, Its History and Natural History* (Ormskirk, 1985).

3. Farrer, p. 113.

4. Farrer, p. 116.

5. L.R.O., DDHe 58/33.

6. V.C.H., vol. vi, p. 120.

7. Proctor, (op. cit.) p. 97.

8. Deane, pp. 49–50.

9. Deane, p. 49; *Lancs Wills*, C.S., n.s. ii, pp. 21–24.

10. Deane, p. 49–50.

11. Deane, p. 50.

12. L.R.O., DDHe 82/15; WCW 1697.

13. L.R.O., WCW; DDHe 122/2.

14. L.R.O., DDHe 105/1, 105/33.

15. L.R.O., DDHe 104/51.

16. L.R.O., DDHe 107; Deane, pp. 66–8.

17. Deane, p. 62–7.

18. L.R.O., WCW 1620 (Will of Robert Hesketh of Rufford).

19. L.R.O., DDHe 54/4.

20. Farrer pp. 116–21; L.C.R.S., *Duchy Pleadings*, vol. iii. xl (1899).

22. L.R.O., DDHe 58/33.

23. L.R.O., WCW 1620 (Will of Robert Hesketh of Rufford).

24. L.R.O., WCW 1599 (Will of Edward Scarisbrick).

25. L.R.O., DDHe 143/23.

26. Farrer, p. 116.

27. L.R.O., DDHe 58/33.

28. L.R.O., DDHe 54/4.

29. L.C.R.S., *Commonwealth Church Survey*, i (1879), p. 110.

30. L.R.O., DDSc 143/23[1].

31. Farrer, pp. 119–21, 32; L.R.O., DDHe 58/33.

32. L.R.O., DDHe 58/53.

33. L.R.O., DDHe 54/4.

34. L.R.O., DDHe 54/2.

35. Farrer, p. 121.

36. Farrer, p. 121–2; L.R.O., DDSc 19/36; L.R.O. DDHe 62/4, 14 Oct. 1798.

37. L.R.O., DDHe 86/11.

38. Farrer, p. 121.

39. L.R.O., DDSc 19/36.

10. Hall i'th'Wood and Samuel Crompton

A. Wadsworth and J. de L. Mann, *The Cotton Trade and Industrial Lancashire* (Manchester, 1931).

C. Aspin and S. Chapman, *James Hargreaves and the Spinning Jenny* (Helmshore, 1964).

E. Roberts (ed.), *A History of Linen in the North West* (Centre for North-West Regional Studies, 1998).

H. Catling, *The Spinning Mule* (David & Charles, 1984).

G. J. French, *The Life of Samuel Crompton* (1859).

Fowler and Wyke, *The Barefoot Aristocrats* (Littleborough, 1987).

Visitor Details

Please note that these details are correct at time of going to press, but the information should always be checked. Neither the author or publisher is responsible for any variations or alterations

Browsholme Hall (Mr C. Parker)
Clitheroe, Lancs, BB7 3DE
Tel: 01254 826719
Email: rrp@browsholme.co.uk
Browsholme Hall welcomes coach parties and group tours by arrangement throughout the spring, summer and autumn. Otherwise the Hall is open to casual visitors on certain days at Spring Bank Holiday, early July and late August. Booked Parties, over 15 in a group including women's institutes, historical societies and school groups are welcome at many other times by arrangement
Admission charge: £4, including guided tour. Parties by arrangement. Toilets. Disabled access to toilets and ground floor. Refreshments by arrangement for parties. Car parking. No interior photography.

Whalley Abbey (Diocese of Blackburn)
Whalley, Clitheroe, BB7 9SS
Tel: 01254 828400
Fax: 01254 828401
Email: office@whalleyabbey.org
Abbey ruins open throughout year, dawn to dusk
11.00–17.00, shop etc. open daily Jan.–Dec. Closed Christmas and New Year weeks.
Admission Prices: £2 Adults £1.25 Senior Citizens 50p Children
Coffee Shop open daily 10.00–17.00 (Jan.–Dec.)
Guided tours and parties by arrangement. Disabled access limited; preliminary contact advised. Toilets. Car parking. Photography permitted. The House/Conference Centre open occasionally, at other times by prior arrangement.

Stonyhurst College
Stonyhurst, Clitheroe, BB7 9PZ
Tel: 01254 826345
Fax: 01254 827040
Opening times: 13.00–17.00
College open only in late July and August.
Grounds open July to September (during summer vacation).
Closed Fridays (except Bank Holidays).
Admission to college and grounds £5.50 (£4.50 children and seniors).
   Grounds only £1.
Guided tours only. Parties by prior arrangement. Tea Room. Very
   restricted disabled access. Toilets. Cark parking. No interior
   photography.

Samlesbury Hall (Samlesbury Hall Trust)
Preston New Road, Samlesbury, Preston, PR5 0UP
Tel: 01254 812010 or 01254 812229
Fax: 01254 812174
Email: samlesburyhall@btconnect.com
Open every day except Saturday from 11.00 to 16.30
Closed from 24 December to 28 December and 1 January to 3 January
Admission: Adults £3 Children £1.
Guided tours available if booked in advance, parties of 20 and over at
   special rates by arrangement. Restaurant. Disabled access to ground
   floor and restaurant. Toilets (inc. disabled). Car parking. Interior
   photography by arrangement.

Turton Tower (Lancs. C.C. Museums)
Chapeltown Road, Turton, nr Bolton, BL7 0HG
Tel: 01204 852203
Fax: 01204 853759
Email: turtontower.lcc@btinternet.com
Closed December to January.
Open March, April, October. Saturday to Wednesday 14.00–17.00
May to September, Monday to Friday 10.00–12.00 noon and 13.00–17.00
Saturday and Sunday 13.00–17.00 only.
February and November, Saturday and Sunday only 14.00–17.00
Admission 90p (students and children 40p) Family ticket £2.30 two adults
   and three children under 16. Guided tours for parties by arrangement.
   Tea room in season, weekends only at other times. Toilets. No disabled
   access to house. Car parking. No photography in house.

Towneley Hall (Burnley Museums)
Towneley Hall, Towneley Park, Burnley, Lancashire BB11 3RQ
Tel: 01282 424213
Fax: 01282 436138
Email: TowneleyHall@burnley.gov.uk
Open all year, except Christmas day.
Open Monday to Thursday 10.00–17.00
Closed Fridays (pre-booked groups only)
Saturday and Sunday 12.00–17.00
Admission free. Guided tours by arrangement and at a charge. Tea Room
   adjacent in Park every day in summer, weekends only in winter. Car
   parking. Disabled access to ground floor and upper floors, including Art
   Galleries. Toilets including disabled. Interior photography by
   arrangement.

Swarthmoor Hall (Society of Friends)
Ulverston, Cumbria, LA12 0JQ
Tel: 01229 583204
Fax: 01229 583283
Email: swarthmrhall@gn.apc.org
Website: www.swarthmoorhall.co.uk
Open all year for group or individual accommodation, self catering or
   B&B and for visiting gardens and grounds.
Open March to October for tours at 14.30 on Thursdays, Saturdays and
   Sundays, and by arrangement at other times for individuals or groups.
Admission £3.50 (Concessions £2.50)
Disabled access only to ground floor.
Refreshments by arrangement. Toilets. Car parking. Interior photography
   permitted.

Speke Hall (National Trust)
The Walk, Speke, Liverpool, L24 1XD
Telephone 0151 427 7231
Fax 0151 427 9860
Email: spekehall@nationaltrust.org.uk
Closed December to April.
Closed Mondays (except Bank Holidays).
Tea Rooms and gardens 13.00–17.00
Admission to Gardens only 70p. House and Gardens £3.50. Parties of 15
   or more £2.50. Family ticket £8. Guided tours by arrangement. Tea
   room open as Hall. Disabled access to tea room, ground floor of house
   and most of the gardens. Toilets (including disabled). Car parking. No
   interior photography.

Rufford Old Hall (National Trust)
Rufford, Nr Ormskirk, L40 1SG
Tel: 01704 821254
Fax: 01704 823823
Email: ruffordoldhall@nationaltrust.org.uk
Closed November to April. Closed Thursday and Friday. Open Bank Holidays and Good Friday. Hall open 13.00–17.00 (last admission 16.30). Gardens, Tea Room/shop weekdays 12.00–17.00 Sundays normal admission times.
Admission prices for 2005 to be announced. Parties by prior arrangement. Guided tours by arrangement. Toilets (including disabled and baby changing). Car parking. No interior photography.

Hall i' th'Wood (Bolton Museums)
Hall i' th'Wood Museum
Green Way, off Crompton Way, Bolton, BL1 8UA
Tel: 01204 332370
Closed September to April.
Closed Mondays (except Bank Holidays).
Opening hours Wednesday to Sunday 11.00–16.15 (last admission).
Sunday 14.00–16.45
Admission £1.55 (child and OAP 75p). Parties of fewer than 20 by arrangement. No refreshments, toilets (no disabled). Car parking. Non commercial photography permitted.

Index

Whalley 24, chapter 2 *passim*, 73, 132
    parish 7, 58, 73
Whalley Abbey 7, chapter 2 *passim*, 56,
    57, 87, 135, 203
Whitewell 6, *7*, 8, *8*, *17*, 19
Whitewell Chapel *6*, 7
Wilkinson, William of Skippool 80, 92
Windle 80
Winwick 57, 58, 86
Wolsey, Cardinal Thomas 53

Woods, John *186*, 195
Worsley 230
Worthington of Blainscough 68
Wright, Fortunatus 194
Wrightington 203, 206, 212
Wyatt Jeffry (Wyatville) *2*, 25, *26*, 135,
    139
Wyre, river 66
Wyresdale 4